Stageco

Bringing the bus out of the dark ages

Keith A. Jenkinson

An Autobus Review Publication

First published December 1996

ISBN 0 907834 36 1

Printed by Bakes & Lord Ltd.
Beacon Road, Bradford BD6 3NB.

AUTOBUS REVIEW PUBLICATIONS LTD.
42 Coniston Avenue, Queensbury,
Bradford, West Yorkshire BD13 2JD

Transferred from Stagecoach South's Coastline fleet to Stagecoach Devon in the spring of 1996, Plaxton Premiere Interurban-bodied Dennis Javelin 800 (M101CCD) leaves Exeter at the start of its journey to Torquay on express service X46. (John L. Hobbs)

INTRODUCTION & ACKNOWLEDGEMENTS

Following its phenomenal growth since its humble beginnings in 1980, few people can fail to have heard of Stagecoach, a company whose buses are to be seen across a large part of Britain as well as in a number of overseas locations. Having taken an interest in Stagecoach since its early years when its vehicles could be counted on the fingers of one hand, it has given me much pleasure to watch its development over the last sixteen years, and equally as much enjoyment putting together this history which it is hoped will give some insight into the company's expansion, its philosophy and its strategy. Having diversified from being an operator of long distance coach services to one concerned mainly with local bus operations and more recently railways, Stagecoach's growth over such a brief period of time is almost beyond belief. As the title of this book so rightly states, it has brought the bus out of the dark ages into an era of efficient, clean transport which is the envy of others within the bus industry. This history of the company's activities and development would, however, have been impossible without the help of others who have provided information and photographs etc. for inclusion within the following pages. Whilst space does not allow each to be mentioned personally, I would like to record special thanks to Derek Scott, formerly finance director of Stagecoach and now company secretary, for reading through the draft text and making several corrections and numerous suggestions, Tim Archer, Rod Bailey and Jerry Davison for providing a wealth of information and photographs relating to the company's overseas developments and Neil Renilson for his continuing flow of information from north of the border over many years. Despite having an extensive library of photographs relating to the Stagecoach Group, illustrating the book would have been extremely difficult without the help of many others to whom I extend my sincere thanks, and in particular Campbell Morrison, Terry Blackman, Murdoch Currie, Pete McElroy and Tim Carter.

I hope that the following pages will provide much of interest to all who read them and to those wishing to keep up to date with the future developments of the Stagecoach Group, such information is regularly included in the monthly magazine 'Bus Fayre'.

Keith A. Jenkinson.
Queensbury, Bradford. *November 1996*

STAGECOACH HOLDINGS PLC PORTFOLIO

A1 Service Limited.
Aberdare Bus Company Limited.
Armstrong Galley Coaches Limited.
Bayline Limited.
Blue Bus Services (Newcastle) Limited.
Bluebird Buses Limited.
Burnley & Pendle Borough Transport Company Limited.
Busways Travel Services Limited.
Busways Travel Services (1986) Limited,
Cambus Limited.
Cambus Holdings Limited.
Charterplan Travel Limited.
Cheltenham and Gloucester Omnibus Company Limited.
Cheltenham District Traction Company Limited.
Chesterfield & District Transport Limited.
Chesterfield Borough Transport Limited.
Chesterfield Omnibus Limited.
Chesterfield Transport Limited.
Chesterfield Transport (1989) Limited.
Circle Line Limited.
City Busways Limited.
Citylink (Hull) Limited.
Cleveland Transit Limited.
Cleveland Transit Coach Travel Limited.
Coastline Buses Limited.
Coronet Tours (1993) Limited.
Cumberland Motor Services Limited.
Devon General Limited.
E & T Johnson Coaches (Hanslope) Limited.
Eastern Valley Bus Company Limited.
East Kent Road Car Company Limited.
East London Bus & Coach Company Limited.
East Midland Buses Limited.
East Midland Motor Services Limited.
East Sussex Buses Limited.
Economic Bus Services Limited.
EK Worldwide Travel Limited.
Favourite Services Limited.
Fife Scottish Omnibuses Limited.
Frenchwood Holdings Limited.
G & G Travel Limited.
GCT Limited.
Generalouter Limited.
GM Buses South Holdings Limited.
GMS Coaches Limited.
Greater Manchester Buses South Limited.
Grimsby Cleethorpes Transport Company Limited.
Grimsby Cleethorpes Transport Services Limited.
Grimsby Cleethorpes Travel Limited.
Halliday Harte Travel (1988) Limited.
Hampshire Bus Company Limited.
Hartlepool Transport Limited.
Hartlepool Transport (1993) Limited.
Hastings Coaches Limited.
Hull City Buses Limited.
Hyndburn Transport Limited.
Kenya Bus Services Limited.
K.H.C.T. Limited
K.H.C.T. (Holdings) Limited
Kingstonian Travel Services Limited.
Kingston upon Hull City Transport Limited.
Legislator 1060 Limited.
Magicbus (Scotland) Limited.
Maun Buses Limited.
Midland Flexibus Limited.
Midland Red South Limited.
Millers Coaches Limited.
Millers Tours & Travel Limited.
Milton Keynes City Bus Limited.
MK Metro Limited.
National Travel Tokens Limited.
Newcastle Busways Limited.
Pegasus Express Parcels Limited.
Peterborough Bus Company Limited.
Peterborough Car Care Limited.
P. Phythian & Son Limited.
Porterbrook Leasing Company Limited.
Porterbrook Leasing Company MEBO Limited.
Premier Travel Services Limited.
PSV Claims Bureau Limited.
Rainworth Travel Limited.
Red & White Services Limited.
Retford and District Transport Limited.
Ribble Motor Services Limited.
Rigby's Coaches Limited.
Sandown (Burnley) Limited.
Sharpton Limited.
South Coast Buses Limited.
Southdown Motor Services Limited.
South East London & Kent Bus Company Limited.
South Shields Busways Limited.
South West Trains Limited.
Stagecoach Devon Limited.
Stagecoach East Kent Limited.
Stagecoach Europe Limited.
Stagecoach Express Limited.
Stagecoach Glasgow Limited.
Stagecoach Graphics Limited.
Stagecoach International Services Limited.
Stagecoach Kenya Limited.
Stagecoach Malawi Limited.
Stagecoach (North West) Limited.
Stagecoach Rail Limited.
Stagecoach (Scotland) Limited.
Stagecoach (South) Limited.
Stagecoach West Limited.
Stagecoach Western Scottish Limited.
Sunderland Busways Limited.
Sussex Coastline Buses Limited.
Swindon and District Bus Company Limited.
Teeside Transit Limited.
Tees Valley Limited.
The Quayside Busway Limited.
The Valleys Bus Company Limited.
The Viscount Bus & Coach Company Limited.
Transit Advertising Limited.
Transit Motor Services Limited.
Transmedia Advertising Limited.
Tyne & Wear Omnibus Company Limited.
United Counties Omnibus Company Limited.
Vanguard Bus and Coach Sales Limited.
Vanguard Coaches Limited.
Viscount Central Limited.
Welcome Passenger Transport Limited.
Wellington City Transport Limited.
Western Buses Limited.
Western Scottish Holdings Limited.
Western Travel Properties Limited.
Western Valleys Bus Company Limited.
Whites World Travel Limited.

Some of the companies listed above are currently dormant. Not included are the various pensions and ESOP companies owned by Stagecoach Holdings plc.

LAYING THE FOUNDATIONS

From its humble beginnings in March 1980 when its fleet comprised a solitary Ford Transit minibus, Stagecoach has grown to become an international company employing around 30,300 staff and operating more than 12,000 buses and coaches on four continents as well as over 1,000 trains. Now listed on the London Stock Exchange, Stagecoach has made a number of major advances in recent years and not least in the number of new vehicles it has purchased to ensure that its operations can maintain and improve the quality of service for passengers.

The roots of the company date back to 1976 when Ann Gloag and her husband, Robin, began a small self-drive motor caravan rental business under the title of Gloagtrotter from their home at 166 Glasgow Road, Perth. As the venture grew, it became necessary for Ann to give up her job as a theatre sister in the burns unit of a local hospital in order to be able to devote more time to their business and before the end of the decade, self-drive minibuses were also added to their 'fleet'. Seeking further expansion, Gloagtrotter turned its sights towards passenger vehicle operation in its own right and in March 1980 purchased a secondhand Deansgate-bodied Ford Transit minibus for use on private hire duties which were carried out under the title of GT Coaches. Soon after this diversification took place, Ann's brother, Brian Souter joined the partnership and, being an accountant by profession, his financial expertise soon began to make its mark on the fortunes of the embryo company. Although his knowledge of the public transport industry was minimal at that time, whilst undertaking his accountancy studies he had worked as a conductor for Central SMT during his holidays and thus he could claim to have at least some experience of passenger needs! Upon learning of a party who intended making an overland trip to China, GT Coaches purchased its first full-size vehicle to enable it to quote for this unusual journey. A former Bristol Omnibus Co. ECW-bodied 45-seat Bristol MW5G, this was acquired for the princely sum of £425 with the intention of reseating it with a set of secondhand coach seats, but in the event, the China trip never materialised and instead the bus, still in its original form and NBC green livery, was used on a contract gained to transport between Perth and Pitlochry workers who were employed on a big road-building scheme. As a result of this, the £425 purchase price was recouped within three weeks, thus starting the story of success which was to continue for the next sixteen years and hopefully beyond.

Where it all began. The original headquarters of Gloagtrotter and GT coaches at 166 Glasgow Road, Perth.

Filled with enthusiasm, GT Coaches further expanded its fleet in April 1980 with the purchase of a thirteen year-old dual purpose Alexander-bodied Leyland Leopard which had started life with North Western and had latterly been operated by National Travel West. This was given GT's new light blue and cream livery and fleetname and was immediately put to use on private hire and contract work. During the summer of that year, Ann and Brian's father Iain was made redundant from his job as a bus driver with Scottish Bus Group subsidiary Alexander Midland in Perth and, wishing to help his son and daughter to forge ahead in their new business, he placed his severance pay in their hands. This, together with their pooled savings and modest profits from their embryo company, enabled them to purchase two more secondhand coaches in September - a fourteen year-old 39-seat ECW-bodied Bristol MW6G and a five year-old 53-seat Duple-bodied Volvo B58. Whilst the former received GT Coaches livery and fleetname, the Volvo at first retained its former owner's colours. Meanwhile, the birth of the new 1980 Transport Act which allowed operators to run express services of over 30 miles in length without the need to gain the customary authorisation from the Traffic Commissioner, provided GT Coaches with the means to further expand its business. To this end, it was decided to adopt a new trading name and after considering various suggestions, that dreamed up by Ann and Brian's brother David was chosen and thus Stagecoach was born. Plans were quickly drawn up to operate an overnight service from Dundee to London via Glasgow and in preparation for this, a secondhand 57-seat Plaxton-bodied AEC Reliance was purchased, this and the Volvo B58 coach being put into a new livery of cream and red and lettered 'The Stage Coach Dundee Glasgow London'. The new service which commenced on 9 October 1980 ran southbound on Thursday, Friday, Saturday and Sunday nights, leaving Dundee at 8.20pm and arriving at St.Pancras Coach Station, London at 7.30am the following morning with the return journey being undertaken on Friday, Saturday, Sunday and Monday nights. The fare charged was £9.50 single from Dundee to London or £6.75 from Glasgow, this undercutting that charged by the Scottish Bus Group by £2. Despite neither coach being fitted with onboard toilet facilities, the service was nevertheless well patronised from the start and on 26 January 1981 a twice daily service was added from Aberdeen to Glasgow, one journey of which

GT Coaches blue & cream-liveried ex.National Travel West Alexander-bodied Leyland Leopard KJA261F collects its passengers in Glasgow in September 1981. (Andy Izatt)

Stagecoach's Executive Director Ann Gloag and Executive Chairman Brian Souter.

Although still painted in GT Coaches blue livery, ECW-bodied Bristol MW6G coach HDV639E had gained a small Stagecoach fleet name when photographed arriving in Blairgowrie on the stage carriage service from Spittalfield in August 1987. Still owned by Stagecoach, this vehicle is now in its preserved fleet. (Ian Train)

connected with the London coach at Dundee. At the same time, the London service was expanded to operate on five nights each week and a few weeks later, on 22 February, a new overnight service was inaugurated between Aberdeen and Newcastle-upon-Tyne. Running nightly except on Saturdays southbound and Fridays northbound, this in actuality only operated as far as Berwick-on-Tweed where it connected with a service from Berwick to Newcastle run by Craigs of Amble and in preparation for these new routes, a secondhand Plaxton-bodied Volvo B58 coach had been acquired in December. This was joined on 4 February 1981 by the first brand new coach to be purchased by the company, a 50-seat Duple Dominant III-bodied Volvo B10M, and being fitted with an onboard toilet this was immediately put to work on the London service where its additional facilities must have been a relief to those travelling over this long journey. In addition to being the first new vehicle to be purchased, the Volvo - FES831W - introduced a new livery which, designed by David Souter, was to become Stagecoach's standard scheme as still applied today. Primarily white, it had along its skirt a red, mustard and blue stripe which was angled upwards in a chevron at the rear while the Stagecoach name was added to each side and across the front.

In those early days, Stagecoach was regarded as something of a joke amongst larger operators, an inexperienced company running elderly vehicles on a shoestring and yet believing that it had a future. Many predicted that it would not last above a few months and would never be able to take on the might of the establishment. Indeed the full Scottish Bus Group board, besuited gentlemen of the 'old school', even turned out to laugh at the first departure from Waverley Bridge, Edinburgh to Aberdeen which was maintained by the 1966 Bristol MW6G, bemused by the sight of a young Brian Souter clutching a carrier bag containing his business papers and allegedly wearing red shoes. They may have laughed then, but were they still laughing ten years later?

Having gained much valuable experience through its London service, GT Coaches had also turned its attention to the local bus scene and on 22 December 1980 taken over A. & C. McLennan's stage carriage service from Perth to Errol. This at first was technically run on hire to McLennans until they surrendered their licence at the end of January 1981 and although no vehicles were involved in the deal, McLennan's Errol depot was taken over to provide an additional base for GT's growing operations. This diversification into local bus services brought the first double decker into the GT fleet when again in December 1980 a former Central SMT Bristol FLF6G Lodekka was purchased, although the Leyland Leopard and the Bristol MW6G coach were also frequently used when the need arose. Towards the end of the year, GT Coaches/Stagecoach obtained a new operating base at Friarton Road, Perth alongside the harbour and although this mainly comprised an open parking area, a small garage was also included which was able to be used for maintenance purposes. Above its door, an amusing board proclaimed that this was the Stagecoach Stables as well as the registered office!

Early in 1981 it was decided to discontinue the GT Coaches name in favour of Stagecoach, although the former remained visible on some of the company's vehicles for several more months and thus Stagecoach

Resting at Kings Cross coach station, London in November 1980 prior to its return journey to Scotland is Duple-bodied Volvo B58 LYS457P which wore a cream livery with deep red band and was lettered 'The Stage Coach Dundee Glasgow London'. (K.A.Jenkinson)

The first brand new coach to be purchased by Stagecoach was Duple Dominant III-bodied Volvo B58 FES831W which is seen here at Kings Cross coach station, London in 1982 ready to collect its Aberdeen-bound passengers. Rebuilt by Duple to Dominant I specification in 1987 it is now part of the company's preserved fleet. (T.W.W.Knowles)

had now truly arrived. Already regarded as an innovative company, it came as no great surprise when in April 1981 two convertible open-top Bristol FS6G Lodekkas were purchased for operation on a proposed new summertime Perth City Tour, although in the event its inauguration was temporarily deferred and instead the two buses were put to use, complete with their tops, on more mundane duties. A new service which did start, however was that from Aberdeen to Blackpool which ran at weekends throughout the summer providing a new link for the many Scottish holidaymakers who favoured this popular Lancashire resort. By now, the original Bristol MW5G had left the fleet to join a new owner and in its place, two more ex.Central SMT Bristol FLF6G Lodekkas were purchased in August 1981 for use on contract duties and the Perth - Errol service. These were often used additionally on the express service between Perth and Glasgow when loadings were high and on a few occasions even ventured as far as Aberdeen.

1982 heralded the start of a service in conjunction with Perth Tourist Association for the benefit of skiers during the winter months. Inaugurated on 9 January between Perth and the ski slopes at Glenshee and operating only when skiing conditions were favourable, a return fare of £2.50 was charged. Following this, Stagecoach suddenly found itself in a competitive situation when, on 1 April, Allander Coaches of Milngavie and Newtons of Dingwall began a joint service from Glasgow to Perth and Newton additionally started to operate between Perth and Edinburgh. This led Stagecoach to convert the licence for its Glasgow to Aberdeen service from express to limited stop stage carriage with picking up points being added at Cumbernauld, Stirling, Arbroath, Montrose and Stonehaven. Three daily journeys were operated in each direction and despite objections being laid before the Traffic Commissioner by Central, Tayside and Grampian Regional Councils, Alexander Northern, Alexander Midland and British Rail, the new licence was granted at the end of June. Not satisfied with the Commissioner's decision, however, the objectors immediately lodged an appeal with the Secretary of State for Transport, Tom King, and after lengthy deliberations he announced in September 1983 that he was allowing the appeal. As a result, Stagecoach had to revert its Glasgow to Aberdeen service to express operation, much to the disgust of its established passengers. Furious about this, the company decided not to let the matter rest there and challenged it in the Court of Session later in the year. Unfortunately, however, its brave challenge - which proved to be the first of many - failed and it had no option but to continue to maintain the service under express licence conditions.

Meanwhile, in the spring of 1982 Stagecoach decided to free itself of its origins to enable full concentration to be given to the development of its bus and coach activities. As a result it sold its Gloagtrotter motor caravan and minibus hire business and thus released much needed capital for its future plans. Requiring still more finance, however, to allow further expansion, Ann and Brian's uncle, Fraser McColl, the Scottish-born president of a large Canadian oil company, took a £16,000 (40%) stake in the Stagecoach business as well as acting as guarantor for two new luxurious Neoplan Skyliner double deck coaches, the first of which -

Peeping out from the doorway of Stagecoach's depot at Friarton Road, Perth is Duple Dominant III-bodied Volvo B58 JSR43X. Note the amusing board above the doorway which describes the premises as Stage Coach Stables. (Ian Train)

Still adorned with the original style of Stagecoach fleet name, Bristol FLF6G 084 (HGM334E) which had been owned by the company since August 1981 rests in the yard of Hobden Street depot, Glasgow in March 1990 only four months before it was withdrawn from service. (K.A.Jenkinson)

The first Neoplan Skyliner to join the Stagecoach fleet was LSP222X which made its debut in May 1982. Seen soon afterwards, it was re-registered 4009SC in 1983 and LES295X two years later, prior to its sale in September 1985 to Yelloway of Rochdale.

- LSP222X - was delivered on 27 April. After quickly settling down on the London service, these two coaches were used to launch a new operation between Aberdeen and London which commenced on 1 July under the title of 'Superstage'. Running on Thursday, Friday, Saturday and Sunday nights southbound and returning overnight on Friday, Saturday, Saturday, Sunday and Monday, instead of travelling via Glasgow, this new service operated via Birmingham and an onboard meal was included in the £15 single (£26 return) fare. Despite the introduction of Superstage, the original service between Aberdeen and London continued to flourish with extra journeys being added between Aberdeen, Perth and Glasgow, each of which was well patronised. The infamous rail strike of July 1982 came as a shot in the arm for Stagecoach who soon found that the demand for its services greatly exceeded its fleet and in order to maximise its enviable position, it hired a number of vehicles, complete with drivers, from A. & C. McLennan of Spittalfield particularly for operation between Perth and Edinburgh. Meanwhile, on 3 May local operator McDonalds Coaches of Perth had begun a new schooldays service from Perth to Auchterarder on behalf of Tayside Regional Council, and after a few months this was taken over by Stagecoach, thus strengthening its own growing number of contracts around Tayside. Stagecoach now held licences for the operation of 14 vehicles and as 1982 progressed, plans for further expansion were implemented. Amongst these was an additional return working between Perth and Edinburgh which commenced on 1 November and several 'shorts' running daily between Aberdeen, Perth and Glasgow and pending the arrival of more vehicles, a Plaxton-bodied Ford R1114 coach was borrowed from a dealer and a Marshall-rebodied Daimler Fleetline single decker was hired from Tayside Regional Transport during December 1982/January 1983. Following the experience gained with its two Neoplan Skyliner double deckers, a further pair were purchased new in December 1982 to add to a pair of Bristol FLF6G Lodekkas acquired in the spring, followed in August by a secondhand ECW-bodied Bristol VRLLH double deck coach. The latter proved problematic from the start, however, and few tears were shed when it departed in February 1983 to eventually find its

An extract from the summer 1982 timetable leaflet.

THE STAGECOACH STORY

People often ask - who really is the Stagecoach Company? Well, we thought that we would take this chance to tell everyone -

"STAGECOACH IS A FAMILY BUSINESS"

But most companies say that! However the beginnings of Stagecoach are to be blamed on Iain Souter who was a Perth based bus driver for many years with W Alexander & Son - well he didn't exactly start it, but he had children and they in turn wanted to be bus drivers "just like daddy". Years later their childhood ambitions were to be realised proving that diesel still pumped through their veins.

In October 1980, the Government changed the laws about public transport breaking the monopoly that the National Bus Group had enjoyed for so long and the first Stagecoach rolled from Dundee to London. We started with two five year-old coaches and a lot of faith - now in under two years we run a fleet of sixteen vehicles and are launching a Superstage Service using two neoplan double decker luxury coaches never used before in this country. These provide videos, hot meals, kitchen and toilet facilities and raise the standard of coach travel to a new level. All of this has happened because we believe that people needed cheap rapid transport with a personal touch and you, the public, agreed and travelled with us.

So now to meet the people involved in running a STAGECOACH OUTFIT. First there's Brian THE SHERIFF who should keep the peace but sometimes causes a riot between being accountant, traffic manager and general fac totem (that's Indian language), there's sister Ann who runs THE BUNKHOUSE, at least she says it often feels like that, whilst managing the office and everyone else at the same time. Brother-in-law Robin keeps THE LIVERY STABLES going, making sure that the horses are fit and rarin' to go. David, the RANCH FOREMAN actually has two real calves on his farmstead but handles the publicity. The important thing is that we all have one job in common and that is driving the buses - we started that way and mean to go on that way.

Granny and Paw (remember him - its all his fault) provide THE VICTUALS, an ever-growing mountain of rolls, snacks and supplies required daily by the passengers. As the work grew we had to hire in more RANCH HANDS each one a character in his own right, but, at the wheel, a professional driver. Behind the scenes there is a loyal little group of office staff, mechanics and cleaners who keep it all going - so that's THE STAGECOACH FAMILY.

Now do you believe that we really are a family business?

way to the USA. Also leaving the company in December 1983 following the breakdown of his marriage was Robin Gloag, one of the founders of Gloagtrotter, GT Coaches and Stagecoach. Taking with him a Plaxton-bodied Volvo B58 coach and a car, he set up a new company under the title of Highwayman Coaches from an office within Stagecoach's Friarton Road premises which he used as his headquarters until the summer of 1984 when he moved to Errol.

Spreading its wings yet further, Stagecoach reached Inverness on 17 March 1983 when it began operation of a new daily service between that Highland town and Glasgow via Perth and a new overnight service from Inverness to London via Perth and Birmingham. The journey time on this new long route was 13 hours 15 minutes and as the Birmingham to London section was timed to coincide with the Aberdeen - London service, on occasions when passenger loadings were light, passengers were transferred onto one coach at Birmingham, thus enabling mileage to be saved. At this same time, a new service was started from Inverness to Edinburgh which was timed to replicate the Perth to Edinburgh part of the service from Aberdeen. In a similar fashion to the London services, this allowed passengers to be transferred to one Edinburgh-bound coach at Perth when there was insufficient demand to warrant two vehicles running through. To further boost its income, Stagecoach entered into an agreement with Coachfreight Ltd., a company which had previously exclusively used National Express to carry parcels on its services between London and Scotland. During the spring, the company moved its registered office and booking facilities from Friarton Road to new accommodation in Brian Souter's house at 24 Marshall Place, Perth, closer to the city centre and soon afterwards began the operation of a Perth City Sightseeing Tour in conjunction with the Tay Queen pleasure boat which it had originally planned to start the previous year. Widening its interests in the leisure market, on 22 June 1983 it introduced a number of day tours under its new 'Fantasia Tours' banner from Crieff, Perth and Dundee to places such as the Trossachs and Loch Lomond. On some of these, a Neoplan Skyliner or one of the three Van Hool Astromega double deck coaches which had been purchased new in March was used and, to add a further touch of finesse, lunch and tea were included in the price and served onboard!

Later in 1983, on 29 August, yet another new Stagecoach service was launched, this being an inter-city express operation between Waverley Bridge, Edinburgh and Park's City coach station, Glasgow. With 12 journeys per day in each direction on Mondays to Saturdays and 12 journeys on Sundays, the scheduled running time between the two cities was 1 hour, although in reality this was often longer due to heavy traffic on the fringe of Edinburgh. A single fare of £1.30 was charged and for an extra 40p, passengers could enjoy a continental breakfast onboard their coach and on Friday, Saturday and Sunday nights an additional journey was operated at 12.20am from Glasgow which returned from Edinburgh at 1.20am. The regular performers on this service were the Van Hool Astromegas or Neoplan Skyliners which were better quality vehicles than those provided by the Scottish Bus Group on its competing X14 service on which the fares were quickly reduced to £1.25 in order to undercut Stagecoach. A similar fares war developed on the Inverness corridor through which the company operated in competition with the Scottish Bus Group, Allander of Milngavie and Newton of Dingwall. This resulted in Stagecoach offering the journey for £5 in order to undercut its rivals and such was its success that pending the arrival of further additions to its own fleet it was found necessary for a few weeks in March to hire coaches from Rapsons of Brora to cope with the increasing numbers of passengers. Seeking an operating base in the Glasgow area from which it could maintain its new inter-city service to Edinburgh, Stagecoach took the lease on a small, but modern workshop/depot at North Canal Bank Street, Port Dundas close to the city centre. This included a spacious open-air parking area and later in the decade was destined to play a further role in the company's development in western Scotland. Later in 1983, Stagecoach began a search for a suitable site in Perth on which it could build a new coach terminal and in November acquired premises between Murray Street and Foundry Lane for this purpose. Soon after planning permission had been granted for the proposed new terminal, however, it was learned that after the new Transport Act took effect Stagecoach would be able to use the Scottish Bus Group bus station in the city and as a consequence the new site was resold during the summer of 1985 before any construction work had begun.

Meanwhile, it was announced on 11 November 1983 that the business of Adamson & Low (Adamson Coaches) of Edinburgh had been purchased. Included in the deal was Adamson's 17 coaches, its depot and its private hire and contract operations, many of the latter being schools workings in the South Queensferry area. During the next few months most of Adamson's predominantly Ford coaches were replaced by newly-acquired secondhand vehicles or some transferred from the Stagecoach fleet and although these were licensed separately under the Adamson name, rather than being repainted into that company's maroon and white colours they were given Stagecoach livery and fleet names to enable them to be transferred between Edinburgh, Perth, Errol

Passengers could be excused for being confused as to the ownership of Plaxton Supreme-bodied Volvo B58 9039RU which, painted in Stagecoach livery carried its own fleet name on its side panels, Adamson in its below windscreen destination aperture and the name of its previous owner, Hunter's in its roof dome panel. It is seen here leaving Adamson & Low's Stenhouse Mill depot in March 1984. (P.McElroy)

and Glasgow whenever the need arose. Not content with the purchase of Adamson & Low, Stagecoach at the end of November took over the operation of Park of Hamilton's Glasgow to London service, although on this occasion no vehicles were involved in the deal and instead, Park continued to provide the coaches, fitting them with removable Stagecoach name panels. A few days earlier, on 18 November, Cotters of Glasgow had extended its Coachline network northwards with a twice-daily and once-nightly service from Aberdeen to London which competed directly with that operated by Stagecoach, but as its fares were slightly higher than those charged by the Perth-based company, the latter suffered little or no abstraction of passengers.

Although 1983 had now almost ended, Stagecoach continued to roll onwards in its continuing quest for expansion and in December purchased the Ardrossan to Glasgow service of Bennett, Kilwinning along with two of that company's Leyland Leopard coaches. This gave Stagecoach its first foothold in Ayrshire, although it was eleven more years before it developed this further. Looking ahead in preparation for a possible increase in its leisure activities, on 29 December a new company was incorporated under the title of Stage-Coach Holidays Ltd., although in the event expansion in the tourist market was never pursued.

By the end of 1983 the fleet total had grown to 61 vehicles of which 47 had been added since the start of the year (including 6 Neoplan Skyliners), 17 being new and the remainder secondhand. In addition to these, several coaches were hired for short periods during the busy summer season from Greyhound of Arbroath while a Duple-bodied and 2 Caetano-bodied Volvos were hired for several months from Whytes of Newmacher and repainted into full Stagecoach livery complete with fleet

Seen at Park's City coach station, Glasgow shortly before joining the Stagecoach fleet is Bennett of Kilwinning's blue-liveried Duple-bodied Leyland Leopard PCS861X. (W.McGregor)

Painted in Stagecoach corporate livery but without fleet names, Adamson & Low's Duple-bodied Volvo B10M A272GJU is seen at Park's City coach station, Glasgow in April 1984 whilst working the Glasgow - Edinburgh shuttle service. Note the array of Stagecoach posters on their office in the background. (P.McElroy)

Park of Hamilton's Van Hool Astromega OAA357 is pictured fitted with a detachable Stagecoach name board on its upper deck side panels whilst on loan to the company in the spring of 1984 for use on the Glasgow - London service acquired from Park in November of the previous year. (Coachmart & Bus Operator)

names. During the autumn, the company purchased three 'cherished' registration numbers - 4009SC, 5142SC and 8000SC - which it placed on a trio of its Neoplan Skyliners and in 1984 it acquired a further six 'SC' numbers - 2345, 4040, 4585, 5889, 7376 and 9492. On the debit side, Stagecoach lost one of its Bristol Lodekkas when former Eastern National AEV812F was destroyed by fire in November.

After the events of 1983, the following year proved to be comparatively uneventful with Stagecoach concentrating on consolidating its position as a major Scottish independent operator. This did not mean, however, that the company was prepared to stand still and whenever an opportunity presented itself it was firmly grasped as another stepping stone towards the future. Stagecoach's service network continued throughout 1984 with few changes except for passenger loadings which grew continually, particularly on its Anglo-Scottish routes. Following its earlier court battle concerning its Glasgow - Aberdeen service, another lengthy conflict loomed on the horizon when it applied for a licence to operate a stage carriage service between Edinburgh and Inverness. Following opposition from several Scottish Bus Group subsidiaries and Fife and Lothian Regional Councils, it appeared as if Stagecoach was heading towards another drawn-out confrontation, but before the application came before the Traffic Commissioner, behind the scenes discussions resolved the situation and after the company agreed certain restrictions, the objections were withdrawn and the service was able to commence in September. Two months later, a new competitor, Tay Valley Coaches began new services from Aberdeen to Glasgow and Edinburgh, marketing these under the title 'Autobus Express', but as the fares charged on both were higher than those of Stagecoach, passengers voted with their wallets and the company's loadings continued to be maintained at their established level. Perhaps the most notable event of 1984, however, was the transfer of the fleet and headquarters of Stagecoach from Friarton Road and Marshall Place to magnificent premises at Walnut Grove on the outskirts of Perth where spacious office accommodation was set alongside a well-equipped workshop and large outdoor parking area. Following the sale of the Friarton Road base in August, the fleet and garage equipment were moved to their new base on 1 September while the transfer of the head office was undertaken on 12 November. During the intervening period the former McLennan nissen hut depot at Errol was also vacated, although it survived unoccupied until September 1987 when it was finally demolished to make way for a new housing development. The fleet changes taking place during the year were fewer than those of 1983 with only four new coaches - all Neoplan Skyliners - being purchased together with two secondhand examples from Trathens (one of which sadly was burnt out on the M6 motorway four months later while undertaking an Anglo-Scottish journey) and half a dozen Bristol Lodekkas, these replacing the three Van Hool Astromega double deck coaches which had proved to be rather unsuccessful and a couple of older Lodekkas. For the company's Adamson & Low subsidiary, however, the story was somewhat different as the need to quickly replace the coaches inherited with its purchase caused the acquisition of a pair of Leyland PD3A double deckers which had started life with Leicester City Transport, three coaches and two single deck buses along with several vehicles transferred from Perth. In the meantime, even though Robin Gloag was now regarded as a competitor since he had started operations under the Highwayman name, when his business experienced some temporary financial difficulties in April 1984, Stagecoach offered him a hand of friendship by repurchasing the Volvo coach that he had taken with him when he left the company allowing him to continue to use it until such time as his problems were resolved. After returning to a position of stability three months later, he bought the coach back and was thus able to continue his business as before from his base at Errol.

Hired from Whyte of Newmachar, Caetano-bodied Volvo B58 WCO733V was painted into Stagecoach livery for the duration of its twelve month sojourn with the company. It is seen here in 1985 leaving Glasgow at the start of its journey to Aberdeen. (P.McElroy)

Stagecoach's headquarters and depot at Walnut Grove, Perth. (K.A.Jenkinson)

In contrast to the previous year, 1985 proved to be one of many changes as far as Stagecoach was concerned. One of the most significant developments was the arrival in Perth during January of five former London Transport Routemasters, the first of this type of double decker to be purchased by an operator north of the border or indeed, outside the capital except for Northern General. Initially, all were placed in store at Walnut Grove and it was not until March that the first made its debut in revenue-earning service. Still wearing its London red livery, it looked somewhat out of place on the rural roads traversed by the Perth to Errol service but soon proved popular with passengers and crews alike who found it to be a comfortable and reliable vehicle. By the time that the other four entered service in May/June, a further five buses of this type had been bought and their arrival allowed the release of a number of Bristol Lodekkas which were quickly despatched to Edinburgh for use on Adamson & Low's various contract operations.

The first ex.London Transport Routemasters purchased by Stagecoach in 1985 were put into service in the Perth area still wearing their former owner's red livery. 847DYE speeds through snow-covered countryside towards Errol whilst working an early evening journey on the service from Perth in March 1985. (Ian Train)

Following tentative enquiries made as long ago as May 1983 to the Traffic Commissioners for permission to pick up and set down passengers at the various motorway service areas south of the border on its Anglo-Scottish express services, Stagecoach gained the necessary authorisation from all the relevant service area operators except those controlling Watford Gap and Rothersthorpe on the M1 and appeared thus set to break new ground in the field of long distance coaching. The Department of Transport thought differently, however, and upon refusing permission and quoting from the Highways Act, informed Stagecoach that in its opinion it was not in order for motorway service areas to be used as 'bus stops'. Having already successfully used the Harthill service area between Glasgow and Edinburgh on the M8 motorway for some considerable time on its service between those two cities, Stagecoach decided to 'test the water' in March 1985 by lodging a formal application with the Metropolitan Traffic Commissioner for pick up and set down facilities at Scratchwood services on the M1. Despite there being no objectors and Brian Souter presenting an excellent case at a public sitting to consider this matter, the application was refused and the company's innovative plan thus never materialised. Despite this setback, Stagecoach still persued its objective of gaining more than 25% of the lucrative Scotland-England express market which it remained confident of achieving in the fullness of time. In the meantime, however, following increased competition from the Scottish Bus Group and British Rail, the express service between Glasgow and Edinburgh had been discontinued from 10 March and as a consequence the depot at Port Dundas was closed. Obviously with future plans in mind, the company decided to retain the lease on this property which was to remain unoccupied for more than a year. Towards the end of that same month, a contract arrangement was reached with Crawford of Neilston for that company to take over the day to day operation of the Glasgow to Ardrossan service which Stagecoach had gained with its purchase of part of the business of Bennett of Kilwinning. Under the terms of the agreement, Crawfords were to provide the vehicles and crews while the revenue was to be shared between the two companies. In a converse move, Stagecoach gained a further foothold in the Dundee area when it took over the licence for a service between Dundee and Errol from Tayside Regional Council.

After a period of rapid expansion, Stagecoach decided to further consolidate its operations and placed its Edinburgh-based Adamson & Low subsidiary into voluntary liquidation in May. Surprisingly, this was repurchased together with 3 coaches by G. Adamson, one of the company's original owners, the remainder of the fleet being transferred back to Stagecoach at Perth. Despite having withdrawn from several operations during the early part of the year, on 1 June Stagecoach took over the control of Park's City Coach Station in Glasgow from Park of Hamilton, but as the Perth-based company had already been staffing the terminal for around a year, there was no visible sign of change and the station continued to function in exactly the same way that it had done previously.

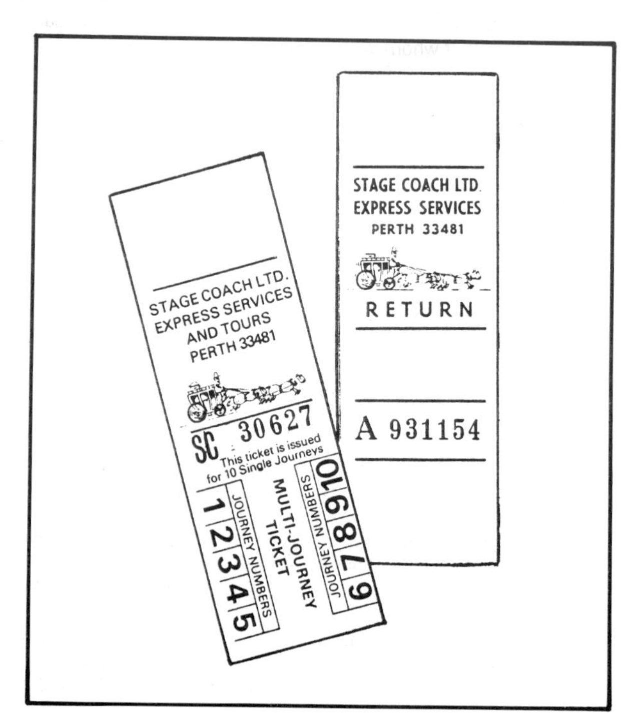

NEW HORIZONS

Following a period of comparative calm and some retrenchment, Stagecoach suddenly expanded again on 7 November when it purchased the whole of the assets and operations of A. & C. McLennan of Spittalfield, a company which had served the communities of rural Perthshire for more than forty years. In addition to giving Stagecoach another operating base and a large number of stage carriage and contract services, it provided a further 26 buses and coaches of which 9 were double deckers. Although Stagecoach would have preferred to retain the McLennan name and livery for its recently acquired business, the trustees of the late Alexander McLennan requested that this should be discontinued within eighteen months. In the event, due to their advancing years none of the inherited fleet was ever repainted into Stagecoach colours, instead being progressively withdrawn with the last example being removed from service in July 1987. Surprisingly, amongst the first to go were the 9 double deckers (1 Daimler CCG5 and 8 Fleetlines) which within a few weeks of their acquisition were replaced by Bristol Lodekkas transferred from Perth while all the inherited services and contracts continued to operate on McLennan discs until April 1986 when they were officially reassigned to Stagecoach.

As a consequence of an incident which had occurred on 7 July 1985, Stagecoach was summoned before Perth Sheriff's Court in March 1986 accused of causing danger through the overloading of one of its vehicles. The charge arose after one of the company's Neoplan Skyliner double deckers operating on the service from Dundee to Perth was stopped before reaching its destination and found to be carrying 97 passengers, 10 of whom were standing in the lower saloon, 5 sitting on the stairs and a further 5 standing upstairs. This, it was stated resulted from there being too many passengers able to be legally accommodated on the two single deckers and one double decker allocated to this particular evening journey and the fact that the relief single decker called for to take the overspill breaking down at Longforgan on its way to Dundee from Perth. Rather than leave any passengers behind, the conductress in charge, perhaps foolishly, opted to take them onboard the Skyliner, thus causing its overloading. After an adjournment to 20 May due to various technicalities of the case, and despite Neoplan forwarding a telex to the court showing that the stability of the coach would not have been affected by the extra passengers, Stagecoach ultimately pleaded guilty to the charge laid against it and was fined £500.

Although still wearing the dark blue & white livery of its former owner, A & C McLennan whose name it still carries below its windscreens, Duple-bodied Bedford YLQ AGG934S had gained a Stagecoach name on its front roof dome when photographed at Spittalfield depot in March 1987. (P.McElroy)

Caught in the act, Brian Souter removes two traffic cones preventing the progress of Magicbus Routemaster WLT504 as it attempts to reach the St.Enoch Square, Glasgow stance of route 20 to Castlemilk to take up the inaugural journey on 26 October 1986. (P.McElroy)

With the deregulation of local bus services looming on the horizon as a consequence of the new 1985 Transport Act, Stagecoach, like most operators throughout Britain, began to look at ways in which it could use the new legislation to its advantage. The ability to be able to operate local services without their applications being able to be blocked by other operators led the company to register three routes in Glasgow, Scotland's largest city and for this purpose it formed a new company under the title of Magicbus (Scotland) Ltd. Although it was incorporated on 10 February 1986 with its registered office at 1 Canal Bank Street, Glasgow, it did not become operational until 26 October (D-day) upon the commencement of services 18 from Glasgow to East Kilbride, 19 Glasgow to Easterhouse and 20 Glasgow to Castlemilk. Unusually, the Easterhouse route was operated on an express basis via the M8 motorway and to maintain these new services the depot at Port Dundas was reopened. Magicbus began its operations with 21 vehicles transferred from Perth comprising 14 Routemasters (including two ex.Northern General front entrance examples), 2 Bristol Lodekkas and 5 Volvo B58 coaches, all of which were painted in standard Stagecoach colours with Magicbus fleetnames. Additionally two schools contracts were gained from Strathclyde PTE in Cumbernauld and Dumbarton, taking the company's vehicles into yet more new areas. Although it had been intended to start the new Castlemilk service from St.Enoch Square bus station, the first bus to operate on service 20 was prevented from gaining access to the terminal by a row of traffic cones and a posse of Strathclyde Buses inspectors and instead it had to pick up in nearby Dixon Street. Determined not to be thwarted by the major operator, a megaphone was used - by Brian Souter - to attract Strathclyde Buses' passengers to the new service, a measure which proved highly successful. On the following day when the East Kilbride and Easterhouse services commenced operation from Buchanan Bus Station a different ploy was used to bring awareness of the new company and routes with a 'magic bunny' dispensing pens, beakers and appropriately coloured Magicbus-lettered rock to passengers. The 18 and 19 were not the first Stagecoach services to use Buchanan Bus Station, however, as on the previous day the company's long distance coach services were transferred to the terminal upon the closure of the nearby Park's City coach station. At this same time, as a consequence

A very dirty SCS361M still in the livery of its previous owner, Boyden of Castle Donnington, prepares to leave Buchanan bus station, Glasgow on the Magicbus service to Easterhouse on 12 December 1986. As can be seen, in addition to having gained a Magicbus fleet name below its windscreens, it carries the legend 'Hire a Budget Bus' in its front destination screen. (P.McElroy)

of deregulation, Crawford of Neilston registered the service from Glasgow to Ardrossan in its own name and thus its franchise agreement with Stagecoach was discontinued.

Prior to the implementation of deregulation, Stagecoach on 15 August began what was believed to be the first ever night service in Perth, this running on Saturday night/Sunday morning between midnight and 3.0am and serving Letham, Tulloch and North Muirton and normally maintained by a Bristol Lodekka. Three days later, Stagecoach took over the operation of the Perth - Pitlochry and Pitlochry - Aberfeldy services previously run by Scottish Bus Group subsidiary Strathtay Scottish who had not registered them to continue after 26 October and following an agreement reached with the latter, the Stagecoach vehicles employed on these two services were technically operated on hire to Strathtay Scottish until D day. Earlier in the year on 5 May, Bennett of Kilwinning cheekily began a new service between Saltcoats and Glasgow via Ardrossan over the route it had sold to Stagecoach in December 1983 and which had latterly been operated under franchise to Crawford of Neilston. However, competing also with A1 Service and Scottish Citylink, Bennett's new venture survived only a week or so before being withdrawn, allowing the status quo to be restored. Meanwhile, Stagecoach's express service network was expanded with the addition of a new weekend daytime service from Inverness to Manchester and on 4 September another new company was set up under the title of Stage-Coach (Holdings) Ltd.

Approaching its terminal at St.Enoch Square, Glasgow at the end of its journey from Castlemilk. Magicbus Routemaster 628DYE carries a poster alongside its front destination screen to promote cheap fares for UB40 holders. (K.A.Jenkinson)

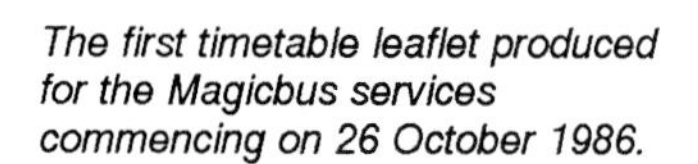
The first timetable leaflet produced for the Magicbus services commencing on 26 October 1986.

MAGICBUS

TIMETABLE

FROM 26th OCTOBER, 1986

FOR BUSY SPELLS
AND QUIET SPELLS
MAGICBUS SPELLS VALUE!

PHONE:
041 - 332 - 4100
FOR ENQUIRIES & MORE TIMETABLES
FOR YOUR FRIENDS & NEIGHBOURS.
Picks up from Strathclyde Bus Stops.

Leaving Buchanan bus station, Glasgow in March 1987 is ex. Northern General front entrance Routemaster RCN695 which wore its former owner's livery and fleet names throughout its brief life north of the border. (Campbell Morrison collection)

EXPANSION OUTSIDE SCOTLAND

Another aspect of the 1985 Transport Act was the sale to the private sector of all the National Bus Company subsidiaries and ultimately the Scottish Bus Group and seeing this as a means of expanding, Stagecoach set its sights on acquiring one NBC company and, as soon as it was placed on the market, the whole of the SBG. A start was immediately made towards achieving this goal when it submitted a bid for City of Oxford Motor Services, although this unfortunately proved unsuccessful and the company was sold to its management. Undeterred by the failure of its first attempt, Stagecoach on 26 November 1986 formed a new company under the title of Skipburn Ltd. the directors of which were Ann Gloag, Brian Souter, and their uncle Fraser McColl who were later joined by Dawson Williams who was general manager of Hampshire Bus. Not unexpectedly, Skipburn immediately lodged a bid in respect of Hampshire Bus and its associated Pilgrim Coaches and in February received the news that this had tentatively been accepted. Thus, on 2 April 1987 Stagecoach, through its Skipburn company, gained its first former NBC subsidiary and its first foothold in England, increasing its combined fleet by 216 vehicles in the process. At the time of its privatisation, Hampshire Bus operated a mixed fleet which included Ford Transit and Iveco minibuses, Leyland National, Leopard and Tiger and Bristol LH single deckers and Bristol VRT and Leyland Olympian double deckers together with a number of Daimler Fleetlines which had been acquired from London Transport, and maintained depots at Andover, Basingstoke, Eastleigh, Southampton and Winchester. Its livery was equally mixed with some vehicles still retaining their old NBC poppy red colours and others wearing the newer red, blue and white scheme. Under its new ownership, it was expected that various changes would soon be made and the first of these took place on 26 April when Pilgrim Coaches ceased trading and its coaches were transferred to Hampshire Bus. Almost before the dust had settled, the company's premises at Grosvenor Square and Bedford Place, Southampton and its bus station in the city were sold for redevelopment, although agreement was reached for the continued use of its depots for nine months in order to allow time for their relocation.

Pictured at Basingstoke still wearing its Hampshire Bus red, blue & white livery is ECW-bodied Bristol VRT 3370 (RPR716R). (Travelscene)

Seen in Cheltenham whilst operating a school tour is Pilgrim Coaches Plaxton-bodied Leyland Leopard UBW788. (C.F.Martin)

Back across the border, following intense competition from the established operators paralleling Magicbus service 18 to East Kilbride, this was withdrawn on 24 January, the buses released then being used to double the frequency on the more successful service to Easterhouse. Unfortunately, during February one of Magicbus's Bristol Lodekkas on its way to take up a schools contract suffered extensive damage when it fell from a flyover at Cumbernauld. Luckily no passengers were onboard at the time and the driver escaped without serious injury. Across country in eastern Scotland, two new services were inaugurated on 23 March running from Perth to Newburgh and Pitlochry to Blair Atholl and as a result of the former, SBG subsidiary Fife Scottish reduced its fares on its established route between these two points in an attempt to stave off the new competition. A week later on 30 March, Stagecoach found itself involved in a battle with Highwayman Coaches who began to operate journeys timed a few minutes ahead of the joint Stagecoach/Strathtay Scottish service between Perth and Errol. This led to a fares war breaking out at the beginning of April between Stagecoach and Highwayman with each continually undercutting the other and within a couple of weeks Stagecoach was offering free travel on its service. Unable to compete at this level, Highwayman conceded defeat and withdrew its service.

In the meantime, the need by Hampshire Bus for additional double deckers led Stagecoach in March/April to purchase 10 Van Hool-McArdle bodied Ailsa Volvos from South Yorkshire PTE, these travelling northwards to Perth or Glasgow for attention before being delivered to their new owner on the south coast. All but one, which was destined to be used for spares, were placed in service on conductor-operated routes 18 and 19 in Southampton on 26 July and whilst most had by that time been repainted into Hampshire Bus red, blue and white livery, a couple still retained their former owner's cream & light tan livery and one even carried Magicbus legal lettering, a sign that it had perhaps originally been considered for use in Glasgow! Following the Ailsa Volvos came 12 ex.London Routemasters, all but one of which were despatched to Hampshire Bus at Eastleigh, the other joining the Magicbus fleet in Glasgow. This was required as a replacement for one of the ex.Northern General front entrance Routemasters which had been destroyed by fire at Hamilton whilst travelling to take up a schools contract. Surprisingly, the Routemasters sent to Eastleigh, despite being repainted into Stagecoach corporate colours, were immediately placed in store and were never operated by the southern-based company. Prior to the

Plaxton-bodied Volvo B58 LUB508P, the coach Robin Gloag took with him as part of his settlement when he left Stagecoach in 1983 is seen here in his Highwayman Coaches ivory & orange livery. (Campbell Morrison)

Resting in Carlisle bus station in September 1987, Cumberland ECW-bodied Leyland Atlantean 1483 (TRN483V) still wore NBC poppy red livery, double-N logos and Carlislebus fleet names and passenger information telephone number. (T.W.W.Knowles)

Parked in the yard of Port Dundas depot at Glasgow in April 1987 are two of Magicbus's front entrance Routemasters - ex.British Airways NMY643E and former Northern General FPT590C. As can be seen, NMY634E has yet to receive a front destination box. (S.A.Jenkinson)

above taking place, Stagecoach (Holdings) Limited acquired the McColl family interests in Skipburn in July 1987 followed by those of Dawson Williams in December.

Right from the start, Stagecoach had regarded pricing as a key part of its strategy and whilst many operators increased fares, often well above inflation, the Perth-based company preferred to keep its fares down by cutting its costs. Its belief was that offering a better service at a cheaper price ultimately led to an increased share of the market and that stability in the market promoted growth in both the short and long term. Stagecoach described the bus industry in 1980 as one that was in general decline 'characterised by increased bus miles, declining patronage, rising costs per passenger and general inadequate profitability'. Seeking to stop this slow decay, it introduced measures which controlled costs, improved standards and began to encourage people back to public transport and by applying its own ideas and rigidly sticking to them it proved that the decline could ultimately be reversed.

Seeking further expansion in England, Stagecoach (Holdings) Limited purchased its second NBC subsidiary on 22 July, this being Cumberland Motor Services who operated from depots at Carlisle, Keswick, Maryport, Millom, Whitehaven, Wigton and Workington. This, it was claimed, made Stagecoach the largest independent bus operator in Western Europe with 560 vehicles, 1,400 staff and a group turnover in excess of £24 million. Almost immediately, Cumberland's new owner undertook a review of Carlisle's operations and began planning a number of changes including a reduction in the city's minibus fleet, an increase in the frequency of a number of local services and the reintroduction of crew operation. Amongst the first priorities, however, was to eliminate the Bristol RELL as soon as possible and within a week of taking control, Cumberland's vehicles of this type had been reduced by half, the remainder being withdrawn at the end of August. Although Cumberland's livery was in the process of being changed from NBC poppy red to Ayres red and sandstone when the company was privatised, the Bristol RELLs retained the NBC leaf green colours in which they had been received from Bristol Omnibus Co. and were confined to internal services within the Sellafield nuclear power station complex. Also leaving the Cumberland fleet in September were 17 of the full-height ECW-bodied Bristol VRTs which migrated to Hampshire Bus in exchange for its 10 ex.London Daimler Fleetlines and 4 of its Ailsa Volvos which were all put to work on Carlisle city services.

Magicbus, after successfully tendering for the Strathclyde PTE supported evening service between Bridgeton Cross and Castlemilk, took over this operation in August and later, on 2 November following

One of eight Routemasters acquired by Cumberland in 1987 for operation on Carlisle city services, 906 (WLT875) passing through the city's pedestrianised area had previously been part of the troubled Kelvin Scottish fleet since leaving its native London. Looking immaculate in its Ayres red & sandstone livery, this bus along with its sisters is still owned by Cumberland, albeit no longer in service although, now painted in Stagecoach corporate livery it was removed from storage in 1996 and despatched to Busways at Newcastle for occasional use. (K.A.Jenkinson)

Still painted in the red, blue & white livery of Hampshire Bus, ex.London Daimler Fleetline 1917 (OUC39R) is seen in Carlisle city centre on 26 October 1987 after joining the Cumberland fleet. Following it are one of Cumberland's Mercedes Benz L608D minibuses and an ECW-bodied Leyland Atlantean. (K.A.Jenkinson)

Acquired with the express services of Cotters Coachline, Glasgow were seven Van Hool-bodied Volvo B10Ms which were placed under the control of Magicbus but retained their original orange & white livery as illustrated by TGD767W. (M.J.Turner)

Kelvin Scottish's retrenchment in the Glasgow area, revamped its Easterhouse service to run cross-city to Milton on a ten minute frequency. A week later, Magicbus started another new service from St.Enoch Square to Castlemilk via Victoria Road, this competing with both Strathclyde Buses and Central Scottish and marking the start of yet another new bus war. To meet its increased vehicle requirement, Magicbus gained a further 20 Routemasters, 9 of which came from Hampshire Bus and the remainder direct from London Transport. Joining these were two of the ex.South Yorkshire Ailsa Volvos which had previously been used by Cumberland at Carlisle but unlike the Routemasters which had all been painted in Stagecoach/Magicbus livery, these retained their Hampshire Bus colours to which Magicbus fleetnames were applied.

Meanwhile, on 3 October Hampshire Bus sold its Southampton operations and 82 vehicles to Musterphantom Ltd., part of the Southern Vectis group, who traded as Solent Blue Line. This represented a loss of around 40% of the Hampshire Bus fleet and left only 117 operational vehicles with the company. As one door closed, another one opened, however, and on 12 October Stagecoach surprisingly purchased Glasgow-based Cotter's Coachline express services together with 8 Van Hool-bodied Volvo B10M coaches and that company's spacious garage at Warroch Street, Glasgow. Cotter's tours business was not included in the deal, this being purchased along with its Watsons of Dundee subsidiary by Wallace Arnold Tours two days later when Cotter's called in the receiver. This new acquisition gave Stagecoach two additional daily and two more nightly services in each direction between Glasgow and London and although placed under Magicbus control, these continued to be operated under the Cotter's banner, the Volvo coaches retaining their former owner's orange and cream livery and fleetnames. With the Warroch Street depot being more spacious than the Magicbus premises at North Canal Bank Street, the latter was vacated before the end of October and its fleet transferred to the former Cotter's base.

The promised revisions to Cumberland's Carlisle services were implemented on 26 October when several of the city's local services were reorganised and crew operation was reintroduced with the arrival of 8 Routemasters, 2 of which came from Hampshire Bus, the remaining 6 from Kelvin Scottish. Painted in their new owner's Ayres red and sandstone livery, these immediately proved popular with passengers and crews alike and were to remain part of the Carlisle scene for over three years. A modest reduction in fares levels was also introduced at the same time, partly in answer to local criticism and partly to offset competition from local independent Palmer.

After failing in its bid to gain a third NBC subsidiary following several unsuccessful bids, Stagecoach (Holdings) Limited ultimately achieved its goal on 18 November when it acquired United Counties Omnibus Co. Ltd. whose operations were based on Northamptonshire, Bedfordshire and part of Cambridgeshire. Like the other former NBC companies joining the group, United Counties retained its own livery which was dark green with orange relief and operated a fleet of 249 buses and coaches mainly comprising Leyland Nationals, Leopards and Olympians, Bristol VRTs and Iveco 49.10 minibuses.

In addition to expanding its area of operation, Stagecoach also enhanced its Scottish-based fleet with the purchase of a number of new and secondhand vehicles for both its coaching and local bus operations. These included 2 new Duple 320 and 6 Plaxton Paramount-bodied Volvo B10Ms which together with a pair of new Neoplan Skyliner coaches were put to work mainly on the Anglo-Scottish express services, whilst among the secondhand acquisitions were some front entrance Routemasters for Magicbus, 8 ex.Kelvin Scottish Leyland Nationals for Cumberland and 8 Bristol Lodekkas for Perth, although 4 of the latter never entered service and were instead used for spares. More unusual, however, was the return to its native Spittalfield of a McLennan-bodied half-cab Leyland PS1 coach which was purchased by Stagecoach for preservation. After being repainted into the white and blue livery of its original owner whose fleet names it was also given, it was made available for use on special duties and occasionally was also used in service. The surprise of the year, however, as far as the fleet was concerned was undoubtedly the purchase from Kelvin Scottish of no fewer than 35 Alexander-bodied Leyland Leopards. These arrived at Spittalfield between October and December and although a few were pressed into service by their new owner before the turn of the year, most were placed in store to provide a reserve fleet which could be mobilised if and when necessary. In the event, only 21 were placed in service, the remainder being progressively cannibalised for spares before eventually being sold for scrap. By now, the effect of being members of a large group was starting to show amongst Stagecoach's former NBC companies with vehicles being loaned or transferred from Perth to one or another whenever the need arose and it was not uncommon to see buses and coaches in unfamiliar liveries hundreds of miles away from their more usual haunts. 1987 also witnessed the disappearance of the GT Coaches livery from the fleet when the last vehicle to wear it, Bristol MW6G HDV639E received Stagecoach colours in January. The requirement on particular duties for a high-capacity single decker led Duple Dominant III-bodied Volvo B10M coach FES831W to be returned

Wearing its pre-Stagecoach dark green, orange & cream livery, United Counties ex.Hampshire Bus Bristol VRT 974 (KRU852W) rests in Luton bus station. (T.G.Walker)

Buses mean business

Immaculately restored in the white & dark blue livery of its original owner, A & C McLennan, preserved 1950 Leyland PS1/1 657 (DGS625) which was acquired by Stagecoach from Davies of Pencader in 1987 is fitted with a body built by McLennan. (D.Robinson)

Having been given a new Duplo body with bus seating in 1987, Stagecoach's first brand new vehicle, Volvo B58 FES831W loads in Perth for Dundee on the service jointly operated with Strathtay Scottish in August 1989. Still owned by Stagecoach in 1996, this vehicle is now part of its preserved fleet. (Murdoch Currie)

in the spring to its builder for refurbishment, and during this process it was rebuilt to Dominant II specification and fitted with 59 bus-type seats while later in the year sister coach JSR42X underwent similar treatment but retained its coach seats. Although Stagecoach had since 1981 regularly purchased brand-new coaches, it had relied solely on the secondhand market for its stage carriage vehicles and it thus came as something of a surprise when, in November 1987, it was announced that an order had been placed for 30 new Alexander-bodied 2-axle Leyland Olympians plus 3 Jumbo variants with 3-axles. Except for one of the latter which was to be allocated to Magicbus, all the others were for operation by Stagecoach's English companies.

The start of 1988 found Magicbus locked in a rapidly escalating battle with Central Scottish and Strathclyde Buses in Glasgow which resulted in it withdrawing its service to Castlemilk via Victoria Road and the Milton extension of its Easterhouse route on 20 February. As some small consolation, however, Magicbus was successful in gaining the Strathclyde PTE contracts for the two services (numbered 67 and 68) to Lennoxtown and Kirkintilloch previously maintained by Kelvin Scottish, each of which ran every two hours. During its Glasgow battle, in order to supplement its fleet Magicbus had gained the remaining 6 of Hampshire Bus's Ailsa Volvos, all of which were placed in service still wearing their previous owner's colours. Never popular with crews, they tended to be only used at peak times, however, and in view of this it was more than a little surprising that following the service withdrawals on 20 February, these were retained and instead a number of Routemasters were taken out of service. In the event, the Ailsas were not destined to survive long though and by the end of April all had been withdrawn following the reinstatement of some of the Routemasters. Meanwhile, in an attempt to attract more passengers to its services, Magicbus introduced a wide range of fares options with adult journeys within Castlemilk and Easterhouse being offered for 20p and a maximum fare of 55p being charged to either from Glasgow. Children were charged half the adult fare to the nearest 5p while UB40 holders and students were offered 5p off 35p fares and 10p off all those above. For senior citizens, the cost of any journey was a mere 10p and additionally a 'Magicgran' ticket could be purchased (on the bus) which offered a whole week's travel for 50p. Disabled travellers could ride for 15p for any journey while for other passengers a £4.00 weekly travel ticket was available which offered 10 journeys anywhere on any route. Although it was difficult to promote so many schemes on the buses themselves, all the Routemasters carried posters at each side of their front destination screens to publicise the special UB40 and senior citizen fares.

Following the success of Routemaster operation in both Glasgow and Carlisle, it came as no surprise when at the behest of Brian Souter, a strong supporter of this type of vehicle, United Counties announced in January that it was to introduce 16 of these former London buses as part of a reappraisal of its operations in Bedford and Corby. Repainted into their new owner's livery and bearing the legend 'Routemaster' on each side, the front and rear, the first example made its debut on 18 January for driver training purposes and on 1 February was joined by 7 more which together took over the cross-Bedford 101 service (Woodside to Kempston) and reintroduced crew operation to the company. It was not until 11 April that the remaining 8 entered service, these being allocated to Corby for use on two new local services, one of which operated during the daytime, the other in the evening. Smoking was prohibited on both decks of the Routemasters just as it had been on the

Having had Magicbus fleet names applied to its red, white & blue Hampshire Bus livery, Van Hool McArdle-bodied Ailsa Volvo LWB380P (which was new to South Yorkshire PTE) stands in the yard of Warroch Street depot, Glasgow in February 1988. (K.A.Jenkinson)

Having been on loan to Hampshire Bus from January to May 1988 for operation on its 300 service, Stagecoach's Duple-bodied DAF MB230 C892CSN retained its promotional route number for a few weeks after its return to its native Perth. It is seen here leaving Buchanan bus station, Glasgow on a journey to Dundee in June 1988. (Campbell Morrison)

company's Street Shuttle minibuses and from 29 February the ban was extended to all United Counties vehicles, the only exception being those employed on Coachlink services. Also joining the United Counties fleet at the start of the year were 5 Bristol VRTs transferred from Hampshire Bus which, together with the Routemasters allowed the withdrawal of six older VRTs and 10 Leyland Nationals, while on 11 April the first daytime Street Shuttle minibus services were introduced to Wellingborough. Meanwhile, on the south coast Hampshire Bus took over Solent Blue Line's Winchester to Southampton service on 3 January along with 7 of the Bristol VRTs which had passed to Blue Line three months earlier with the Southampton area operations. Soon afterwards, Hampshire Bus launched a new high-profile service in February between Basingstoke and London, marketing this as the 'Stagecoach 300'. For its operation 4 Duple Caribbean-bodied DAF coaches were transferred from Perth, but after passenger loadings failed to reach their projected level, the service was discontinued from 25 May and the four coaches were returned from whence they came.

Except for a few inter-fleet vehicle transfers, the purchase of the Routemasters for United Counties and the withdrawal of several older buses and coaches, the combined fleet witnessed little change during the early months of 1988 although in January an unusual 24-seat Wright-bodied Dodge minibus had been purchased from Strathclyde PTE. Fitted with a wheelchair lift and wearing an all-over light grey livery, it was at first stored at Perth before eventually travelling south (driven to Andover overnight by finance director Derek Scott who was going to Hampshire to meet the auditors!) to join Hampshire Bus by whom, after being repainted into an unrelieved white livery, it was placed in service at Basingstoke in August. Even more unusual, however, was the purchase from McGills of Barrhead on 1 May of two Leyland-DAB articulated single deck buses with the intention of using them on the Magicbus services in Glasgow. In the event, both were instead quickly despatched

Right : Having lost its original livery for one of unrelieved green, United Counties Routemaster 701 (HVS710, originally WLT512) stands in Midland Road, Bedford while working the 101 service to Kempston. (Dave Mockford)

An unusual vehicle within the Stagecoach fleet was former Strathclyde PTE Wright-bodied Dodge D365OSU which was built with a wheelchair lift incorporated into its rear bulkhead. Allocated to the Hampshire Bus fleet in which it was numbered 43, it is seen here in corporate livery at Basingstoke in February 1990. (Travelscene)

A pair of Leyland-DAB bendibuses acquired from McGills of Barrhead, although originally intended for use by Magicbus in Glasgow, instead were placed in service with Hampshire Bus. Seen here picking up its Southampton-bound passengers in Winchester in July 1988 is the first of this duo, 291 (FHE291V). (Travelscene)

Stored at Spittalfield in Stagecoach's strategic reserve fleet in October 1988, Magicbus Routemaster WLT909 displays both its original and new registration number. Six months later, it was despatched to East Midland who placed it in service at Mansfield. (Campbell Morrison)

Following the purchase of Kirkpatricks of Brigham by Cumberland in May 1988, several of the latter's ex.United Counties Willowbrook-bodied Leyland Leopards were repainted into Kirkpatrick's cream & red livery as illustrated by 1152 (UVV152W) seen here at Workington about to be overtaken by similar-liveried 1154 (UVV154W). (Campbell Morrison collection)

Cumberland's Duple Laser-bodied Leyland Tiger 105 (B105HAO) lost its National Express livery in favour of Yeowart's yellow & mustard at the start of 1990. Seen here in Whitehaven depot, this livery was soon afterwards used by Cumberland for its Coachline unit. (B.Pritchard)

to Hampshire Bus where one - in corporate livery - entered service on 19 May at Winchester, the other joining it a day later still wearing McGills' colours. Meanwhile, in Glasgow several of the Magicbus Routemasters were re-registered with A-suffix numbers, releasing their original London marks for sale to private buyers.

Following announcements by the Government of plans to privatise London Buses and the Scottish Bus Group during the next few years, Stagecoach made it known that it would be interested in purchasing either, both or parts of these concerns if given the opportunity and to assist the company with its future plans, at the end of March it appointed merchant bankers Noble Grossart Ltd. of Edinburgh as its advisors. In the meantime Stagecoach continued its expansion by purchasing in May, through its Cumberland Motor Services subsidiary, the businesses of two of Cumbria's major independent bus and coach operators, Yeowarts of Whitehaven and Kirkpatricks of Brigham. Yeowarts had been a thorn in Cumberland's side since October 1981 when it had introduced a competitive town service in Whitehaven while Kirkpatricks had concentrated mainly on coaching operations and contract work. Despite being immediately placed under the control of Cumberland, both the newly acquired businesses continued to operate independently from their own premises and retained their established fleet names and liveries.

Almost before the ink had dried on the Cumbria acquisitions, Stagecoach launched an assault on Harry Blundred's Devon General stronghold of Torquay following an announcement that Devon General's sister company, Thames Transit of Oxford, was to start minibus operations in Basingstoke in Hampshire Bus territory. In an attempt to stave off this new attack, Stagecoach and City of Oxford Motor Services joined forces and declared war on Harry Blundred by introducing a free bus service between St.Marychurch and Paignton Zoo via Torquay's promenade starting on 27 June. Hampshire Bus was given the responsibility of planning and marketing the new operation and providing the vehicles and to this end 8 of the company's Leyland Nationals were repainted into an all-white livery and appropriately lettered with 'Freebus' fleet names for use on this new service which had been carefully chosen to take maximum patronage from Devon General and ran on a ten minute frequency from 9am to 7pm. Additionally, each bus had its front panel adorned with a cartoon character, one of which was 'Happy Harry'! The publicity accompanying the operation was both comprehensive and extremely professional with printed leaflets, each bus stop along the whole of the route being fitted with a timetable holder in which service details were shown and numerous 'Freebus Stop' flags erected alongside conventional Devon General signs. Passengers were also given questionnaires seeking their preferences, for example between

This view of the blockade of Keswick bus station in August 1988 shows some of the vehicles used for this purpose. Visible are a pair of ex.Yeowarts vehicles, two former Hampshire Bus Leyland Leopards, a Magicbus Routemaster and a trio of ex.Southdown Leyland PD3/4s. (K.A.Jenkinson)

Freshly painted in Stagecoach corporate livery and adorned with Hampshire Mini Bus fleet names, Alexander-bodied Renault 41 (E935NBK) stands outside Andover depot in July 1988. (Travelscene)

Former Kelvin Scottish all-white liveried Alexander-bodied Leyland Leopard GMS294S stands in the yard of Perth depot in October 1988 having just returned from Keswick where it had been used in the blockade of the bus station enroute from Hampshire Bus by whom it had been used as a replacement for the Leyland Nationals despatched to Torbay. (Campbell Morrison)

minibuses and larger single deck vehicles. Being far from happy by the invasion of his prime territory, Harry Blundred, after threatening to ban Yelloways Trathens coaches from all Devon General's bus stations if they continued to provide Hampshire Bus with parking and maintenance facilities at their depot, issued High Court writs against Hampshire Bus and City of Oxford on 7 July for 'conspiracy in that they had combined with each other to operate a free bus service in the Torbay area, maliciously and/or with the real or predominant purpose of thereby injuring the plaintiff's business'. As a result of this move, the two companies concerned had no option but to immediately cease their operation despite having originally planned to continue it for six to eight weeks. By the following morning all signs of the service had disappeared completely with all the publicity material having been removed and the vehicles having returned to their native Hampshire surrounds. According to Devon General, the invasion had cost around £100,000 in lost revenue while the 8 Freebus Leyland Nationals had between them covered 10,000 service miles during their eleven days in Torbay.

Having failed to dissuade Transit Holdings from proceeding with its plans to invade Basingstoke, Hampshire Bus made plans to retaliate in the town concerned, recruiting 14 new drivers for minibus training and drafting in 15 new minibuses in preparation for the forthcoming battle. Due to a mix-up by the Traffic Commissioner, however, the newly created Basingstoke Transit was unable to commence its operations as planned on 4 August and had to defer these until 2 September, thus reducing the pressure on Hampshire Bus for a further month. During this reprieve, Stagecoach Holdings through its Hampshire Bus subsidiary entered into talks with Harry Blundred and towards the end of August purchased Basingstoke Transit before it had chance to make its debut, thus avoiding the bus war which had been looming on the horizon for several weeks. Meanwhile, following the return of the Freebus-liveried Leyland Nationals to their native surrounds, the 8 ex.Kelvin Scottish Leyland Leopards which had been drafted into the fleet from Perth to cover for their departure to Torbay were able to be returned northwards, although not across the border. Stagecoach was now at the centre of a new controversy, this time in the heart of the Lake District. As a protest against local planning permission for the redevelopment of Keswick bus station being given by the council to the local business Caterite rather than to Stagecoach's choice, Condor Developments, Cumberland blocked its bus station in August with more than 20 withdrawn buses to prevent its use by coaches bringing visitors to the town. As a result, the tourist coaches were forced to park some three miles away from the town centre, causing a great deal of inconvenience as well as a loss of business for many local traders. The buses used in the blockade were drawn from several sources and included the 8 Leopards returning home from Hampshire Bus, a trio of vehicles acquired with the Yeowart business, some withdrawn Magicbus Routemasters and 3 recently-acquired ex.Southdown full-fronted Leyland PD3s. Another development in Cumbria was the withdrawal by Brownriggs of Egremont on 21 September of its competitive 'Country Bus' services in Whitehaven and Workington which it had started as a result of deregulation. Although Brownriggs was to continue in business mainly as a coach operator, its five minibuses and two coaches made surplus by the withdrawal of its local bus services were quickly purchased by Cumberland.

In order to make it easier to transfer vehicles between its various operating companies and also to present a unified image, it was decided to abandon the individual liveries applied to vehicles of its English subsidiaries in favour of that used by Stagecoach in Perth and thus during the early summer of 1988 a start was made in the repainting of Cumberland, Hampshire Bus and United Counties vehicles into the new corporate scheme. Soon afterwards the first of the new double deckers to be purchased by Stagecoach Holdings (Alexander-bodied Leyland Olympians) made their debut in England and before their delivery was completed an order for a further 40 was placed for arrival in 1989 thus indicating the importance that was now being placed on the upgrading of the fleet. Additionally, no fewer than 47 V and W-registered Bristol VRTs were purchased from Devon General toward the end of 1988 and early in 1989 to enable older vehicles to be replaced more quickly and thus further enhance fleet standards. More unusual, however, was the acquisition of a 6-seat Cessna light aircraft which was obtained mainly for use by the Group's directors to enable them to more speedily visit the scattered outposts of their rapidly expanding empire. Housed at Scone airfield, it was rumoured that in true Stagecoach manner the plane had been procured in exchange for a batch of 6 buses!

The field adjoining the former McLennan's depot at Spittalfield was used for the storage of a large number of surplus vehicles during 1988 including some reserve fleet and withdrawn Bristol Lodekkas and several cannibalised ex.Kelvin Scottish Leyland Leopards. (K.A.Jenkinson)

Seen soon after returning to Hampshire Bus following its brief sojourn in Torbay, all-white liveried Leyland National 746 (FPR62V) still retained lettering for the Babbacombe to Paignton Zoo service on its cove panels and The Pony Express name and logo on its front panel when caught by the camera in August 1988. (Travelscene)

Acquired by Cumberland with the local bus operations of Brownriggs of Egremont, MCW Metrorider E317BRM is seen in Workington in September 1988 still sporting a Country Hopper fleet name despite its recent change of ownership. (K.A.Jenkinson)

Painted in the original Street Shuttle livery of United Counties, Robin Hood-bodied Iveco 49.10 39 (D39DNH) is seen here in Bedford bus station in May 1989. (T.G.Walker)

VENTURING OVERSEAS

On 21 July 1988, Stagecoach undertook its first overseas venture when it registered a new company under the title of Stage-Coach International Ltd. primarily for a new project in which the company had become involved in Sri Lanka. Under this new banner it was proposed to export 40 former London Buses Routemasters to that country, and to provide their new owner with expertise on maintenance and operation of buses of this type, former Midland Fox general manager Peter Lutman was recruited by the company. Prior to this, in the spring of 1988 Brian Souter and Ann Gloag whilst on a visit to Hong Kong for the purpose of viewing the operations of the renowned Kowloon Motor Bus Company met up with Clement Lau Ming-Chuen, an engineer who on 27 June 1986 had set up a company under the title of Speedybus Services Ltd. to supply former Kowloon Motor Bus double deckers to various municipal operators in the Peoples' Republic of China. Seeing an opportunity to become involved in the bus industry in this part of the Far East, Stage-Coach International Services Ltd. struck a deal with Clement Lau on 15 November 1988 which resulted in the birth of Speedybus Enterprises Ltd. in which each party held a 50% share. In addition to supplying buses to China, Speedybus Enterprises entered into an agreement with a Hong Kong-based advertising agency whereby most of the buses supplied were painted in all-over advertising liveries, thus further enhancing the new company's finances. In the meantime, back at home Stagecoach made a bid for Portsmouth City Transport but was pipped to the post by neighbouring Southampton CityBus. Also joining Stagecoach Holdings in December 1988 as a non-executive director was Ewan Brown, a merchant banker by profession and a former director of the Scottish Transport Group. His knowledge and

One of a number of former Kowloon Motor Bus Metsec-bodied Daimler CVG6s supplied under contract to the Peoples' Republic of China by Speedybus Enterprises, this all-over advertising liveried example is seen followed by an articulated single deck trolleybus in Guangzhou in December 1990. (C.Lau)

valuable skills together with those of Derek Scott who had joined the board as Finance Director in 1987 were subsequently to play a major role in the shaping and growth of the company and one of the first

Awaiting their fate at Stagecoach's Spittalfield graveyard in August 1988 are seven of Magicbus's ten Van Hool McArdle-bodied Ailsa Volvos all of which still retained the livery of their previous owner, Hampshire Bus. (K.A.Jenkinson)

Standing in Buchanan bus station, Glasgow in July 1989 displaying London Kings Cross 300 in its destination aperture, Duple-bodied DAF C895CSN had lost its Stagecoach livery in favour of an all-white scheme with Magicbus Londonlink lettering for operation on the service competing with Bruce of Airdrie. (K.A.Jenkinson)

moves made by the expanded management team was the private placing in 1988 of a quantity of Stagecoach shares with seven institutional investors - Murray Ventures plc; TSB Scotland plc; Noble Grossart Investments Ltd; The Standard Life Assurance Co.; Scottish Development Agency; The Scottish Investment Trust plc and Scottish Eastern Investment Trust plc - which raised £5 million to enable further expansion to be achieved. Following the assurance of this financial backing, Stagecoach entered into exploratory talks with Strathclyde Regional Council in the hope that it might be able to purchase that undertaking's bus operations, although these were soon abandoned following the council's privatisation plans being put on hold. Additionally, letters were sent out to most of the remaining 50 municipal bus operating companies in the UK expressing an interest should they be offered for sale.

After a period of comparative calm with few changes being made to Stagecoach's Scottish fleets, a start was made in November 1988 on the disposal of the large number of surplus vehicles which had been built up at Spittalfield during the previous twelve months. This clearout was not unconnected with the fact that most of the buses concerned were parked on land which was not owned by the company and the subsequent discovery of this fact by the site's rightful proprietor. Although many of the buses removed were sold for scrap, several found new owners who returned them to service both north and south of the border. At this same time, Stagecoach experimentally introduced the Bristol VRT to its Perth-based fleet when it borrowed an example from Cumberland and put it to work on several services including that from Pitlochry to Aberfeldy. Although it was returned to Cumberland after three or so weeks, it reappeared at Perth in January 1989 where it remained active still in the NBC poppy red livery in which it was received until its eventual withdrawal in October. At this same time it was joined by four buses of the same type acquired from Devon General and by a Leyland National which was transferred from Hampshire Bus and which was placed in service by Magicbus in Glasgow on the 18th of that same month.

Seeking to improve its prestigious Glasgow and Edinburgh to London services which had been acquired following the collapse of Cotters Coachline, Stagecoach introduced a new two-tier service on 7 November 1988 on which passengers could choose between standard or super service. For this purpose, four of the company's Neoplan Skyliner coaches were converted with their 14-seat lower decks being fully partitioned and carpeted for 'super service' passengers each of whom was given free newspapers and magazines. For 'standard service' passengers the upper deck had 6 seats removed to improve leg room and along with 'super service' all were offered free tea and coffee and could purchase sandwiches, pastries and cold drinks from the hostess onboard. In London the terminal was altered from Kings Cross to Victoria Coach Station in order to provide better facilities and Stagecoach proudly claimed that not even British Airways could match their new service which was given a reduced running time between termini. Additionally, a new 'Weekender' service was introduced from London to Glasgow, Edinburgh, Cumbernauld, Livingston, Dunfermline, Stirling, Perth and Dundee with timings which were more convenient for weekend trips, one of which left London at 2.30pm and reached all its Scottish destinations before midnight. No sooner had the new operation got underway, however, than Bruce of Airdrie announced that it was to start a new daily service under the title of 'Londonliner' from its home base to London via Glasgow at the end of November. Far from pleased by this intrusion, Stagecoach immediately laid retaliatory plans for the introduction of an identical service which was to be operated by Magicbus. For this purpose, its 4 Duple-bodied DAF coaches were repainted into an all-white livery to which 'Magicbus Londonlink' names were added.

Following an uneventful start, 1989 soon began to show signs of being a year of further expansion when in February the fleet and operations of Highwayman Coaches were purchased from Robin Gloag, one of the founders of Gloagtrotter, the company from which Stagecoach was born. Although all Highwayman's 5 coaches were involved in the deal, its depot at The Hideout, Errol was retained by Robin Gloag as the base for his new vehicle body repair business and as part of the agreement, Stagecoach guaranteed an initial one year contract for repair work to its growing fleet.

As part of its continuing drive to improve travelling conditions, Hampshire Bus followed United Counties example by banning smoking on all its stage carriage services, thus becoming the second of Stagecoach's subsidiaries to make such a move. Meanwhile, Cumberland received its much-publicised 3-axle Alexander-bodied

One of a large number of UTM buses painted in all-over advertising liveries, 1983 vintage Country district AUT-bodied single door Leyland Victory Mk.II 761 (BF2215) fitted with a roof-mounted luggage carrier is seen in Blantyre early in 1990. (R.Bailey)

UTM Cityline's two-tone blue liveried dual door AUT-bodied Leyland Victory Mk.I 342 (BE5104) was new in 1978. Here it picks up its passengers - and their luggage - near Nguluoi in 1990. (R.Bailey)

Displaying the legend 'Ride a Roadrunner) across its front panel, East Midland's MCW Metrorider 808 (E808EDT) hurries away from Chesterfield in July 1989 bound for Hollingwood. (D.J.Stanier)

coach-seated Leyland Olympians in February while early in March Hampshire Bus gained 3 new Duple bus-bodied Dennis Javelins for in-service evaluation. The flow of new Iveco minibuses continued apace with examples being placed in service by United Counties and Hampshire Bus while the latter opened a new outstation at Botley and reopened its former outstation at Petersfield in March and April respectively.

Further expansion was achieved when, after renaming Stage-Coach International Ltd, Stage-Coach International Services Ltd., Stagecoach (Holdings) stepped into Africa on 31 March by purchasing United Transport International's 51% stake in Malawi's national transport company, the remaining 49% of which was held by the Malawi Government. With its headquarters in Blantyre, United Transport Malawi Ltd. operated a fleet of 258 single deck vehicles, the majority of which were Leyland Victory Mk.1 and Mk.2 models fitted with locally-built bodywork. These maintained a wide range of urban and inter-urban services throughout the country which was operationally divided into three regions, each of which applied its own livery. Founded in 1947 as the Nyasaland Transport Company, in addition it initially operated a fleet of heavy lorries for general haulage work, although these were sold in 1982 to allow UTM to concentrate solely on its passenger-carrying activities. The acquisition of United Transport Malawi came as no great surprise as it had been known for some time that Stagecoach had been cautiously considering overseas diversification and had looked at several countries which drove on the left, spoke English and had some UK expats.

Following its sortie in Africa, Stagecoach once again turned its attention to further expansion in England and on 7 April purchased the former NBC company, East Midland Motor Services Ltd. together with its subsidiaries Frontrunner (SE) Ltd., Frontrunner (NW) Ltd. and its 50% stake in East Midlands Transport Advertising. Only days before its acquisition by Stagecoach, East Midland had purchased a share in Forrest of Mansfield - a removal and storage company - and also acquired Rainworth Travel of Langwith, an independent bus and coach operator. Based at Chesterfield and with an operating area covering Derbyshire and North Nottinghamshire, upon deregulation East Midland had opened a new base in Essex where it gained several tendered services. After a few weeks, these were placed under the control of a new subsidiary named Frontrunner (SE) Ltd. and similarly, after gaining a number of tendered services in the Greater Manchester area, another subsidiary was formed under the title of Frontrunner (NW) Ltd. Almost

Picking up its passengers in Chesterfield, East Midland ECW-bodied Leyland Olympian 312 (UDT312Y) had Mansfield & District fleet names applied to its green & cream livery. (D.J.Stanier)

Passing the Friendship Centre on Glasgow's massive Easterhouse estate in August 1989, Magicbus Alexander-bodied 3-axle Leyland Olympian F110NES displayed lettering on its side panels proclaiming it to be 'Britain's Biggest Bus'. (K.A.Jenkinson)

immediately following its change of ownership, East Midland's service network came under scrutiny in order to provide improved and more profitable operations and in conjunction with this one of United Counties' Routemasters was hired for service trials in Mansfield. Its success led to its stay being made permanent and it was ultimately joined in 1991 by more buses of this type cascaded from Magicbus. Meanwhile, a new express service was inaugurated between Sheffield and Nottingham under the title of 'Steel Arrow Express' and the existing three days a week service from Mansfield to Liverpool which was operated jointly with

Acquired by East Midland with the business of Rainworth Travel, former London Country Plaxton Supreme IV Express-bodied Leyland Leopard NPA221W is seen here still painted in its former owner's white & blue colours. It was ultimately numbered 12 in the East Midland fleet. (Campbell Morrison)

Hulleys of Baslow was increased to become daily. Although East Midland and the two Frontrunner companies all shared the same two-tone green & cream livery, the Rainworth Travel fleet which retained its individual identity continued to use its established white & dark blue scheme until repainting into Stagecoach corporate colours commenced. Not all the news was being made south of the border, however, as in Scotland Magicbus received its new 3-axle bus-seated Alexander-bodied Leyland Olympian, placing it in service on 11 April. Christened the Megadekka, it had seating for 110 passengers and was claimed to

Arriving at The Battery on Morecambe's promenade enroute from Heysham to Lancaster, Ribble Leyland National 866 (LFR866X) still wore its pre-Stagecoach red & light grey livery. (K.A.Jenkinson)

Hurrying away from Stockport bus station in September 1989 is Bee Line Buzz yellow-liveried Freight Rover Sherpa D249OOJ adorned like most vehicles in that fleet with prominent advertising for Embassy cigarettes. (K.A.Jenkinson)

Transferred from Perth to Glasgow for operation on the former Cotters service to London and painted in Stagecoach corporate livery with Coachline fleet names, Neoplan Jetliner 4585SC (originally A216LWD) rests between its duties in Warroch Street depot, Glasgow. (S.A.Jenkinson)

be Britain's largest bus, a legend it proudly displayed in large letters on its upper deck side panels.

No sooner had the dust settled on the East Midland acquisition than it was announced that Stagecoach Holdings had, on 21 April, purchased Ribble Motor Services Ltd. of Preston from its management together with its Manchester area subsidiary Bee Line Buzz and its stake in National Transport Tokens Ltd. In this instance, however, Ribble's extensive property portfolio was not all included in the deal and much of it remained with Dimples Estates Ltd., a company owned by three of the of the original team who bought Ribble from the NBC in 1988 and two property developers. With a massive fleet of some 838 vehicles and an operating area which stretched throughout Lancashire, Ribble's acquisition gave Stagecoach a major presence in north-west England from the Scottish border to Manchester and additionally the former United Transport Bee Line Buzz and Zippy operations made it Britain's largest minibus operator. At the time of the takeover, Ribble's standard bus livery was red, white and grey while its Zippy and Bee Line fleets were painted in yellow with red relief.

Continuing to seek further consolidation, Stagecoach through its Cumberland subsidiary acquired the 10-coach business of Stephensons of Maryport on 2 May and immediately placed this under the control of its Kirkpatricks division. Stephensons' taxi and limousine hire business was not, however, included in the deal and remained with its original owner who also retained its existing premises in Maryport. Of the coaches acquired, on this occasion several were immediately placed in store pending a decision on their future and were ultimately sold without being used by their new owner.

After several months of speculation as to its future following its rejection of an acquisitive bid by Ribble in September 1988, the local authority-owned Barrow Borough Transport was placed in administrative receivership in December of that year. Seeing the position in which BBT

Ribble's Robin Hood-bodied Iveco 49.10 056 (D736YBV) seen here at Preston bus station still wearing the predominantly yellow livery and Zippy fleet names of its former owner was one of a number of minibuses acquired with the United Transport Buses business in 1988.

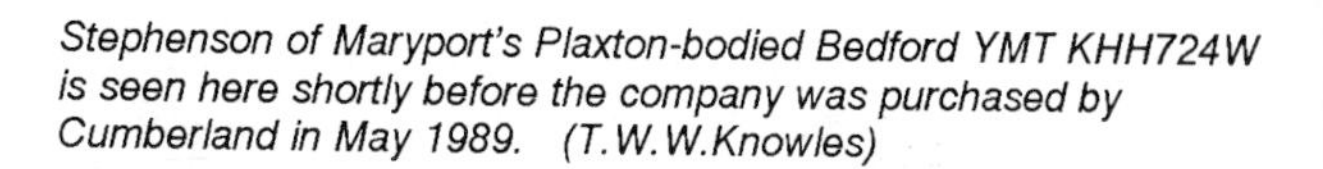
Stephenson of Maryport's Plaxton-bodied Bedford YMT KHH724W is seen here shortly before the company was purchased by Cumberland in May 1989. (T.W.W.Knowles)

now found itself led Ribble to increase its competition in the town in the hope that it might eventually succeed in its attempt to gain control of its rival and, following the collapse of negotiations between Barrow Borough Council and Holt Drive Hire of Bolton, its goal was achieved on 26 May. The £1.2 million deal included Barrow Borough Transport's premises and its bus fleet but excluded the company's van hire business or the right to trade as successors to BBT. Immediately following the takeover, Ribble modified a number of its services to take account of BBT's disappearance although no additional routes were introduced and no extra vehicles were drafted in. Barrow Borough Transport's 24 buses were instantly removed from the town and placed in store, although a few days later some were reinstated at Preston still in their previous owner's cream & blue livery albeit with the addition of Ribble fleet names and on 11 June Ribble moved its fleet from its Emlyn Street base to the depot acquired from Barrow Borough Transport in Hindpool Road. During this period, Ribble had been busy reorganising its activities and as part of its rationalisation plan, it transferred all its Lakeland and South Cumbria operations, its depots at Barrow, Kendal and Ulverston and its outstations at Grange over Sands and Sedburgh to Cumberland Motor Services on 18 June. At this same time it announced that it was to close its central repair works at Preston and transfer all maintenance work to its major depots.

In addition to the now customary transfer of vehicles between Stagecoach Group companies continuing unabated, United Counties surprisingly despatched one of its Plaxton Paramount 3500-bodied Leyland Tigers to Africa on 22 May to join United Transport Malawi for use primarily on its long distance express service from Blantyre to Lilongwe. UTM also received its first double deckers in the form of 12 former Kowloon Motor Bus Metsec-bodied Daimler CVG6s which were supplied by Stagecoach's Hong Kong associate, Speedybus Enterprises. Shipped from Hong Kong to Durban, these buses then had to drive overland through Zimbabwe and Mozambique in order to reach Blantyre, a long and arduous journey, and before entering service in their new home, all were repainted in all-over advertising or Stagecoach corporate livery.

Still painted in the cream & crimson livery of its former owner, Stagecoach's ex.Devon General Bristol VRT FDV819V picks up its passengers enroute from Pitlochry to Perth in March 1989. Repainted soon afterwards in corporate colours, it is still owned by the company, albeit Inverness Traction to whom it was transferred in April 1996. (Campbell Morrison)

Resting at Lilongwe depot in the autumn of 1991 is Stagecoach Malawi Coachline Duple-bodied Leyland Leopard 8 (BF9002) which began life in the UK with Wallace Arnold (registered XWX179S) and was acquired by UTM in 1984. (J.Davison)

United Counties Unique Famos-Ensign Charisma S315.21 coach 100 (G100JNV) in National Express livery was caught by the camera at Woburn in September 1989 whilst visiting the Showbus rally. (J.Whitmore)

Being hoisted aboard ship in Hong Kong harbour on 22 March 1990 at the start of its long journey to Africa is former Kowloon Motor Bus Metsec-bodied Daimler CVG6 D543 which was to become 1046 in the fleet of Stagecoach Malawi. As can be seen, one of its sisters is already stowed in the hold.

Of the eight ex.Greater Manchester NCME-bodied Leyland Atlanteans acquired by Magicbus from Ribble in January 1990, five were returned from whence thay came after less than three months service in Glasgow. The remaining trio of which 119 (KBU914P) and 118 (LJA636P) are seen here at Hobden Street depot, Glasgow, remained in use - mainly on schools services - until April 1992 when they were sold to Kelvin Central Buses with Magibus's Glasgow operations.

Meanwhile, north of the border Stagecoach was preparing, amidst great secrecy, an attack on Strathtay Scottish who at that time was in line to become the first company to be offered for sale in the Scottish Bus Group privatisation programme. For this purpose, a quantity of Leyland Nationals travelled northwards to Perth from Hampshire Bus, United Counties, Cumberland and East Midland and were placed in store to await developments while across in Glasgow, Magicbus introduced changes to its Easterhouse service on 30 May under which one-person-operation was to be implemented after 7.00pm each day. As a result, the Routemasters which maintained the daytime service had to be replaced after the evening peak with vehicles suitable for OPO and for this purpose a further 4 ex.Devon General Bristol VRTs were acquired and allocated to Warroch Street in Stagecoach corporate colours. Additionally, as a result of the inability of Scottish Bus Group subsidiary Central Scottish to operate its services due to continuing strike action by its employees, Magicbus gained a temporary licence to run a new service, numbered 53, from Buchanan bus station in Glasgow to Birkenshaw and Larkhall a few days before the strike ended on 27 May. Having found this service to be reasonably lucrative, after its short period of operation ended Magicbus registered it in its own name to commence on 3 July, although not proving as profitable as had been originally expected, it was discontinued on 6 August. As far as Stagecoach's express services were concerned, on 1 May that running from Glasgow to Aberdeen had a southbound 'Breakfast Express' journey added each morning and a 'Supper Express' northbound journey each evening seven days a week upon which a full range of hot foods was available ranging from an 85p burger to a £1.70 full airline-style meal. At this same time, all the Anglo-Scottish journeys were converted to 'Super Service' and in conjunction with ABC Travel supported by Buckinghamshire County Council, a free connecting service was provided between junction 14 of the M1 motorway and Milton Keynes. Additionally, as a result of its ever-increasing popularity, Magicbus's nightly Londonline service was expanded with the introduction of a daytime operation. Still regarding leisure travel as an important part of its portfolio, Stagecoach continued its programme of full-day tours from various parts of Tayside to a number of areas of scenic beauty, running these to a different destination on Mondays to Thursdays each week from June to mid-September. Costing between £8.00 and £11.90, a novel feature of these tours was that the price included all admission charges (where applicable) to the places visited as well as lunch and afternoon tea which was again served onboard the coach. Meanwhile, in southern England, Hampshire Bus participated in Hampshire County Council's 'Sunday Rider' scheme under which a county-wide ticket enabled travel on the buses of 15 different operators as well as on 3 ferries. Launched on 21 May, this scheme which continued until 3 September proved extremely popular in attracting numerous additional passengers to the county's previously under-used Sunday bus services.

After having chosen Hampshire Bus to evaluate the Group's new Dennis Javelin buses, it came as no surprise when Cumberland Motor Services, due to its close proximity to the Leyland plant at Lillyhall, was

The only Leyland Lynxes purchased new by Stagecoach were a trio for Cumberland in 1989 and an ex.Leyland demonstrator. One of the former, 253 (F253KAO) is seen here at Barrow in Furness in April 1992 operating a local town service. (Murdoch Currie)

With its route details painted on its destination screen glass and along its cove panels, Leyland National 204 (RFM884M) picks up its passengers during the first week of Perth Panther's operations when its services were operated free of charge.
(Campbell Morrison)

Locked in battle with Strathtay Scottish on Perth city services, Perth Panther Leyland National 210 (GFX974N) is overtaken by Strathtay Scottish Routemaster SR25 (WTS333A) in Kinnoul Street, Perth in August 1989.
(K.A.Jenkinson)

selected to conduct the in-service trial of 3 new Leyland Lynx single deckers which made their debut in July. Also evaluated by Cumberland for three weeks was an Optare Delta demonstrator, although in the event neither of these types was included in future orders from the Stagecoach Group.

Following the creation by Stagecoach on 9 June of a new company, Perth & District Buses Ltd., the attack on Scottish Bus Group subsidiary Strathtay Scottish which had been carefully planned for several weeks was launched on 19 June when the assembled fleet of Leyland Nationals sporting new Perth Panther fleet names and displaying a route diagram on their cove panels took to the road on two new services which shadowed Strathtay's most lucrative routes and upon which cheaper fares were charged. Running cross-city on a 7/8 minute frequency from Muirton and North Muirton to Letham and numbered 'A' and 'B', both were initially operated free in order to gain maximum publicity and patronage. Not surprisingly, Strathtay Scottish responded quickly and on 3 July began a new service from Perth city centre to Letham which matched the frequency of the Perth Panthers and for which 6 of its Routemasters were repainted into the old Perth City Transport colours of red & cream with appropriate old-style fleetnames to give the impression to intending passengers that two new operators had appeared on the city's streets rather than one! Having firmly established itself on routes 'A' and 'B', Perth Panther on 17 July introduced its third service which ran to a figure 9 pattern from William Low's superstore via Tulloch, Perth city centre and Moncrieffe with clockwise journeys being lettered 'C' and those running anti-clockwise 'D'. Again using Leyland Nationals and charging a flat fare of 30p (15p for children and 10p for Tayside pass-holders), all four services accepted the Panther Pass, a £3.25 weekly ticket which permitted unlimited travel and could be purchased on the bus. Still not content with its rapidly-growing share of the market in Perth, a new hourly service was inaugurated between the city centre and Pitcairngreen, again in direct competition to Strathtay Scottish, operated by Leyland Leopard or Volvo coaches from the Stagecoach fleet which were suitably adorned with Perth Panther fleetnames. All the new services ran on Mondays to Saturdays only, leaving Strathtay to maintain all the city's unremunerative Sunday services. Determined to fight back, Strathtay repainted a couple of its Leyland Leopard coaches into a new livery upon which was added on each side 'This is the Pitcairn GREEN BUS', but this was to little avail. Stagecoach continued to register a new Tayside area bus service each week for the following two months and the effect on morale at Strathtay Scottish as the weekly announcement of which route was next was dramatic!

Still wearing its Frontrunner South East two-tone green & cream livery, NCME-bodied Leyland Atlantean 1670 (KBU915P) had gained Ribble fleet names by the time it was photographed in Blackburn bus station in September 1989.

Seen in Derby bus station in October 1990 displaying Rainworth Travel fleet names is East Midland Mellor-bodied Ford Transit 951 (D552URM) which was acquired from Cumberland in September 1989. (D.J.Stanier)

On the reverse side of the coin, after experiencing increasing difficulty in maintaining services some 150 miles away from its home base, East Midland sold its Frontrunner South-East subsidiary to Ensign Bus of Purfleet on 30 June. In reality, Ensign had in fact been operating services 248, 252 and schools service 550 for a week before their official transfer due to the unavailability of Frontrunner crews and early in July it resold four of its inherited Essex County Council services to County Bus & Coach of Harlow as these did not fit into its own plans for the future. Although all Frontrunner South-East's ex.Greater Manchester Leyland Atlanteans passed to Ensign Bus, agreement was reached that these would be exchanged for a similar number of dual-door buses from within the Stagecoach Group as soon as possible and by the end of August all had departed to join Ribble with a number of that company's Atlanteans and Bristol VRTs and 4 East Midland Bristol REs taking their place. Upon their arrival back in Lancashire, the ex.Frontrunner buses were immediately placed in service by their new owner still wearing the two-tone green & cream livery in which they had been received, albeit with the addition of Ribble fleet names. Further north, Cumberland converted a number of its Barrow town services to minibus operation while in Kendal, competition was eliminated when Lancaster City Transport withdrew its town services on 29 July. Overseas, a further 8 ex.Kowloon Motor Bus Daimler CVG6 double deckers were added to the fleet of United Transport Malawi to bring the total to 20, although it was not until 25 July that the first of these were placed in revenue-earning service. Used on the busy Blantyre - Limbe - Kamuzu Highway corridor, they were at first viewed with some trepidation by passengers who, not being familiar with double deckers, were extremely reluctant to travel on the upper deck not knowing to where the stairs led, and after mounting them, being frightened by 'not being able to see the driver'. Happily such fears quickly disappeared and within a few weeks the upper deck proved more popular than the lower saloon! By now the repainting programme into Stagecoach corporate livery was well underway although local and regional fleetnames such as Cityline, Coachline, Expressline and Southern etc. continued to be applied. Additionally, vehicles of the various operating divisions were given different coloured front roof domes in order to maintain ease of identification to prospective passengers.

East Midland painted its Routemasters in a variety of different liveries including the company's original biscuit, cream & brown which was applied to RM1164 (NSG636A). (B.Newsome)

EXPRESS DEPARTURE

August had barely begun when it was surprisingly announced that in order to be able to give total concentration to its local bus operations, Stagecoach had sold its entire Perth-based express coach operation, its headquarters and depot at Walnut Grove and 31 coaches (one of which was being cannibalised for spares) to National Express who formed a new subsidiary for this purpose under the title of Tayside Travel Services Ltd. The deal signed on 4 August 1989 allowed Tayside Travel Services, who were to trade under the name of Caledonian Express, to use the Stagecoach name for a period of two years in order to assist the new company to establish itself in Scotland. In addition, a clause was inserted into the agreement which allowed Stagecoach the continued use of its Walnut Grove premises until alternative accommodation could be found. All Stagecoach's other operations on Tayside were transferred to Magicbus (Scotland) Ltd. whose legal lettering was applied to all the vehicles remaining in the company's ownership, although this was not used as a fleet name except on the buses operating in Glasgow. The decision to sell its express coach operation had not been reached easily, but after finding that there was little opportunity to further expand this side of the business, the only viable options were to either buy National Express or sell to them. As National Express was not for sale, however, the option became academic.

Arriving at Buchanan bus station, Glasgow on a journey from London to Dundee in 1988 is Neoplan Skyliner 7878SC which began life registered C727JTL. (Campbell Morrison)

Climbing up Manchester Road out of Bradford enroute to Glasgow in the summer of 1990 is Tayside Travel Services ex.Stagecoach Plaxton Paramount-bodied Volvo B10M D446CNR which sported both Stagecoach and Caledonian Express fleet names. (K.A.Jenkinson)

Carrying lettering to promote Southdown's Gold Card monthly bus pass is Bristol VRT 685 (EAP985V) pictured at The Hard bus station, Portsmouth in the autumn of 1989. (J.Whitmore)

Still in Top Line yellow & black livery albeit with the name of its new owner above its destination screen, Hastings & District ex.Eastbourne Buses East Lancs-bodied Leyland Atlantean 518 (GHC518N) is seen here at Down Farm, Ore. (T.S.Blackman)

Stagecoach's unrelenting battle with Strathtay Scottish escalated further on 7 August with the introduction of a new service from Perth to Crieff and Comrie while a week later, on 12 August, two more local cross-city services were started operating on a circular basis between Scone and Burghmuir every 20 minutes in each direction with hail and ride facilities on some parts of the route and passengers being carried free on the first two days of their operation. Once again these competed directly with routes maintained by Strathtay but on this occasion they were operated by new Iveco minibuses carrying the Perth Panther fleet name. In response, Strathtay replaced its conventional buses on its challenged services with some new Dodge minibuses painted in Perth City Transport livery and adorned with 'City Nipper' logos.

During this period of attrition in Perth, Stagecoach took the opportunity to further strengthen its position on the south coast of England by purchasing Southdown Motor Services on 16 August from under the nose of Alan Stephenson's AJS Holdings who had been attempting to add this important company to its portfolio for several weeks. The acquisition of Southdown was viewed with great importance as its western boundary butted up to Hampshire Bus and in addition to adding another 250 or so vehicles to the Group's combined fleet it also gave Stagecoach an area of operation which stretched from Hastings to beyond Southampton. Included in the deal was Sharpton Ltd. who owned all the company's depots, offices and bus stations, and Southdown's 51% share in Hastings Topline Buses Ltd., a company formed in March 1988 by Southdown and Eastbourne Buses. Shortly after gaining control of Southdown, Stagecoach purchased Eastbourne's 49% stake in Top Line to give it total control but although it was placed under the control of Southdown for administrative purposes, it was retained as a separate subsidiary with its distinctive yellow & black livery. Sadly, however, the change of ownership of Southdown marked the end of the company's attractive green & cream livery which had for so long been a feature of this part of the south coast.

Although the Tay Tiger fleet name was applied to Perth Panther Leyland National 209 (GFX973N), it was never seen in service and was removed after only a couple of days following complaints by Tayside Public Transport Co. (Campbell Morrison)

Being unable to use the Tay Tigers fleet name on the buses employed on its services from Dundee, Stagecoach instead added its own name to some of its Leyland Nationals as illustrated by 222 (GTL355N) seen in May 1990 preparing to leave for Carnoustie.

Still painted in Frontrunner North West livery and complete with that company's fleet name, Alexander-bodied Leyland Atlantean KSA186P had become a member of the Southdown Portsmouth fleet when photographed in Portsmouth in February 1990 working the local 42 service to Petersfield. (T.S.Blackman)

Back in Scotland, the battle with Strathtay Scottish moved northwards on 21 August when Stagecoach inaugurated its first local service in Dundee, cheekily giving this the same number as the Strathtay service it copied. Running from the city centre to Monifieth, it was maintained by 6 Leyland Nationals which it had been planned would carry 'Tay Tigers' fleet names. At the last minute, the buses concerned had their new names replaced by the Stagecoach title, however, following complaints from Tayside Buses, who were at that time negotiating a sponsorship deal with Tay Tigers Ice Hockey team. A week after Stagecoach had arrived in Dundee it commenced a second service from the city centre to Carnoustie which again mirrored a Strathtay route and copied its number and, in order to save dead mileage to and from Perth or Spittalfield, accommodation was obtained for its buses at the Dundee depot of Greyhound Coaches close to the city centre.

Meanwhile, the previous year's trading results to 30 April 1989 showed that the company had achieved a pre-tax profit of £3,458,000 on a

The Ford Transit minibuses hired by Stagecoach from Devon General were all transported the long journey from their home to Scotland by rail as seen here.

Preparing to leave Mill Street, Perth in October 1989 while operating Perth Panther service 1 to Letham is C675FFJ, one of twenty Carlyle-bodied Ford Transit minibuses hired by Stagecoach from Devon General. (K.A.Jenkinson)

turnover of £36,757,000 which indicated the success of its expansion programme coupled with the rationalisation of its operations. Amongst the numerous new vehicles purchased by the Stagecoach Group was a surprise acquisition by United Counties of a new Famos S315.21 coach (marketed in the UK as the Ensign Charisma) which was painted in National Express Rapide colours for use on that company's contracted services to London.

Having now had time to assess Southdown's operations, its depots at Horsham and Haywards Heath which had been closed prior to their purchase by Stagecoach were now regarded as being surplus to requirements and were offered for sale while that at Hayling Island was closed and used as a temporary store for withdrawn vehicles. All but two of the Eastbourne Buses Leyland Atlanteans which had remained in service in the Topline fleet since its acquisition were replaced by Southdown Leyland Nationals on 24 September and returned to their rightful owner while on the following day the local bus operations of Cedar Travel of Worthing were purchased by Southdown. This provided the company with six additional services in Worthing and 8 minibuses, all of which it was intended would retain their existing white, orange & brown livery and fleet names and would be operated as a separate unit on their established routes. Cedar's coaching interests were not included in the deal and remained with their original owner.

Continuing its vigorous activities towards further rationalisation, Stagecoach sold its Ribble subsidiary, Bee Line Buzz, the majority of Ribble's operations in Manchester and its East Midland subsidiary Frontrunner North-West to the Drawlane Group on 30 September together with 44 full-size buses and coaches, 186 minibuses and its depots at Stockport, Tintwhistle and Manchester. As part of the deal, Drawlane subsidiary North Western Road Car Co. Ltd. who had since June 1988 been competing with Ribble on a number of services in and around Blackburn, withdrew from that area on 11 September and passed the services concerned to the Stagecoach company. At this same time, Ribble closed its Burnley depot and transferred its small allocation to the Burnley & Pendle Transport depot in the town where outside parking space was rented. Also sold to Drawlane at this same time was the company's Cessna aeroplane which had been replaced a few weeks earlier by a larger, and more comfortable, Cessna 410-type 8-seater registered G-JEMS. In an attempt to tidy up its empire mainly for accountancy purposes, Stagecoach created a new division known as Stagecoach South under which both Hampshire Bus and United Counties were placed.

The vehicle replacement programme continued with the arrival in September of 23 new minibuses (15 Reeve Burgess-bodied Iveco 49.10s and 8 Reeve Burgess-bodied Mercedes Benz 811Ds) and 7 coach-seated Alexander-bodied Leyland Olympians and in addition, a large number of existing vehicles were moved between fleets to satisfy new needs. Also moved to new pastures, albeit only temporarily, was one of Cumberland's 3-axle Leyland Olympians which was loaned to Greater Manchester Buses for evaluation purposes from 4 to 11 September. During its stay it became the subject of much publicity, not for its superb riding quality, however, but when it was used as a getaway vehicle by a bank robber who had just stolen £2,000 from the Hazel Grove branch of the TSB. The driver was unaware of the situation until the villain's shotgun fired accidentally in the upper saloon and as might have been expected, the local press headed the story relating to the incident with the headline 'Bank bandit shoots up a Stagecoach'.

After gaining 5 Bristol LH6L single deckers from East Midland, 4 ex.Trent Leyland Leopard coaches from Cumberland and 3 coach-

Pictured in its new home in Malawi is former Magicbus Bristol FLF6G Lodekka KPW487E which joined the UTM fleet in November 1989 after taking a load of medical supplies an other gifts from Blantyre in Scotland to Blantyre in Malawi. (R.Bailey)

seated Bristol VRT double deckers from Hampshire Bus for its expanding Perth service network, 8 Ford Transit minibuses were hired from Devon General from 25 September. Surprisingly, rather than being driven north from their native Devon, these little buses travelled by rail from Exeter, letting the train take the strain out of their 500 mile expedition and a further 12 vehicles of this type made a similar journey on 2 October. Prior to this on 7 September, one of Stagecoach's Bristol FLF6G Lodekkas unexpectedly left the fleet when it began its long journey to Malawi. Suitably adorned with legends bearing good wishes etc., it first visited the Scottish town of Blantyre where, after it was loaded with medical supplies and gifts for the Queen Elizabeth Central Hospital in Blantyre, Malawi, it was given an official 'send off' at a special 'hands across the water' ceremony. Leaving Southampton seven days later, its journey was by sea to Durban from where it travelled by road through Zimbabwe and Mozambique, arriving at its final destination on 3 November. Its cargo was presented by Ann Gloag to a high-ranking official of Malawi's Ministry of Health during the following week after which the Lodekka then joined the United Transport Malawi fleet for occasional operation. The connection between the two Blantyres dates back to David Livingstone, the explorer/missionary, who was born in Blantyre, Scotland and eventually 'discovered' what is now Malawi.

Back home, Stagecoach Holdings became the subject of complaints to the Office of Fair Trading by both Lancaster City Council and Strathtay Scottish - Lancaster alleging that its operating arm was being put under undue pressure to contract its operations, Strathtay Scottish complaining that the tactics adopted in the Tayside bus war were anti-competitive. Before the OFT could complete its investigations into these matters, Stagecoach subsidiary Ribble reached agreement with Lancaster City Transport to reorganise its services in Lancaster and Morecambe to provide a better service to passengers and both operators agreed to the interavailability of their tickets on shared routes. Additionally Lancaster withdrew its services to Preston and Blackpool and all the changes were implemented on 2 October. Early in October, Brian Cox who in addition to being managing director of Hampshire Bus was also responsible for Stagecoach's operations in Scotland, relinquished the latter and instead took up the position of managing director of Southdown. His Scottish duties were then taken over by Neil Renilson who was no stranger to the area having been managing director of Strathtay Scottish until joining Stagecoach earlier in the summer. Other moves saw Tony Cox, commercial manager of Ribble's northern area take up the position of traffic manager at United Counties whilst Maurice Titheridge, Hampshire Bus's chief driving instructor was seconded to UTM in Africa for ten days after having spent six weeks in Scotland helping to set up the Perth Panther operation, confirming Stagecoach's commitment to bus operation and the career development of its staff. The company's success was now growing rapidly and in her

The hub of the Stagecoach empire. The company's new headquarters at Charlotte House, Perth also incorporates a travel office on its ground floor. (K.A.Jenkinson)

Despite having operated for Stagecoach at Perth for several months, ex.Cumberland Bristol VRT HHH273N retained its NBC poppy red livery and CMS posters throughout its time north of the border. After its withdrawal from service it was used as a store room at Stagecoach's new depot at Inveralmond, Perth where it is seen in October 1989. (S.K.Jenkinson)

Approaching Perth city centre whilst working local service 2 from Tulloch in October 1989, Robin Hood-bodied Iveco 49.10 031 (G31PSR), like its sisters, wore Perth Panther Cub fleet names. (Murdoch Currie)

speech at the Bus & Coach Council conference in Guernsey, Ann Gloag attributed this to the excellent management team the company had assembled. Favouring individual pay negotiations at each company within the Group, she indicated 'no deal' for any union pressure to return to the days of central negotiation. When asked if the company was wise in its policy of closing central maintenance workshops she pointed out that this decision allowed Stagecoach with its massive purchasing power to go to outside concerns and gain extremely good rates and added that virtually every time central workshops had been inherited, these were found to be bastions of union militancy, a paragon of inefficiency, and a definite waste of resources.

Having continued to use the offices and depot at Walnut Grove, Perth since their sale to National Express on 4 August, Stagecoach Holdings at the end of that month found new administrative accommodation at 20 Charlotte Street, Perth in a building previously occupied by Blair Insurance Services who handled Stagecoach's insurance claims. Being much closer to Perth city centre than Walnut Grove, this became the Group's new headquarters and also incorporated a travel office within its reception area. To allow the move from Walnut Grove to be completed, new depot premises were gained on Inveralmond Trading Estate on the northern fringe of the city and became operational on 21 October. The new 'depot' was, in reality, an area of uncovered land upon which the only building was a portakabin. The former Cumberland Bristol VRT which had been withdrawn from service a couple of weeks earlier still wearing NBC red livery and adorned with Cumberland advertising posters was put to use as a store room whilst a withdrawn ex.Magicbus Leyland Leopard was converted to a uniform store and a B & Q garden shed was erected to provide facilities for the cleaners. As the site contained no undercover facility for vehicle maintenance, a small unit was leased nearby on the Estate in which all minibus maintenance was carried out, conventional size buses having to travel to Spittalfield for such work to be undertaken.

In Perth, the Panther network was revised on 9 October when, continuing its pressure on Strathtay Scottish, all the services became identical to those of the SBG subsidiary and were timed to run a few minutes ahead of them. The increased number of vehicles required brought into use the Ford Transit minibuses hired from Devon General whose maroon & cream livery they continued to wear, and in addition to these, 8 new Iveco 49.10 minibuses were also put into service. Across the border on 2 October, Ribble had closed its small depot at Garstang and reallocated its vehicles to Preston while East Midland successfully gained a number of South Yorkshire PTE tenders in the Doncaster area, partly at the expense of Yorkshire Traction. These were rebranded as 'Dearne Valley' and at the same time the company's new coach-seated Olympians were put to use on a revised Sheffield to Nottingham express service. Later, on 16 October, Ribble recast several of its services after reaching a territorial agreement with Preston Borough Transport and withdrew all its Zippy minibus routes north of the river Ribble. By now, Stagecoach's corporate livery was becoming increasingly common within all of its various operating companies and after devising a new Stagecoach Holdings logo which, based on the geographical outline of Great Britain, formed the letters SCH, this began to be applied to all the corporate-liveried vehicles as well as to publicity material and timetable leaflets etc.

Undoubtedly the major news of October, however, was the purchase on the 20th of Portsmouth CityBus, a former municipal undertaking in which Southampton CityBus held a 75% share and StartRight (the Portsmouth CityBus workforce) owned the remaining 25%. An ailing company, Portsmouth CityBus together with its Red Admiral minibus operation had for some considerable time been facing ever-increasing competition from both People's Provincial and Southdown and it was clearly evident that a great deal of reorganisation would be required in order to improve its trading position. Immediately placed under the control of Southdown, the first priority was to rationalise the services of both companies to eliminate duplication and wastage. Thus in early November it was announced that all the services within the city would be placed under the Southdown Portsmouth banner and would be centred on the CityBus depot at Eastney which had been secured on a three-year lease from the city council. This would allow Southdown's Hilsea depot to be closed and sold for redevelopment and looking to the longer term, negotiations were already taking place in an attempt to extend the lease on the Eastney premises. As part of the deal struck with Southampton CityBus during the purchase process, it was agreed to transfer two Hampshire Bus routes - the half-hourly stopping inter-urban 47 between Winchester and Southampton and Southdown's share of the joint Southampton - Portsmouth express service - to the council-owned company early in 1990.

After expressing an interest in Ulsterbus and with the dust having barely settled on the south coast, Stagecoach turned its attention to north-west Scotland when, on 11 November through its Magicbus subsidiary, it acquired the business of Inverness Traction from the receiver. With this business came a number of Inverness town services, 22 Freight Rover Sherpa minibuses and 6 Leyland Leopards, 2 of the latter having only been purchased from Stagecoach four months earlier. Ironically, the Inverness operation was placed under the control of Neil Renilson who, whilst managing director of Strathtay Scottish, had sent buses free of charge to SBG subsidiary Highland Scottish to help it attack Inverness Traction soon after its formation and now had to repair the damage he had helped to cause! Apart from the Leyland Leopards, all the other inherited vehicles were leased and as their new operator was keen to return them to their rightful owner as quickly as possible, it was not long before replacements were drafted in from other Group companies to allow their release. Amongst these were the 10 ex.Zippy tri-axle Talbot Pullman minibuses which had been in store with Cumberland. Still wearing their former owner's yellow and red livery, these provided a total contrast to the grey used by Inverness Traction and considerably brightened up the town's narrow thoroughfares.

Having gained a Strathclyde PTE contract to provide the Sunday operation on a Glasgow area service running from Clydebank to Parkhall, Stagecoach once again turned its attention to Tayside where, on 27 November, it started a new route from Dundee to Blairgowrie which copied that of Strathtay Scottish and used the same number (57). To attract passengers to this new service, adverts were inserted in the local press which in addition to showing the times and fares included two free travel vouchers which could be used up to and including 9 December. Since the start of the Tayside bus war some five months

Acquired by Southdown with the operations of Portsmouth Citybus, Leyland National 204 (THX219S) which began life with London Transport still wore the cream & red livery and fleet names of its former operator as it approached The Hard, Portsmouth in July 1990. (T.G.Walker)

Wearing the grey livery of Inverness Traction, Dormobile-bodied Freight Rover Sherpa G277TST which was withdrawn from service in October 1989 following accident damage awaits a buyer at Stagecoach's Spittalfield depot in March 1990. (Campbell Morrison)

Mercers of Longridge operated former South Yorkshire PTE MCCW-bodied Leyland Fleetline OKW512R on its services running into Preston where it is seen here in November 1989. (T.W.W.Knowles)

earlier, as a result of Stagecoach's policy of undercutting fares, Strathtay Scottish had been forced to reduce many of its charges by up to 50% and although neither operator could claim to be making a substantial profit from these operations, Stagecoach was continuing to strengthen its position while the travelling public had never had it so good either in terms of fares or frequency of service. Meanwhile, in Lancashire, peace had returned to Blackburn on 20 November following an agreement being reached between Ribble and Blackburn Transport in respect of their service networks under which wasteful competition was eliminated while on 13 November East Midland had achieved significant economies after recasting its services in the Worksop and Bassetlaw areas and operating them with more new Mercedes Benz 811D minibuses.

Competition was further eliminated in north-west England when on 26 November the local bus operations of Mercers of Longridge were purchased followed on 1 December by those of W.A.Palmer of Carlisle. Although an old-established coach operator, Mercers had not entered the stage carriage field until October 1986 but since that date had built up a fleet of 20 buses (10 double deckers, 6 single deckers and 4 minibuses) and a network of local services including several Lancashire County Council contracts. Although all the buses passed to Ribble under this deal, Mercers retained its depot at Grimsargh and coach fleet which it intended to expand while all Palmer's 8 vehicles, although taken into stock by Cumberland, were immediately withdrawn and offered for sale. The acquisition of W.A.Palmer gave Cumberland seven additional services including its first which operated across the Scottish border to Gretna Green and Longtown. Further south, East Midland was in the meantime facing disruption of its services when the National Union of Railwaymen imposed an overtime ban following the dismissal of a fitter.

South Coast Buses coach-seated MCW Metrorider 2909 (419DCD) which was originally registered F565HPP and joined the company via Southdown with the Cedarbus business was unusually fitted with a sliding entrance door. (T.S.Blackman)

Opposite page :

Left column, top to bottom :

Having only recently been acquired by Ribble from Lancaster City Transport, East Lancs-bodied Leyland Atlantean 1214 (A214MCK) although still in the livery of its former owner had just been given Ribble Buses fleet names at Blackburn depot on 7 September 1993 prior to making its debut in service with its new owner at Preston. (K.A.Jenkinson)

Picking up its Chesterfield-bound passengers in Pond Street bus station, Sheffield in 1990 is East Midland Leyland National 531 (WNO552L) which had been acquired from Eastern National two years earlier. (T.G.Walker)

Although still painted in the green & yellow livery of Alder Valley, Bristol VRT 964 (WJM824T) had gained corporate-style Stagecoach Hants & Surrey fleet names when caught by the camera in Guildford in December 1992. (T.S.Blackman)

Typifying Busways' fleet of Bristol REs now operated by its Blue Bus Services division is 1818 (JMW167P), an RESL6G acquired from Thamesdown Transport in January 1988. (Paul Savage)

Right column, top to bottom :

Still adorned with the livery in which it was received from Ayrshire Bus Owners but having gained Stagecoach A1 Service fleet names, Alexander-bodied Leyland Atlantean 814 (NCS15P) rests at Ardrossan depot in February 1995. (K.A.Jenkinson)

One of Cheltenham & Gloucester's five ex.South Midland (and originally Greater Manchester PTE) Park Royal-bodied Leyland Titans, Swindon & District-liveried 110 (GNF10V) is seen at Latton Cross returning from Cirencester to Swindon on its first day in service in April 1990. (Travelscene)

With less than a month to go before its withdrawal from service, Cumberland's ex.London Routemaster 903 (ALD983B) which was acquired from Kelvin Scottish in 1987 is seen in Carlisle city centre in November 1992. Still owned by Cumberland and now repainted into Stagecoach corporate livery, it is currently held in reserve and has never operated in its new colours. (K.A.Jenkinson)

Passing Glenrothes bus station in August 1992 on the X59 service to Dundee is Fife Scottish 905, a coach-seated Alexander-bodied Volvo Citybus still wearing its pre-Stagecoach livery. (K.A.Jenkinson)

000
Littlewoods £2Million won't change me.
HOLLYWOOD
A214 MCK

Stagecoach
ATLANTEAN
NCS 15P

50
EAST MIDLAND
WNO 552L

62
WINDON
GNF 10V
Latt
village

NEWS AND MAIL
20A
Guildford
JOBS, CARS, HOUSES, AND LOCAL NEWS
Stagecoach
WJM 824T

61
CITY CENTRE
903
ALD 983B

BBS Newcastle
1818
BLUE BUS SERVICES
JMW 167P

Fife SCOTTISH
DUNDEE

Operating service 21 at Malvern Way, Hastings is Park Royal-bodied AEC Regent V 946 (MFN946F) which was new to East Kent and later passed to Hastings & District in whose blue, cream & yellow livery it is still maintained.   (T.S.Blackman)

New to South Yorkshire PTE, East Lancs-bodied Bristol VRT 771 (OWE271K) despite still wearing its old Hastings & District blue, cream & yellow livery had gained Stagecoach-style Hastings Buses fleet names when caught by the camera in June 1992. (T.S.Blackman)

Former Kowloon Motor Bus Metsec-bodied Daimler CVG6s D425 & D431 (AD7331/7) which never entered service in their new home in Malawi are seen here being scrapped at Chichiri depot, Blantyre together with UTM Leyland Victory 216 from its Country (Southern) fleet. (J.Davison)

In an attempt to keep services running normally during this troubled period, East Midland's managing director George Watson quickly assembled a troubleshooting squad by importing relief drivers from other Stagecoach subsidiaries including a bus load of volunteers from its Scottish depots. For a couple of weeks the Mansfield town services were then maintained by a combination of Inverness Traction inspectors and Perth Panther and Magicbus drivers, giving Highland and Strathtay Scottish a brief respite as a result of all duplication being withdrawn to free drivers temporarily transferred to East Midland. In addition to climbing behind the wheel himself, George Watson was joined by Brian Souter who also took on a driver's role and drove several journeys on the Chesterfield - Nottingham service. Accommodation for the 'imported' crews was provided by the company in local hotels, motels and guest houses during their period 'away from home' and as a result of this swift

With its roof heavily patched, ex.Kowloon Metsec-bodied Daimler CVG6 1052 (BH6752) displaying Cityline and Stagecoach fleet names stands at Stagecoach Malawi's Lilongwe depot.   (J.Davison)

response the NUR subsequently dropped its action to allow normality to return to the area.

Following much speculation during previous months of the possible sale of Hastings Topline Buses to Milton Keynes City Bus who was at that time attempting to take over Hastings & District Transport Co. Ltd., Southdown suddenly stepped in on 8 December and purchased Formia Ltd., owners of Hastings & District, Hastings Coaches Ltd., Eastbourne & District Transport Ltd. and Cinque Ports Travel Ltd., thus further strengthening its position along the south-east coast. Included in the deal was the Hastings & District fleet, all its services and depots at Rye and Silverhill (St.Leonards-on-Sea) and at the time of the acquisition two different liveries were used, one being ivory & crimson, the other blue, yellow & cream.

Having found its double deckers to be a great success, Stagecoach's African subsidiary United Transport Malawi acquired a further 5 former Kowloon Motor Bus Daimler CVG6s together with 5 Duple-bodied Albion EVK55CL-type coaches from this same source, although one of the latter was cannibalised for spares rather than being placed in service. By now, double deck operation had resulted in a growth in patronage of more than 60% with a negligible increase in the number of kilometres operated and as a result their operation was extended to several other services in the Blantyre area. During the period since Stagecoach had gained its controlling interest in the company, a large number of its services had been revised and several of those discontinued earlier had been reinstated while of necessity, some of the 'country' routes had to operate to different timetables during the wet and dry seasons. Additionally, two new international services had been introduced, one from Lilongwe to Lusaka in Zambia, the other from Lilongwe to Harare with the former, which had a journey time of 13 hours including a 90 minute break at the Mwami border point, being operated jointly by UTM and UBZ of Zambia running outbound from Lilongwe on Sundays and Wednesdays, returning on Tuesdays and Thursdays. Another service with an unusual operation was that from Blantyre to Lilongwe which took up to 8 hours 30 minutes between termini, as on this, two of its daily journeys were operated by Leyland Victory Mk.2 buses hauling freight trailers.

ROLLING INTO A NEW DECADE

Compared with the events of the previous year the new decade opened quietly, although this proved to be but a brief respite before the wheels of change were put into motion again. On 2 January Hastings & District ceased the practice of outstationing one of its Eastbourne & District minibuses at Pevensey while twelve days later Top Line moved from its premises at Farrants Yard to the Hastings & District depot at Silverhill where space was made by the removal of a number of delicensed and stored vehicles to the Coach Station and Bulverhythe. Despite having vacated Farrants Yard, a shed was retained there in which more withdrawn vehicles were able to be housed. Along the coast, Portsmouth CityBus was fully merged with Southdown on the night of 20/21 January and immediately all the former CityBus vehicles had their legal lettering altered to show Southdown as their new owner. Although those buses repainted in corporate livery were fitted with new Southdown Portsmouth fleetnames, those still in the old CityBus colours of cream & red retained their existing names and it was some considerable time before these disappeared completely. Meanwhile, Cedar Travel who had sold its local bus operations to Southdown in September of the previous year cheekily re-entered the field with a new cross-town service in Worthing and another to Midhurst. On 22 January Hampshire Bus relocated its Botley outstation to the yard of Hills Transport and on that same day Stagecoach fired new shots at Strathtay Scottish by extending its Dundee - Carnoustie service (74) to Arbroath and altering its 75 service in Dundee to run via Broomhill Drive and Ashludie Hospital. Together these two routes provided a 10-minute frequency between Dundee and Monifieth presenting Strathtay with an even greater challenge on its lucrative Tayway services bearing these same numbers, while somewhat unexpectedly, on the final day of January East Midland despatched four of its MCW Metrorider minibuses on loan to London Buses for driver training purposes, two of them being allocated to Hounslow garage, the other two to Fulwell, and it was not until March that these were returned to their rightful owner.

February had barely begun when, on its second day East Midland took a 50% holding in Maun International Coachways of Sutton-in-Ashfield, thus reducing the competition it had faced on a number of routes including that from Mansfield to Newark. Maun International Travel Consultants Ltd. and Maun Crusader Tours Ltd. were, however,

Next page :
Left column, top to bottom :

Wearing Stagecoach's original GT Coaches-style double deck livery and still sporting the aeroplane picture on its side panels which it carried when it was received from Bristol Omnibus Co. in April 1981 is convertible open-top Bristol FS6G 866NHT, seen here in June 1982. (P.McElroy)

The penultimate Neoplan Skyliner to join the Stagecoach fleet was E92VWA which did so in December 1987. Here it leaves Glasgow's Buchanan bus station on a journey to Aberdeen in April 1988. (S.K.Jenkinson)

New to Grampian Regional Transport and later serving with East Midland's Frontrunner North West subsidiary, Alexander-bodied Leyland Atlantean KSA189P ultimately joined the Southdown fleet and, after gaining Stagecoach corporate livery was given Portsmouth fleet names for use on the services acquired with Portsmouth Citybus. It is seen here working a journey to Southsea in March 1990. (Travelscene)

Stagecoach South added stripes at each side of the destination screen of both its double and single deck buses as illustrated by South Coast Buses Leyland National 102 (AYJ102T) seen at Hastings railway station in 1993. (T.S.Blackman)

Right column, top to bottom :

Purchased from Park of Hamilton for use in the Adamson fleet, former Leicester City Transport MCCW-bodied Leyland PD3A/12 LJF27F seen here in 1984 had received Stagecoach's new livery whilst the FLF6G Lodekka in the background still wore the GT Coaches-derived colour scheme.

Resting at Friarton Road depot, Perth still painted in GT Coaches livery is former Western National (Royal Blue) ECW-bodied Bristol MW6G HDV639E. (G.Martin-Bates)

Fitted with its original Duple Dominant III body, Volvo B58 JSR42X seen here in 1983 was later given a new Duple Dominant I body in December 1987. (W.McGregor)

Painted in Stagecoach South's customary livery with its additional stripes around its front destination aperture and front side panels, an immaculate former Hastings & District Bristol VRT (760 : BKE760T) is seen in Hastings in July 1993. (T.S.Blackman)

Freshly repainted into corporate livery, Stagecoach Hartlepool NCME-bodied Dennis Falcon 28 (B28PAJ) traverses Church Street, Hartlepool in April 1995. (K.A.Jenkinson)

Painted in the colourful red, orange, yellow & green livery of Maun of Mansfield, Alexander-bodied Leyland leopard TSU642W passed with its owner's business to East Midland early in 1990. After being repainted into Stagecoach corporate livery and numbered 411 by its new owner. (P.T.Stokes)

STAGECOACH
STAGECOACH
PERTH 33481
866 NHT

MICHAEL JOHN FOR CARPETS
LEYLAND

STAGECOACH
STAGECOACH
E92 VWA

GLASGOW
STAGECOACH
VOLVO
JSR 42X

PORT
Portsmouth
SOUTHSEA 11
Portsmouth

400
SUMMER SEASON 93
Stagecoach
Stagecoach

99 HASTINGS
102
AYJ 102T

14 CHALLONER ROAD VIA MULGRAVE ROAD
Stagecoach
Stagecoach
B28 PAJ

UNI=SPRINT
Stagecoach

250 Ellon
Northern Scottish

PREMIER
PREMIER TRAVEL SERVICES
'Columbus'
J448 HDS

8 City Centre
SCARLET O'HARA

53 HOLLINGTON
Tesco
TOP LINE
TOP LINE
BCD 822L

"I ate the bit my Gran couldn't finish"
CAMBUS
761
CAMBUS
PTT 92R

X15 Coventry
via Kenilworth
LONDON £20.00 RETURN
ANY TRAIN, ANY TIME
FROM WARWICK OR LEAMINGTON
Ron Ingram
C962 XVC
X12 University of Warwick
G&G TRAVEL
WDA 994T

Hackney Shoreditch
Liverpool St. Bank
St Paul's Aldwych
26
WATERLOO STN.
Stagecoach
KYV 311X

Pictured in Chichester on March 1990, Southdown's corporate-liveried Robin Hood-bodied Iveco 49.10 920 (G420RYJ) carried Coastline fleet names on either side of its body. (Travelscene)

Southdown Robin Hood-bodied Iveco 49.10 923 (E233JRF) seen in Worthing in April 1990 was painted in a white livery with orange relief band and fitted with corporate Stagecoach-style Cedarbus fleet names. (T.S.Blackman)

excluded from the deal which added 19 single deckers and minibuses, 4 double deckers and 6 withdrawn vehicles to the East Midland fleet and gave it an operating base at Sutton. Many of the vehicles acquired were condemned immediately mainly due to their age or condition and to compensate, several vehicles were transferred from the East Midland fleet. In view of East Midland only owning a half-share in the company, Maun was operated independently and retained its colourful green, orange, cream & red livery. Further north Cumberland closed its Ulverston depot on 16 February, moving its 6-vehicle allocation to the yard of Cumbria Commercials in the town while in Barrow Cumberland began to fit its buses with coloured destination blinds using a different colour for each route and thus reintroducing an almost forgotten practice. For some inexplicable reason, during February several Hastings & District buses had green Southdown names and logos added to their front panel, although these were all removed before the end of the month, disappearing almost as quickly as they had appeared. Simultaneous with this move, Southdown on 25 February introduced two new minibus services between Chichester and Witterings in order to retaliate against Westrings of West Wittering who had for some time offered competition on this corridor. The new routes both adopted the new 'Coastline' brand name which was also applied to the park & ride service won on tender by Southdown and during the next few weeks, the Coastline name was extended to all the company's minibuses operating in Chichester and Bognor in the same way that the Cedarbus name was used in Worthing.

In Scotland, Magicbus moved on 25 February from its old depot at Warroch Street, Glasgow (which had been sold to Robert Maxwell whose Daily Record print facility was sited nearby) to new premises at Hobden Street in the Springburn area of the city. Comprising a modern workshop and large open-air parking area, the new site provided the company with much improved facilities and greater space even though it was further away from the city centre. In the meantime, in Tayside a breakthrough in the fierce bus war was finally achieved following talks between Stagecoach and Strathtay Scottish which produced an agreement from both parties to share operations on all the services involved in Perth on a 50/50 basis and co-ordinate their timings. The first route to be subject to the new pact was that operating through the city centre from Scone to Hillend and it was agreed by both companies that further co-operation would become a reality in the months which lay ahead. This marked a major achievement for Stagecoach who had thus gained a 50% share of the Perth bus market after just seven months.

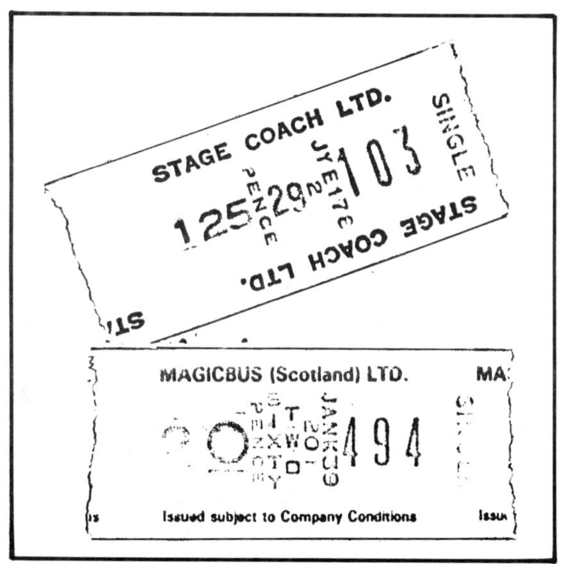

Previous page :
Left column, top to bottom :

One of a number of buses repainted into Uni-sprint livery for operation on services from Morecambe to Lancaster University, Ribble Alexander-bodied Leyland Olympian 2192 (H192WFR) leaves Lancaster bus station in October 1996. (Travelscene)

Cambus Holdings coaching subsidiary Premier Travel Services operate a number of coaches in a variety of liveries. Seen at the Cowley Road, Cambridge depot in April 1996 is 414 (J448HDS), a Plaxton Premiere 350-bodied Volvo B10M acquired from Park of Hamilton in 1993. (K.A.Jenkinson)

Wearing the later version of the Top Line livery and also sporting a small Southdown fleet name below its windscreens is Leyland National 22 (BCD822L) seen at Hastings in March 1990. (Travelscene)

Still painted in Stratford Blue livery and named 'Ron Ingram', Midland Red South ECW-bodied coach-seated Leyland Olympian 962 (C962XVC) stands alongside G & G Travel's ex.West Midlands Travel MCCW-bodied Leyland Fleetline 1958 (WDA994T) at Leamington depot in October 1995. (K.A.Jenkinson)

Right column, top to bottom :

Awaiting its departure to Ellon at Aberdeen bus station in the summer of 1991 is Northern Scottish Alexander-bodied coach-seated Leyland Olympian 063 (C463SSO). (Travelscene)

Travelling towards Peterborough bus station in June 1996 is Viscount Buses ex.Keighley & District Bristol VRT 775 (PWY45W) which is painted in Peterborough Bus Company livery. (K.A.Jenkinson)

Approaching Drummer Street bus station, Cambridge in June 1996 is Cambus ECW-bodied Bristol VRT 761 (PTT92R) which joined the fleet from Red Bus, North Devon in 1986. (K.A.Jenkinson)

Still adorned with a white centre band but having gained Stagecoach East London fleet names, Leyland Titan T311 (KYV311X) makes its way towards Waterloo Station in the spring of 1995. (M.Salmon)

Taking a break at Tamworth motorway services is Midland Travel 87 (D550MVR), a Van Hool-bodied Volvo B10M acquired from Shearings Holidays. Note the Coachstyle names across the top of its windscreens. (G.T.W.Carter)

Having gained its initial objective, Stagecoach's attention was then directed towards scaling down the level of over provision that had built up during the protracted battle. In the meantime, the company had received 20 more new Alexander-bodied Mercedes Benz 709D minibuses for operation in Perth and Inverness which, upon their arrival allowed the replacement of a number of the hired Devon General Ford Transits and some of Inverness Traction's tri-axle Talbot Pullmans.

On 5 March East Midland and Rainworth Travel combined their coaching and travel agency activities and Rainworth's bus operations into a new division of East Midland which operated under the title of Rainworth Travel Ltd. but used the trading name 'Midland Travel'. The new operation and its combined 35-vehicle fleet used East Midland's Shirebrook depot as its base, thus allowing the old Rainworth premises at Langwith to be closed and offered for sale. Soon after this reorganisation took place, the 4 MCW Metroriders loaned to London Buses were returned and in their place another 4 were despatched to the capital to continue the driver training work. March also proved to be a month during which Stagecoach faced criticism in both Preston and Portsmouth following its takeover of local operators. In Lancashire, concern was expressed by the County Council at the deterioration in the standard of service by Ribble in the Preston area where difficulties had arisen following the acquisition of tendered services from Mercers. The additional pressure on vehicles and particularly the need for more double deckers had severely strained Ribble's resources and as a result the company gave notice of termination of five of the County Council's contracts. In Portsmouth the situation was more serious and it was announced that an investigation was to be mounted by the Monopolies and Mergers Commission into the Group's acquisition of Portsmouth CityBus where the Secretary of State for Trade and Industry believed that this had possible effects on competition in the marketplace for commercial and contracted bus services. The MMC was asked to make its report by 21 May, and although there was confidence in the Southdown camp, the outcome of the report was nevertheless awaited with some trepidation. Meanwhile, Stagecoach was not surprised to learn that the Office of Fair Trading was not going to take up the complaint lodged by Strathtay Scottish relating to the company's competitive activities in the Perth area since the allegation of predatory behaviour was not sustained and in any event the work sharing agreement had now rendered the whole matter irrelevant.

Also during March, United Transport Malawi was renamed Stagecoach Malawi and in addition to receiving a further 6 ex.Kowloon Motor Bus Daimler CVG6s from Speedybus Enterprises, the company placed its first order for new buses. The arrival of the Daimlers allowed double deck operation to be introduced in Lilongwe while the new buses were 28 Gardner-engined ERF Trailblazers which were to be supplied in ckd form for local assembly. It was hoped that these could be bodied by PEW of Malawi, a coachbuilding company in which Stagecoach Malawi had a 14% share, but if this could not be undertaken quickly the bodies would be constructed by AUT of Harare. Operationally the company continued to review its service network and improved the frequency on most of its express routes as well as extending its intercity service to serve several more townships and reintroducing the service from Blantyre to Monkey Bay to cater for lake travellers and tourists.

Back in Scotland, the remaining 8 Devon General Ford Transit minibuses were all taken out of service and returned to their owner on 21 March while several previously withdrawn Bristol Lodekkas were taken out of storage at Spittalfield and returned to service in Perth. More surprising, however, was the repainting into corporate livery of a Lodekka which was equipped as a caravan and had been purchased in that form in December 1986. The purpose of its reactivation was so that it was able to make a two week overland trip to Romania, driven by

Already converted to a caravan when purchased by Stagecoach in December 1986, Bristol FLF6G 074 (FJB738C) was ultimately painted into Stagecoach corporate colours for some overland journeys to Romania loaded with medical and other supplies. In addition to displaying Stagecoach fleet names, it had the logos of the company's other Scottish subsidiaries painted on its staircase panel. (Campbell Morrison)

Standing at the Bowness terminus of Cumberland's Lakeland Experience service to Ambleside is green & cream liveried ex.Southdown open-top Bristol VRT 2038 (UWV620S). In addition to carrying promotional lettering on its upper deck and front panels, it also has a route diagram above its side windows and further material on its lower deck side panels. (T.W.W.Knowles)

37
Middlesbrough
10,000 2 Colour A4 Leaflets for Only £139
Discount Print From
one
Tel: 240 888
TRANSIT
218
B218 OAJ

EASTBOURNE
LONDON FESTIVAL
Abbo
&Abbo
98 HASTINGS
TOP LINE
TOP LINE
ENJ 915V

METRO
C705 FKE

SHIPWRIGHTS ARMS
02
TOWN SERVICE
GCV 461S

2
Red & White
F203 YKG

4487
ALL WALLBANGER NO HARVEY.
TUNGSTEN
BREWED
HUSK FREE
FOR PURITY
143
GMS
GMS
GMS

Routemaster
1
SHIRE ROAD
SAFEWAY
IN CORBY
Routemaster

19
We got them where I get my Smarties.
VISCOUNT Buses
SAFEWAY
VISCOUNT
F510 NJE

Tucked between the buildings in Mill Street, Perth in October 1990, former Ribble and Barrow Borough Transport all-white liveried East Lancs-bodied Dodge S56 353 (D459BEO) was being used as the 'tea bus/rest room' for Stagecoach and Perth Panther platform staff. (K.A.Jenkinson)

volunteers Brian Johnson from Magicbus's Spittalfield depot and Bill Ritchie from East Midland at Harworth and laden with relief supplies. In the event, it made a number of such journeys and on each occasion proved the reliability of this type of bus. Meanwhile, Southdown despatched 4 of its convertible open-top Bristol VRTs to Cumberland who put them to use in May in open-top form still wearing their apple green & cream livery on a new service in the Lake District running from Windermere to Ambleside. Adorned with a route diagram above their lower deck side windows and 'Lakeland Experience' lettering, they quickly became a familiar sight in this tourist area where they proved extremely popular.

Opposite page :

Left column, top to bottom :

With headlights ablaze, Cleveland Transit 1985 NCME-bodied Dennis Dominator 218 (B218OAJ) awaits its passengers in Stockton-on-Tees Market Place in December 1994. (K.A.Jenkinson)

New to East Kent and later passing to Cheltenham & Gloucester, Stroud Valleys Dormobile-bodied Ford Transit C705FKE painted in Metro livery operates a local service in Stroud in March 1994, four months before passing to sister company Midland Red South. (K.A.Jenkinson)

Still adorned in the yellow Bustler livery once widely used by National Welsh on its minibus fleet, Red & White Carlyle-bodied Freight Rover Sherpa passes through Cwmbran in March 1994 while working service 2 to Croesyceiliog. (K.A.Jenkinson)

Typifying the Stagecoach Malawi fleet is ERF Trailblazer 896 (BJ1286) seen here heading towards Lilongwe in 1994. (J.Davison)

Still wearing its original United Counties livery with Routemaster fleet names on its side panel, front roof dome and above its radiator grille, ex.London 714 (685DYE) is seen here at Corby bus station in 1988. (D.Brundrit)

Right column, top to bottom :

Still painted in Southdown's apple green & cream livery but additionally carrying demountable Top Line fleet names is Leyland National 115 (ENJ915V) seen here operating service 98 to Hastings.

Soon after its acquisition of Yeowarts of Whitehaven, Cumberland repainted a number of its Leyland Nationals into that erstwhile independent's mustard & yellow livery. One such bus was 801 (GCW461S) seen here in Whitehaven in August 1988. (K.A.Jenkinson)

Manchester's Piccadilly bus station is the setting of this view of GM Buses South NCME-bodied Leyland Atlantean 4487 (SND487X) painted in the familiar orange livery applied to both GM Buses fleets prior to their sale to Stagecoach and FirstBus. (K.A.Jenkinson)

New to Cambus and passing to Viscount upon its formation, NCME-bodied Leyland Olympian 510 (F510NJE) passes through Peterborough town centre in June 1996 wearing its owner's yellow & white livery. (K.A.Jenkinson)

Evaluated by Stagecoach in November 1990 was G208CHN, a CVE Omni minibus. After only one day in service at Perth, however, it was relegated to 'staff shuttle' duties between Inveralmond depot where it is seen here and the city centre. (Campbell Morrison)

Adorned with Maun Minibuses fleet names, East Midland Reeve Burgess-bodied Mercedes Benz 811D 721 (G821KWF) awaits its departure from Derby bus station to Bakewell in April 1991. (D.J.Stanier)

Following the renaming of Maun International Coachways Ltd. to Maun Buses Ltd on 26 February in order to indicate its separation from Maun International Travel Consultants, East Midland purchased the remaining 50% share of Maun Buses on 7 April to give it complete control of the company, although it continued to be operated as a separate unit. Coincidental with this, appreciable savings were made by East Midland following the implementation a number of service changes in the Chesterfield and Clowne areas whilst gained at this same time was an amount of contracted operations won on tender from Derbyshire County Council. Meanwhile, the investigation by the Office of Fair Trading into Ribble's acquisition of Mercers' local bus interests concluded that it was not necessary to refer the matter to the Monopolies and Mergers Commission. Once again, as there was no case to answer, this decision came as no surprise to Stagecoach.

The co-ordination on Tayside between Magicbus and Strathtay Scottish took another step forward on 16 April when the competitive activities in Perth were further scaled down and on the final day of the month Stagecoach withdrew the Carnoustie to Arbroath extension of service 74 from Dundee which it had added on 22 January. At the other end of Britain, Hastings & District began operating as Hastings Buses on 17 April and, as part of a major rationalisation scheme, introduced a new service network under which all Top Line's routes passed to the Hastings company together with the former's 17 Leyland Nationals. At the same time, the Eastbourne & District minibus operations of Hastings & District were transferred to Southdown's Eastbourne depot who quickly removed the Eastbourne & District stickers from the vehicles involved.

The financial results of the year ending 30 April 1990 showed that the Group had enjoyed another successful year with its profits up by 43.8% to £4.217 million on a turnover which had increased by 167.7% to £98.381 million, its capital employed being up by 19.7% to £24.7 million. During this period the Group had continued its policy of upgrading the fleets of its subsidiaries by the purchase of new vehicles and had undertaken further restructuring as far as maintenance and operations were concerned. The highlight of the year was, however, the announcement that Ann Gloag, Stagecoach Holdings' managing director had been awarded the Institute of Directors-sponsored 'Business Woman of the Year Award' after being an unsuccessful shortlisted candidate the previous year. More usually awarded to someone working in the fashion, cosmetic or retail trades, it was fitting that transport - which was not nearly as glamorous - had at last been recognised and even more fitting that the honour was bestowed on someone who had in such a short space of time done so much to change the face of the bus and coach industry. Not to be out done, during the summer Brian Souter, Stagecoach's chairman, was rewarded for his contribution to the passenger transport industry by being presented with the Scottish Young Business Achievement Award, a well-earned accolade which he richly deserved.

In order to reduce costs and enhance its space, United Counties moved its head office and depot in Northampton from Bedford Road to new premises at Rothersthorpe Avenue on 24 June while back in Scotland Magicbus lost its contract for the provision of a two-bus working on the Glasgow to Lennoxtown route during a new round of tendering in Strathclyde. Fortunately this loss was countered by the gaining of nine bus workings on schools services on Tayside which were won from Strathtay Scottish under new Tayside Regional Council tenders. Surprisingly, despite now undertaking all its repaints in Stagecoach corporate colours, Hastings Buses outshopped one of its three remaining Bristol REs in its old blue, yellow and cream livery while perhaps even more unexpectedly, after removing the Eastbourne & District names from its ex.Hastings minibuses in April, Southdown reapplied these in mid-July to the windows of four Mercedes Benz L608Ds, thus reviving their local identity. Later in the year, the company reintroduced the Eastbourne & District name on a wider scale, however, when it repainted 12 buses (Bristol VRTs and Leyland Nationals) into a special version of Stagecoach's corporate livery with all their stripes being blue rather than the more usual blue, orange and red.

July proved to be less than a happy month for Stagecoach Holdings who fell foul of the Secretary of State for Trade and Industry, Nicholas Ridley. Despite the investigation conducted by the Monopolies and Mergers Commission on Southdown's acquisition of Portsmouth CityBus concluding that although this was against the public interest there had been no adverse effect so far, and recommending that no temporary increase in service frequencies or reduction in fares should be made as predatory retaliation against competitors, Nicholas Ridley almost unbelievably over-ruled the MMC's findings and instructed Stagecoach to sell off part of its Portsmouth operations. The Director of Fair Trading was given two months to negotiate with Stagecoach and if an agreement could not be reached within this period, the Secretary of State would then use his powers to 'enforce appropriate remedies'. Not surprisingly, this decision infuriated the company, especially as Hampshire County and Portsmouth City Councils along with bus-user groups and trade unions had all been in favour of a merger between Southdown and CityBus and the fact that the MMC had found no evidence of anti-competitive behaviour. Indeed, had the merger not taken place, Portsmouth CityBus would have undoubtedly ceased trading, leaving the residents of the city with a much lower standard of service. Almost before the implications of the forced divestment of its Portsmouth interests had sunk home, Stagecoach learned that the Office of Fair Trading was to conduct an investigation into East Midland's acquisition of Maun Buses, while in the meantime although the Monopolies and Mergers Commission had found that Highland Scottish had acted in an uncompetitive manner against Inverness Traction, no remedial action was to be taken against it, ironically as a result of Stagecoach's acquisition of the Inverness independent placing that business in a stronger competitive position!

Towards the end of August, Ribble revised a number of its services and withdrew two of its oldest-established trunk routes, the 150 from Preston to Burnley and the 761 from Blackpool to Liverpool, both of which were in future to be covered by various shorter distance services. This reorganisation enabled no fewer than 11 single deck and 19 double deck vehicles to be withdrawn and thus further improved the company's viability. Cumberland meanwhile decided to discontinue its red & ivory Coachline livery in favour of the yellow and tan previously used by Yeowarts of Whitehaven and at the same time purchased 5 Plaxton Paramount 3500-bodied Volvo B10M coaches from Wallace Arnold Tours, although none of these were immediately placed in service and instead were put into storage at Carlisle depot for several months. 15 new Alexander-bodied Leyland Olympians also arrived and were shared between Ribble and Cumberland while in Perth, the fleet of Leyland Nationals and ageing Bristol Lodekkas was further reduced by the arrival of 4 Bristol VRTs from East Midland.

Although Stagecoach had added no more companies to its ever-growing portfolio since its acquisition of Maun Buses, it was nevertheless still continually searching for further expansion and had submitted bids for all the Scottish Bus Group subsidiaries already placed on the market. In addition, upon hearing of the difficulties at that time facing National Welsh Omnibus Services Ltd., an investigation into this company was instigated with a view to its possible purchase.

Painted in corporate-style livery but with blue stripes instead of red, orange & blue, Southdown convertible open-top Bristol VRT 621 (UWV621S) seen in Terminus Road, Eastbourne in December 1990 carried local identity Eastbourne & District fleet names. (T.S.Blackman)

Unfortunately, however, no agreement could be reached with the National Welsh management and Stagecoach withdrew its interest to leave Western Travel Ltd. free to acquire part of the company, the remainder of which remained with its current owners. Further south, a major storm was created amongst the residents of Lewes when Southdown announced plans to close its bus station in the town centre for redevelopment as a shopping complex. It proposed to relocate its maintenance and overnight parking facilities to a new site outside the town and replace its terminal with bus stops in several of the nearby busy streets, stating that this was necessary in order to reduce costs. Meanwhile, Hampshire Bus had been busy reorganising its premises and on the first day of September closed its Andover depot in Anton Mill Road and moved to new premises at Livingstone Road on the Walworth Industrial Estate. A few days later it reopened its Stockbridge outstation at the site it had vacated in October 1986 while during July and August it had operated open-top double deck tours around Basingstoke and to Wellington Country Park. Maintained by one of its two ex.Southdown convertible open-top Bristol VRTs, these tours proved extremely popular and attracted a healthy number of passengers.

A new innovative venture was the fitting of 6 of the Alexander-bodied Mercedes Benz 709D minibuses used by Magicbus on its Glasgow - Castlemilk service with an internal on-bus moving message advertising system. This used an LED screen fitted at the front above the driver's partition which showed a flow of advertising messages and, of course,

Looking immaculate as it passes through the suburbs of Perth whilst working a local city service is Routemaster 609 (XSL596A) which was originally registered 289CLT.

Typifying Gray Coach Lines fleet is MCI 102A3 2523 which still wore its original white, black & red livery with chrome lower panels when photographed at Toronto in July 1990. (Stagecoach International)

provided the company with additional revenue. As a result of the reorganisation of its services in the Bolton area on 15 October, Ribble was able to further reduced its fleet and withdraw 12 minibuses, 5 single deckers and 4 double deckers, the latter being the final examples of the large number of secondhand vehicles purchased by the company at the time of deregulation in 1986. In the south, in anticipation of the sale of Portsmouth CityBus, all the withdrawn buses stored at Southdown's Hilsea depot were moved to the company's Horsham premises during mid-October while in Scotland, several of the withdrawn Magicbus Routemasters stored at Spittalfield were given a complete overhaul and repaint in preparation for their return to use on Perth city services towards the end of October.

Overseas, the flow of ex.Kowloon Motor Bus Daimler CVG6 double deckers to Stagecoach Malawi continued, bringing their total to 56 and in August these were joined by a 102-seat Metsec-bodied Daimler Fleetline from the same source, this being the company's first rear-engined double decker. By this time, the Malawian fleet had grown to no fewer than 364 buses and coaches and its workforce to 2,750 employees included amongst which were 6 UK expats and managing director Peter Lutman. Major improvements to servicing and maintenance facilities had been carried out at Makata Road (Blantyre) and Lilongwe depots and discussions with several of the country's independent bus operators led to the start of a number of franchising agreements whereby better co-ordinated timetables could be introduced for the benefit of passengers. Due to increased passenger demands, the company applied for permission to operate a second weekly journey travelling through Zambia to Harare in Zimbabwe and after this was granted, Stagecoach Malawi turned its attention to the possibility of starting a new service from Lilongwe to Dar-es-Salaam in Tanzania which, subject to approval being given by the Tanzanian Government, would be operated by the new ERF Trailblazers. To assist with traffic planning, United Counties' commercial manager Ben Colson was sent to Malawi for five weeks to organise two courses which were attended by 30 of the company's staff. Equally as important, however, was Stagecoach's diversification into Canada on 19 October when it purchased most of the assets of Gray Coach Lines from the Toronto Transit Commission and established a new company, Gray Coach Lines Inc. for this purpose. Although 98 MCI coaches were included in the deal, only 85 were actually taken into stock, the remaining 13 having already being sold via Toronto Transit Commission to the Tokmakjian group for resale to South American operators. Having an office at 180 Dundas Street West, Toronto, Gray Coach Lines ran on three main groups of frequent intercity scheduled express routes to Sudbury and North Bay in the north, Kitchener, Guelph and Owen Sound in the north-west and to St.Catherines, Niagara Falls and Buffalo in the USA. In addition, high-frequency coach services were maintained to downtown

East Midland's former Magicbus Alexander-bodied tri-axle Leyland Olympian F110NES was used to tour Britain in November 1990 as part of the Bus & Coach Council's 'Buses mean business' campaign. Members of the public were invited to sign their names upon the exterior panels of the bus which is seen here in Leeds Central bus station.

Toronto from Pearson International Airport as well as the Toronto and Niagara Falls sightseeing tours. Although legal complexities in Canada at first prevented the newly-acquired company from using the Stagecoach name, this was ultimately registered and was applied above the passenger door on all the company's coaches which at first retained their existing white, black & red livery. Operating from Toronto Transit Commission's Lakeshore garage, Gray Coach was unique within the Stagecoach group in not fully undertaking any maintenance of its own, this being contracted out to Toronto Bus Centre Inc. Almost as soon as the ink had dried on the purchase documents, the company began to make plans for its future and on 5 November began a new through service between Toronto and New York City jointly with Adirondack Trailways and Empire Trailways. As will be seen later, this was to be followed by other 'pooled' services running cross-border into the USA.

On the home front, further consolidation was achieved in Cumbria when, on 19 November, Cumberland Motor Services purchased the 3-coach business of Andy Vine of Cleator Moor whose operations comprised mainly works and schools contracts and private hire duties. None of the coaches acquired - an AEC Reliance and 2 Leyland Leopards - were used by their new owner, however, and instead were immediately placed in store to await disposal. Illustrating Stagecoach's continuing support for charity and environmental matters, one of Southdown's NCME-bodied Volvo D10M double deckers toured Britain from 20 to 24 November in connection with the BBC's 'Children in Need' appeal while East Midland's 3-axle Olympian Megadekka was used for a nationwide tour to promote a Bus & Coach Council campaign which advocated the bus as a solution to the ever-increasing problem of urban congestion. Specially repainted for this purpose in an all-over white livery and adorned with the legend 'Buses Mean Business', a trading logo used by Stagecoach for several years and now adopted by the BCC, members of the public were invited to sign their names on its exterior to demonstrate their support.

In a determined effort to retaliate against the growing number of taxis plying for hire in Corby and attract passengers back to the buses, United Counties who already operated its 'Street Shuttle' minibuses in the town launched a new service on 12 November under the title of 'Corby's Magic Minis'. Using 8 ex.Ribble Robin Hood-bodied Iveco 49.10s, all of which were given a striking new livery of black with gold Stagecoach-style stripes and chevrons (which mimicked the livery used on Corby's taxis) and had their seating capacity reduced from 18 to 13 to give more space for shopping and baby buggies etc., the new service operated at intervals of 3-5 minutes from 9am to 6pm on Mondays to Saturdays. Putting together the best features of a taxi with all the convenience of a regular minibus service at prices passengers could afford, the new service immediately proved highly successful. On the leisure scene, having arranged three excursions to London's Christmas Lights on 1, 10 and 20 December, Hastings Buses despatched its open-top Bristol VRT to the capital to operate that end of the tour thus leaving passengers to travel from Kent to London and back in one of the company's coaches in order to provide a high degree of comfort for the longest part of the journey. Continuing the Christmas theme, Hastings Buses also suitably decorated one of its Leyland Nationals which operated from 17 to 24 December with a Santa board attached to its front panel and its driver wearing a Santa costume.

Having waited with bated breath for the Monopoly and Mergers Commission's report on its acquisition of Formia Ltd., when this was published on 20 December Stagecoach was relieved to find that although the report concluded that the deal might be expected to operate against public interest, it did not recommend the divestment of the Hastings operations as this would be likely to lead to one dominant supplier giving way to another and would also risk disruption of services and inconvenience to passengers while the change was being implemented. Instead, a number of measures were recommended which it was believed would be more effective in remedying the adverse

Decorated with a Santa mask on its front panel, embellished with a Merry Christmas pelmet in its windscreens and with its driver dressed in a Father Christmas costume, Hastings & District Leyland National 363 (WNO563L) seen here at Hollington Tesco was sold to Portsmouth Transit in January 1991. (T.S.Blackman)

effects of the takeover. The Secretary of State for Trade and Industry, Peter Lilley, announced, however, that he rejected the MMC's findings and instructed the Office of Fair Trading to hold further talks with Stagecoach over the possibility of divesting itself of part of the Hastings operation to stimulate competition in the area and report back within two months. This led some observers to believe that the company was facing another Portsmouth situation and that it may now lose yet another part of its southern empire during the early months of 1991 despite neither MMC report actually recommending divestment.

Looking back at 1990, Stagecoach had enjoyed another successful year in which opportunities had arisen and been firmly grasped to further develop its ever expanding empire. A number of enquiries had been made throughout the world as far away as the southern hemisphere and particularly encouraging was the attitude of the World Bank who believed that developing countries could benefit from investment by companies like Stagecoach. Against a background of the economy slowing down, it was more important than ever that companies were restored to fighting weight as soon as possible, since the more fit each one became, the better equipped it would be to survive and take advantage of future opportunities. Maintaining its philosophy that the public expected the best service possible and at a reasonable price, Stagecoach firmly believed that it should treat all its customers in a way that it would expect to be treated itself and thus reliability, cleanliness and the right attitude from all members of staff were of paramount importance.

DIVESTMENT AND EXPANSION

By the start of 1991, Stagecoach's activities in the Far East had grown considerably with no fewer than 42 double deck buses having been supplied by Speedybus Enterprises for operation in the Peoples' Republic of China. These comprised 20 Daimler CVG6s and 22 Daimler Fleetlines (including 14 ex.London Buses examples) all of which had previously operated for Kowloon Motor Bus. Before being despatched across the border from Hong Kong, all had been rebuilt to make them suitable for offside boarding and on the Daimler CVGs the entrance doors were repositioned at the centre and rear instead of at the front and centre. This work completed, the majority were then repainted into all-over advertising liveries (for Mild Seven, BIF Furniture, Winston, Weinsen or Ransonic) before they were placed in service in the Chinese cities of Chengdu, Hangzhou, Wuzhou, Fushan, Changchun, Tianjin and Fuzhou.

In Britain, 1991 began with the transfer to East Midland and its associate Maun Buses of the 10 tri-axle Talbot Pullmans which had been in store at Cumberland's Barrow depot since their return from Inverness Traction, while for the holiday season a new coach holiday/minibreak brochure was produced which linked the programmes of Hastings Coaches and Derwyn's Coach Tours and carried both companies names. Meanwhile, on 7 January Hampshire Bus introduced two new minibus services in Winchester, one from the City Centre to Oliver's Battery, the other cross-town from Winnall to Oliver's Battery. Operated by Iveco 49.10s adorned with Stagecoach instead of Hampshire Bus fleetnames, the decision to brand these with the group's name was taken in the hope that Winchester would be chosen as a Bus & Coach Council 'Buses Mean Business' project which would result in significant publicity and thus reflect the Group's commitment to the improvement and wider use of bus travel throughout Britain. Despite implementing numerous changes to its service network in Inverness, Stagecoach found itself facing the possibility of yet another investigation by the Office of Fair Trading following allegations by the Highland Regional Council of route sharing between Inverness Traction and Highland Scottish which effectively ended competition in the town. Although obviously not welcoming the prospect of yet another OFT investigation, both companies were confident that in the event of the Regional Council's complaint being taken onboard, the final result would absolve them of any malpractice.

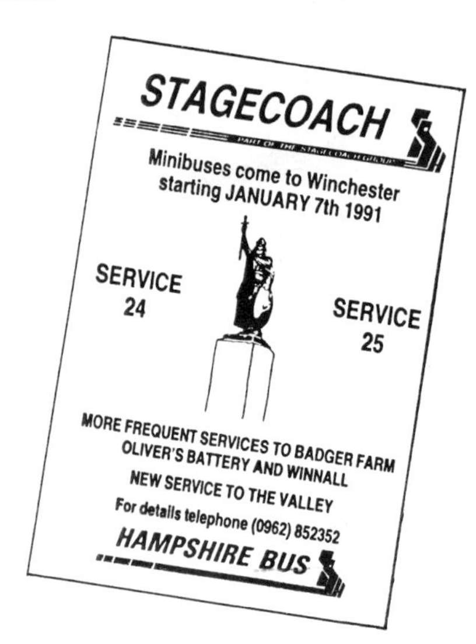

Prepared by Speedybus Enterprises for export to the Peoples' Republic of China, these three ex.Kowloon Motor Bus Daimler Fleetlines already painted in overall advertising liveries await their departure from Hong Kong at the beginning of July 1991. (C.Lau)

Having started life with Bee Line Buzz and later operated for Ribble and Inverness Traction, much-travelled tri-axle Talbot Pullman D82RVM was eventually transferred to East Midland. Numbered 994, it was given Stagecoach corporate livery and Mansfield & District fleet names together with the slogan 'People Going Places'. (P.French)

The long-running saga of Stagecoach's Portsmouth operations was finally resolved on 18 January when the company finalised the sale of Southdown Portsmouth to Harry Blundred's Transit Holdings who had outbid People's Provincial and Southern Vectis. This resulted in the divestment of all the company's services operating between Portsmouth, Waterlooville and Petersfield, those to Paulsgrove, Portchester and on Portsea Island and the services between Portsmouth and Fareham and Havant and Fareham. Also included in the deal was the lease of the former CityBus depot at Highland Road, Eastney and 104 buses and coaches. Southdown, however, retained 30 peak-hour vehicles operating in the Havant area on services to Portsmouth and Waterlooville, stabling them at Havant and Leigh Park and maintaining them at Chichester. Upon the takeover by Transit Holdings on 20 January, the Stagecoach Portsmouth name on all the vehicles concerned was immediately replaced by new Portsmouth Transit, Red Admiral or Blue Admiral vinyls. Except for Southdown's Senior Traveller half-fare passes which were to continue to be valid until May, the interavailability of tickets between the new companies and Southdown ceased on 10 February when the Stagecoach-owned company launched a new multi-journey ticket in the Havant area which was marketed under the title 'Top Ten' and confined to use on Southdown buses. In order to publicise this and identify its buses amongst the plethora of liveries associated with Transit Holdings, Southdown adorned all its buses operating in the area with 'Top Ten Bus' vinyls placed in or near their destination screens and on each side of their bodywork. Although this practice was to continue for several months, it became less important as Transit's conversion to 100% minibus operation was completed. Nevertheless, Southdown put into action a priority painting scheme under which concentration was given to transformation of all its Havant and Leigh Park-based vehicles into Stagecoach corporate colours.

Having been converted from dual to single door layout, Southdown Bristol VRT 648 (AAP648T) received Stagecoach South's version of the group's corporate livery (with stripes around its front upper deck) and was given 'Top Ten Bus' vinyls above its door and windscreens. Looking immaculate, it stands at Havant bus station in September 1991. (T.S.Blackman)

Aware of the difficulties at that time facing Tayside Public Transport Co. which had a projected £1 million trading shortfall and had for some months been the subject of a possible management/employees buyout, Stagecoach contacted the Regional Council with a bid for the undertaking. If it had been successful it would have given the company a major foothold in an area in which it had previously only had a tiny presence and would have compensated for its inability to bid for Strathtay Scottish under the terms applied to the SBG privatisation programme. In the event, the bid was rejected and the Tayside undertaking was sold to its management/employees. Interest was also shown in Scottish Bus Group subsidiary Fife Scottish which, although adjacent to the company's Perth operations was far enough away to not be considered to be creating a monopoly situation.

Meanwhile, overseas developments continued to feature in the news with the Group's Canadian subsidiary Gray Coach Lines operations undergoing a number of significant changes amongst which was an agreement reached on 11 January to sell its northern routes together with 30 vehicles to Ontario Northland Transportation Commission, subject to all the necessary regulatory approvals. After a long period of legal complexities, this deal was never concluded, however, and instead, from 23 June the ONTC provided all the drivers for the northern routes on contract to Gray Coach. Meanwhile, following the success of its joint service to New York City, Gray Coach together with American carriers Empire Trailways and Adirondack Trailways started a new service on 17 March from Toronto to Buffalo and Rochester and with Empire Trailways and Capitol Trailways from Toronto to Washington D.C. In an attempt to further expand its operations, Gray Coach also examined a number of dormant licences in southern Ontario in what is known as the Golden Triangle surrounding Toronto and which would act as feeder services into the Government of Ontario's commuter rail network. Having held the famous Gray Line franchise for the Round Toronto tour and Niagara Falls conducted tour for many years, Gray Coach Lines remodelled these in conjunction with local operator Toronto Tours Ltd. and the previous six separate sightseeing destinations were developed into one 'value for money' Round Toronto Coach Tour. (Gray Line is the Dallas-based worldwide sightseeing organisation for which Gray Coach Lines Inc. held the franchise for Totonto land-based sightseeing tours and although the names are similar, and thus

Standing with Gray Coach Lines Bristol Lodekka 1965 (formerly BHU976C in the UK) and corporate-liveried MCI 102B3 2550 at Toronto in October 1991 are William Verrier (left), Vice Chairman of Gray Coach Lines Inc and the company's President Brian Souter. (Stagecoach International)

The first Bristol FLF6G Lodekka to be exported to join the Gray Coach Lines fleet was former Magicbus BHU976C. Seen in Toronto fitted with an offside door and numbered 1965, it was later joined by five more buses of this type. (Stagecoach International)

Typifying the PCC trams owned by Toronto Transit Commission which were used by Gray Coach Lines for its Vintage Streetcar Tour is this example seen awaiting its passengers in Toronto. (Travelscene)

Purchased by Stagecoach Malawi in January 1991 from Travellers of London with whom it was registered E587UHS, Coachline's Plaxton Paramount 3500-bodied Volvo B10M 4 (BH9604) is seen at Chichiri depot, Blantyre. Note the heavy bumper bars fitted to offer protection to the front panels. (J.Davison)

confusing, there was no ownership connection). Gray Coach Lines also operated a 'Vintage Streetcar Tour' of the city using two sleek PCC 1951-vintage single deck trams of Toronto Transit Commission which were specially painted into the 1921 TTC red livery. Having, however, considered the operation of double deck buses on its sightseeing tour of Toronto, the company acquired a Bristol FLF-type Lodekka from Stagecoach in Perth which had been converted to offside loading by East Midland prior to shipment. Arriving in its new home on 1 May, it was cleared by Customs ten days later and was then despatched to the Concord, Ontario premises of SN Diesel and National Refurbishing Inc. where it was modified to bring it into line with Canadian safety and lighting requirements and repainted into Stagecoach corporate livery before being licensed for its new duties. At this same time, the first of the company's MCI coaches also received corporate colours after which the remainder of the fleet was similarly treated at the rate of approximately one vehicle per week. In addition to the Bristol Lodekka, 3 new MCI coaches joined the fleet at the end of July with a further 2 being ordered for delivery in November and 5 in April 1992. Meanwhile, on 15 May Gray Coach moved its garaging from the Toronto Transit Commission's depot at Lakeshore to Toronto Bus Centre Inc's premises in Cherry Street, about one mile away.

Across the world in Africa, Stagecoach Malawi was experiencing operating difficulties with its Leyland Leopard and Tiger coaches which were fast becoming unreliable and costly to maintain, and acquired 4 Plaxton Paramount 3500-bodied Volvo B10Ms from Travellers of Hounslow as replacements. Painted into Stagecoach corporate livery and fitted with air conditioning before leaving Britain, these coaches were allocated to the Coachline division where they quickly settled down on long distance express services.

After unsuccessfully submitting bids for the first Scottish Bus Group subsidiaries to be offered for sale, Stagecoach achieved its objective on 27 March when it acquired Northern Scottish Omnibuses Ltd., beating its management buy-out team, Go-Ahead Northern and Drawlane in the process. The Aberdeen-based company had, in fact, been 'on the market' since October 1990, the decision on its future having been delayed while the Scottish Bus Group took advice on the Office of Fair Trading's attitude to a possible bid from Grampian Regional Transport. Adding a further 206 vehicles to its Scottish-based fleet, this acquisition gave Stagecoach a major foothold in an area where, except for its

Standing outside Aberdeen bus station is Bluebird Northern Duple-bodied Leyland Tiger 435 (CSU922, originally BSG545W) which joined the fleet from Central Scottish in pre-Stagecoach days. (Murdoch Currie)

Resting at Aberdeen bus station are Bluebird Buses Alexander-bodied Leyland Tigers 422 (A117ESA) and 434 (CSU921, originally WGB176W) together with Alexander-bodied Leyland Olympian 38 (YSO38Y). (T.W.W.Knowles)

One of only two Neoplan Skyliners to be operated by Bluebird Northern, N2 (D319NWG) is seen here at Edinburgh bus station on 26 October 1991 working a Scottish Citylink service from Aberdeen. (Murdoch Currie)

express services prior to their sale in August 1989, it had never had a presence. Within two days of gaining control of its new subsidiary, Stagecoach's corporate livery made its appearance when Alexander-bodied Leyland Olympian LO69 emerged from the paint shops at Aberdeen in its new colours and sporting a traditional Bluebird fleet name and logos. At the helm of Bluebird Northern was Neil Renilson who, as managing director of Stagecoach (Scotland) Ltd. was joined by Ian Mackintosh (operations director), Iain Smart (traffic manager east), Bob Walker (traffic manager west) and Robert Harvey (finance director).

As part of a tidying up process, Stage-Coach Holidays Ltd. was renamed Magicbus (Scotland) Ltd. on 5 March at the same time that the original Magicbus (Scotland) Ltd. was renamed Stagecoach (Scotland) Ltd. On this same date, Hampshire Minibus Ltd. was renamed Hampshire Bus Co. Ltd. while the company already bearing that title was renamed Stagecoach (South) Ltd. Under these arrangements, Stagecoach (Scotland) Ltd. took control of all the Group's Scottish operations excepting those of Northern Scottish (although the Magicbus and Inverness Traction fleetnames continued to be applied to the vehicles operating in Glasgow and Inverness) while Southdown and Hastings Buses were both placed under the Stagecoach (South) Ltd. banner. Later, on the final day of April, Portsmouth CityBus Ltd. was renamed Southdown Buses Ltd. Under these changes, Andy Blackburn (operations manager) and Billy Devlin (fleet engineer) transferred from Magicbus in Glasgow to Stagecoach (Scotland) Ltd. during April to assume similar roles in Tayside with Phil Harper moving to Glasgow.

In addition to preparing its apple green & cream liveried open-top Bristol VRTs and Leyland Atlantean for their re-entry into service on their summer duties on the Lakeland Experience operation from Bowness to Ambleside in conjunction with the Windermere Iron Steamboat Company, Cumberland also repainted three of its Mercedes Benz L608D minibuses into this same livery for use on a new Lakeland Experience service from Bowness to Coniston branded the 'Coniston Rambler'. Further afield, Hastings Coaches produced a new continental excursion brochure covering a number of different destinations while Midland Travel offered weekend breaks between April and November to no fewer that 32 different destinations, all at the amazingly low price of £32. In addition, Midland Travel produced a brochure containing a wide range of day and evening excursions including a number advertised as being 'on a 30 year-old vintage London double decker'. Although East Midland's fleet contained several Routemasters, two buses of this type owned by the company's managing director George Watson were also available for use if required. In order to further develop and expand its activities, the company launched an exclusive Midland Travelclub to which membership was available for an annual subscription of £10. Amongst the benefits members received was advance information on holidays etc., and so successful was this venture that within ten days of its inception more than 1600 members had been enrolled. Another innovative move by East Midland was the monthly publication of 'Passenger News', a series of A5-size leaflets which were aimed at keeping passengers informed of service changes and new timetable leaflets which were available. On the debit side, however, East Midland lost some 4% profitable turnover as a result of the massive cuts made by South Yorkshire PTE to its contracted services while on a happier note, following the success of its Corby Magic Minis operation, United Counties started a second route in the town under this banner on 2 April.

Soon after gaining control of Northern Scottish, the former SBG subsidiary in April acquired the Aberdeen - Banchory service of F. & M. Clark of Banchory together with 3 Leyland Leopards, all of which were quickly sold. Clarks Taxis & Coaches was not included in the deal, however, and continued to operate its other stage carriage services and schools contracts from its existing premises at Dykehead Garage. Later, Northern Scottish after having spent the previous four years building up its city services in Aberdeen surprisingly withdrew the majority of them in June leaving Grampian Regional Transport to fill the gaps. In order to do this, the latter had to switch almost all its resources from the Balgownie, Inverurie and Banchory areas leaving Northern Scottish to pick up what it wanted in those areas. Meanwhile, at the opposite end of Britain Southdown moved its head office from Walwers Lane, Lewes to Lewes Enterprise Centre while one of Hastings Coaches Leyland Tigers was given Derwyns Coach Tours fleet names above its front wheel arch on both sides for use on tours and minibreaks organised jointly between the two companies. Always seeking ways of reducing costs, Ribble closed its Fleetwood depot on 27 April and moved its minibus fleet to an open parking site at the nearby Docks.

Until more recent times the Lakeland Experience Coniston Rambler service was maintained by Cumberland Mercedes Benz L608D which had been specially repainted into apple green & cream livery for this purpose as illustrated by 558 (D558RCK) seen at the Bowness terminus in July 1994. (K.A.Jenkinson)

In addition to carrying Hastings Coaches fleet names, yellow, cream & blue liveried Plaxton Paramount-bodied Leyland Tiger 1001 (401DCD, originally RUF430X) sported a Derwyn's Coach Tours vinyl above its front wheel arch. Parked alongside at Silverhill depot is a company car bearing the registration (404DCD) from another Southdown Queen Mary Leyland PD3/4. (T.S.Blackman)

Enroute to Keswick on an early evening journey from Lancaster, Cumberland 1019 (H119SAO) carried the original-style LakesLink 555 service logo on its side panels. This was later replaced by larger lettering which proved easier to read from a distance. (T.W.W.Knowles)

Following its success in northern Scotland, Stagecoach was delighted to learn on 29 May that it had been given preferred bidder status for Fife Scottish whose headquarters were at Kirkcaldy. Only hours before the announcement was made by the Scottish Office, however, a group of local Central Fife Members of Parliament who had learned of this protested vigorously at the decision and immediately demanded that reconsideration be given to the bid submitted by the management and employees of the SBG subsidiary. As a result, the unusual step was taken to allow the latter to make a revised bid, but although Fife's management team took advantage of this, an announcement made on 10 June reconfirmed that Stagecoach still remained the preferred bidder. This, of course, precluded Stagecoach from purchasing any further SBG subsidiaries which were still to be sold, as under the original rule no company was eligible to acquire more than two of them. The Fife Scottish deal was eventually completed on 23 July giving Stagecoach control of a substantial part of eastern Scotland north of the river Forth as well as an additional 300 buses and coaches and depots at Aberhill, Cowdenbeath, Dunfermline, Glenrothes, Kirkcaldy, Newburgh and St.Andrews. Retaining their positions within the company were managing director Jim Moffat and engineering director Sandy Brydon while Ken Smart, former general manager of Highland Scottish was appointed as operations manager. Meanwhile, the now customary transfer of vehicles between the Group's various subsidiaries continued apace and amongst these a number of Northern Scottish Alexander-bodied Leyland Olympians were sent south to join Ribble, their place in Scotland being taken by several ex.Southdown Mercedes Benz L608D minibuses and a couple of Bristol VRTs.

Looking to the future and following the lead taken by Stagecoach Malawi where an Employee Share Ownership Plan had been set up to purchase 15% out of the Malawi Government's 49% shareholding in the company for the benefit of the local workforce, Stagecoach Holdings prepared a similar scheme approved by the Inland Revenue for its U.K. employees. This was to consist of two trusts - a Warehouse Trust and a Profit Sharing Trust. The Warehouse Trust was the vehicle for the purchase all of the shares which would eventually be owned by UK employees and it was stated that this would initially borrow money to acquire around 10% of the ordinary shares in Stagecoach Holdings from three sources. These were 5% of the company's shares acquired by one of the company's previous bankers in July 1987; an issue of new shares earmarked for the employees which was accepted by the company's institutional shareholders at the time of the successful private placing in December 1988, and a small percentage of existing shares held by Brian Souter and Ann Gloag. The Warehouse Trust, once it became operational, would then offer some of these shares to employees in a Buy One Get One Free ('BOGOF') offer for cash while free shares would be allocated out of future profit and held by the Profit Sharing Trust until they were allotted to employees after a two year waiting period under Inland Revenue rules. The Warehouse Trust would also buy back shares from employees who left the company and wished to divest

Fife Scottish operated a large number of Alexander-bodied Ailsa Volvos, one of which (877 - UFS877R) is seen in pre-Stagecoach livery at Dundee. (T.S.Blackman)

One of Fife Scottish's numerous Alexander-bodied Leyland Leopards, 186 (PSX186Y) leaves Kirkcaldy bus station in April 1995 still sporting its original cream & red livery. (K.A.Jenkinson)

Repainted in Stagecoach corporate livery but retaining its Buzzbus logos, Fife Scottish Alexander-bodied Dodge S56 25 (D825RYS) which was acquired from Kelvin Scottish in 1990 leaves Glenrothes bus station on local service G2 to Newcastle. (S.A.Jenkinson)

Having been hurriedly transferred from Cumberland to Inverness Traction in October 1991, ECW-bodied Leyland Leopard VAO641Y still wore its previous operator's livery and fleet names when photographed at Inverness in November of that year but had received an Inverness Traction vinyl below its windscreens. (Campbell Morrison)

Still painted in NBC poppy red livery and adorned with Cumberland fleet names and NBC 'double-N' logos, Bristol VRT PHH409R is seen in Inverness on 28 September 1991 a few days after being transferred to Inverness Traction for use on services previously operated by Highland Scottish. (Murdoch Currie)

themselves. From 1994, each year the company made a profit, a portion would be given to the Profit Sharing Trust who would use it to buy 'free' shares for employees from the Warehouse Trust or new shares issued for this purpose.

Stagecoach's philosophy towards the provision of better quality vehicles and improved service networks both at home and overseas was highlighted in June when it placed an order for no fewer than 70 new ERF Trailblazer chassis for use by its Malawi subsidiary. These were to be bodied locally by PEW and were to be used as replacements for older Leyland Victories in addition to expanding the fleet. No sooner had their delivery commenced than an order was placed (in September) for a massive 255 9.8m Alexander midibus bodies with an option for a further 100 for use by its UK subsidiaries. Specified for delivery over two years, the chassis upon which these were to be mounted were 55 Dennis Darts and 200 Volvo B6s. During the following month while the previous order for 30 Leyland Olympians was being delivered, a further 46 Dennis Dart chassis were ordered together with 70 more Olympians, this signifying a massive investment which would allow the withdrawal of numerous older members of the combined fleet as well as several non-standard buses and coaches. Meanwhile, as part of its ongoing strategy of rationalisation, Ribble transferred all its Blackburn depot's conventional buses to its depots at Preston and Clitheroe and the outstation at Burnley leaving Blackburn with around 20 minibuses which were employed mainly on local services. Having served their purpose in attracting passengers back on to the buses East Midland withdrew its Routemaster double deckers in mid-June as a consequence of a reorganisation of its services in the Mansfield area and effectively brought two-man operation within the company to a close. Not quite dead, however, the buses concerned were retained for a few more weeks due to the high demand for vehicles during the World Student Games in Sheffield in July. Soon after the Routemaster disappeared from East Midland, it also vanished from the streets of Corby on 2 September when United Counties revamped its services in the town, replacing them with minibuses.

Following the closure by Northern Scottish of its bus station at Stonehaven in July and putting it up for sale, Stagecoach at the same time gained a number of tendered services in the Crieff area previously operated by Strathtay Scottish. This led to the closure of the SBG subsidiary's depot and bus station in the town and to Stagecoach opening a new outstation in the yard of a local haulage contractor. With no fixed allocation, the buses employed from this new base were drawn from Perth where all maintenance was carried out, and although Leyland Leopards were the more usual vehicles to be found operating from Crieff, a couple of double deckers were also needed for certain contracts and the service running to Perth. Later in the year, the company's Spittalfield depot, acquired with the business of A. & C. McLennan in 1985, was closed and its allocation and engineering facilities transferred to Perth, although an outstation was maintained in the village for operational purposes. Continuing its rationalisation north of the border, Fife Scottish closed its engineering subsidiary Transport Industry Engineering at Kirkcaldy early in September following it a month later with the closure of its small depot at Newburgh. It was not only in the Kingdom of Fife where changes were taking place, however, as early in September Inverness Traction had made massive gains at the expense of incumbent Highland Scottish after 60 of the latter's drivers staged a walk-out following the threat of redundancy and offered their services to the Stagecoach subsidiary. This prevented Highland from operating many of its routes and forced it to take the decision to pull out of commercial operations in the town, leaving Inverness Traction to replace these at short notice. After drafting in around 28 vehicles from Stagecoach's other subsidiaries and introducing 8 new Alexander-bodied Leyland Olympians diverted from Cumberland and Stagecoach South, Traction initially ran its new services free of charge for a few days until the Traffic Commissioner granted emergency licences. Several of the Leyland Leopards and Bristol VRTs obtained from Cumberland still wore that company's pre-Stagecoach colours of Ayres red and sandstone and were merely given Inverness Traction logos prior to being pressed into service while those coming from the group's Scottish subsidiaries were already in corporate colours as, of course, were the new Olympians.

In the south of England, Harry Blundred of Transit Holdings and Stagecoach subsidiary Southdown who had earlier been arch enemies in the Basingstoke/Torbay bus war, joined forces to launch 'Buses Mean Business' proposals to combat traffic congestion in Portsmouth and to counter rival People's Provincial's uneconomic light rail initiative. Emphasising their support for the local council's transport plan, the duo

Ribble's former Highland Scottish Alexander-bodied Leyland Olympian 2217 (B893UAS) prepares to join Morecambe promenade near The Battery hotel on a journey from Lancaster to Heysham. Its Scottish-style front destination indicator is reminiscent of Ribble's double deckers in the days of their BET ownership. (K.A.Jenkinson)

also wanted to see the proposed bus priority corridor between Commercial Road and Hilsea implemented without further delay and three Green Routes introduced upon which there would be improved bus stopping facilities, continuous bus lanes and automatic priority for buses at traffic lights. Following this, Hampshire Bus launched a new service on 28 October which provided a bus link between Southampton and Basingstoke for the first time. Although running via the Chandlers Ford bypass, Winchester and the A30 and providing a reasonably quick journey time, the new service was aimed more at the leisure market than commuters who still found the train provided a speedier journey between these points. Prior to this, Hampshire Bus during September had despatched its 3 Duple bus-bodied Dennis Javelins to Ribble in exchange for a trio of Leyland Leopard coaches which were used to replace a couple of dual-purpose Leyland Nationals at Andover depot. Additionally, during the last two months of the year Ribble also acquired 13 Alexander-bodied Olympians and 7 Alexander-bodied Leopards from Highland Scottish, the double deckers being used to upgrade the company's Lancaster and Morecambe area operations.

Despite making a bid larger than that of the management/employee buyout team for West Midlands Travel in October, Stagecoach's offer was rejected by its owners, West Midlands Passenger Transport Authority who preferred the company to go to its workers. This decision prompted Stagecoach to contact the Office of Fair Trading in view of the PTA's apparent under-valuation of a public asset, but the Minister of State for Public Transport, Michael Portillo, declined to intervene saying that the sale of the company was a matter for the PTA and not, in his opinion, one for the OFT. Additionally he warned that if Stagecoach purchased the company it would have 'significant competitive implications'. In response, Stagecoach's chairman, Brian Souter stated that 'competition among bus companies would be seriously affected if West Midlands Travel, one of Britain's largest and most profitable bus companies, was privatised at a very substantial discount'. Despite this and his other forceful criticism, WMT was ultimately sold to its management/employees in December and thus Stagecoach was unable to gain the foothold wanted in the heart of England. As this battle of words continued, the Scottish-based company gained further expansion in Africa when, on 18 November, it purchased the majority shareholding in Kenya's two largest bus operators - Kenya Bus Services of Nairobi and KBS (Mombasa) - from BET subsidiary United Transport International. Under this deal, the Nairobi City Commission retained its 25% share in Kenya Bus Services while the Mombasa City Council kept 49% share of KBS (Mombasa). With 250 and 75 buses respectively, both companies suffered from open competition from independent minibus operators and the government-owned bus company in Nairobi, but having gained valuable experience in Malawi, Stagecoach was confident that it would be able to quickly improve and further develop its newly-acquired operations and play a major role in the country's transport network. Both the Kenyan companies operated typical BET African fleets in which Leyland Victories and ERF Trailblazers predominated.

Painted in Red Arrow livery for use on selected routes as a publicity exercise, Kenya Bus Services dual-door Singh-bodied DAF TB2100 601 (KAA128N) is seen at Eastleigh depot, Nairobi in December 1991. (Stagecoach International)

Well loaded with passengers and still painted in its pre-Stagecoach cream & red livery, Kenya Bus Services (Mombasa) 1985-vintage dual-door Suleman-bodied ERF Trailblazer 51 (KWY053) - since renumbered 981 - prepares to leave the Likoni Ferry terminus on Mombasa Island in December 1991. (Stagecoach International)

Painted in Kenya Bus Services' two-tone blue & white Bluebird Service livery, Singh-bodied Leyland Victory Mk.II 212 (KTJ235) - since renumbered 762 - approaches Kikuyu on a journey from Nairobi in December 1991. (Stagecoach International)

Its passenger carrying days having ended, Southdown Queen Mary NCME-bodied Leyland PD3/4 0292 (FCD292D) gained a life extension as a driver training bus and gained Stagecoach corporate livery. (T.G.Walker)

Picking up its passengers at Stanley whilst operating the service from Spittalfield to Perth, Alexander-bodied Dennis Lancet ND2 was on loan to Stagecoach from Bluebird Northern whose yellow livery it still wore. (Campbell Morrison)

With broad orange, red & blue bands on its lower panels and Hampshire Travel fleet names, Hamphire Bus Plaxton Paramount-bodied Volvo B10M 1006 (896HOD, originally B192CGA) seen here at Epsom on 1992 Derby Day was acquired from Fife Scottish in October of the previous year. (T.S.Blackman)

On the home front, Stagecoach had just completed its first employee share scheme offer (the BOGOF) - which had attracted a £0.8 million investment from more than 1,000 employees. By investing an average of £750 against a minimum of £280, those 20% of all employees now owned 5% of the company which was valued at around £30 million by the Inland Revenue. At this same time plans were also announced for improving the ESOP at the company's Malawi subsidiary where 15% of the shares were owned by a trust on behalf of the 3,000 employees. To reflect the fact that employees now held a share in the company, Stage-Coach (Holdings) Ltd. was re-registered as a public limited company, Stagecoach Holdings plc on 27 September.

Concluding another highly successful year in which, despite some disappointments, further expansion and rationalisation had been achieved, Stagecoach was able to record a healthy rise in its pre-tax profits for the first six months of its 1991 financial year. Announcing this as £3.2 million compared with £2.7 million for the whole of the previous year, the company looked forward to 1992 with confidence, predicting that its fortunes would continue to grow as the new year progressed. There was no doubt that profit generated income which in turn allowed for service improvements which generated new profit.

With the first 20 of its massive order for new Dennis Dart midibuses entering service with Hastings Buses at the start of 1992, it was revealed that the next 60 were to be allocated to Southdown (40) and Hampshire Bus (20) followed by 12 for Inverness Traction, 6 for Magicbus and 3 for Cumberland. This began what was to become a continuous flow of new vehicles throughout the years ahead during revealed that the next 60 were to be allocated to Southdown (40) and Hampshire Bus (20) followed by 12 for Inverness Traction, 6 for Magicbus and 3 for Cumberland. This began what was to become a continuous flow of new vehicles throughout the years ahead during which time Stagecoach made a massive investment in order to provide passengers with new degrees of comfort and reliability. Meanwhile in the interests of improved efficiency, following a network review by Fife Scottish, full-sized buses replaced minis on several daytime services in the Dunfermline area where some evening frequencies were reduced due to minimal patronage. In a further move towards long term financial savings, Stagecoach who, like many other large operators funded the cost of its own accident repairs, developed its own in-house accident management programme under which it used a computer system to analyse all accidents throughout the group by types of incidents in order to see if there were any emerging patterns. To promote greater safety amongst its drivers, it additionally organised a group-wide competition to reward the garages with the lowest record of blameworthy or part-blameworthy accidents and promote a team spirit. By producing quarterly analyses of each depot's performance, it was able to identify habitual offenders and accident blackspots which allowed changes to be implemented in operational methods where necessary. So successful did this revolutionary scheme prove, that within months engineering budgets were able to be significantly reduced and downtime costs minimised.

Hampshire Bus made history when it became the first major bus company in the UK to take advantage of the Government's Profit Related Pay scheme which encouraged employees to have part of their pay linked to company profits, thereby sharing in the company's success. Responsible for implementing the scheme was Debra Topliff, finance director of Stagecoach South. Under PRP a proportion of an employee's wages or salary was allowed to be paid tax free, the maximum annual sum eligible for tax free pay being 20% of gross earnings (less pensions and payroll giving to charity), up to a maximum of £4,000. This enabled a basic rate tax payer to take home approximately 5% more of his/her gross earnings. The Inland Revenue's rules for PRP were quite strict, however, and the company had to make profits to enable it to pay the tax-free PRP. Additionally, a total PRP 'pool' had to be established and this increased or decreased each year as profits rise or fall. Although the key rule was that a minimum of 70% of employees must agree to take part in the scheme, Hampshire Bus decided from the outset that it must be everyone or no-one, a decision with which the company'

DIVERSIFICATION INTO RAILWAYS

Unfortunately, although 1992 had started well in general terms, in February the company found itself facing two Office of Fair Trading investigations, one in Lancashire where a local independent operator had lodged a complaint against Ribble following its post-Christmas cut-price fare offer between Chorley and Blackburn, the other in Bognor Regis where an independent minibus operator complained that Southdown had set its fares at an uneconomic level on a competing service. These were followed in March by another accusation of unfair competition and predatory pricing against Ribble and Hyndburn Transport on their service between Accrington and Blackburn and although all except Bognor Regis were ultimately dismissed, the initial judgement in the case of Southdown was contested by the company before an agreement satisfactory to both parties was finally reached. In the meantime, a reorganisation of Stagecoach's operations in the south of England resulted in the creation of two new companies - East Sussex Buses Ltd. and Coastline Buses Ltd. on 6 March while a month later on 2 April Southdown Buses Ltd. was renamed Southdown Motor Services Ltd; Southdown Motor Services Ltd. was renamed Sussex Coastline Buses Ltd. and Hastings & District Transport Ltd. became South Coast Buses Ltd. In the event, however, neither East Sussex Buses nor Coastline Buses became operational. Other companies to change their identity at around this time were Northern Scottish Omnibuses Ltd. which was renamed Bluebird Northern Ltd. on 3 March; United Transport Passenger Services Ltd. which took the name Stagecoach Kenya Ltd. with its registered office c/o Stagecoach (North West) Ltd., Frenchwood Avenue, Preston on 24 March, and Skipburn Ltd, which became Magicbus (Scotland) Ltd on 25 March when the company already bearing the latter title was renamed Stagecoach Rail Ltd. Stagecoach Rail was set up following a deal between Stagecoach Holdings and state-owned Inter-City under which the former was to take over the responsibility for marketing of 116 seats in each direction on the seated night rail service from London Euston to Edinburgh, Dundee and Aberdeen which without the support of Stagecoach would have been withdrawn by Inter-City. For this purpose, 6 seated railway coaches leased from British Rail were repainted into Stagecoach corporate colours in time for the launch of the new service on 11 May. Thus, at 9.20pm on that evening, the first privately-operated passenger train (or, at least, two coaches thereof) since the railways were nationalised in 1947 left Aberdeen for its historic journey to London. Amongst the specially invited guests on the inaugural run was 77-year old Mrs Isabella McRorie who was Stagecoach's first passenger in 1980 when it started its Dundee to London coach service. As part of the package offered by Stagecoach Rail to its passengers, all fares included one hot and one cold meal, the use of pillows and blankets and, if booked in advance, a guaranteed reserved seat. Additionally Stagecoach, through its Inverness Traction subsidiary, provided a free feeder coach service from Inverness, Aviemore and Perth to connect with this new venture at Edinburgh while passengers within the Bluebird area could also connect free to Aberdeen. At London Euston, Stagecoach Rail rented a small office where equipment was stored during the day and which provided a small base while catering equipment and food etc. was delivered by van each evening to Edinburgh where it was loaded on to the train. Stagecoach Rail's objective was to provide a quality of service meeting the best airline standards and each train carried two stewards/stewardesses, one of whom travelled throughout the complete journey from Aberdeen to London, the other starting at Inverness with the feeder coach and transferring to the train at Edinburgh. Alcohol was

Displaying its new Coastline fleet name below its windscreens and a Coastline Express name centrally above its lower deck windows, Alexander-bodied Leyland Olympian 209 (G809RTS) is seen in Brighton working the Coastline 200 service in September 1992. (T.S.Blackman)

Used to transport refreshments and other supplies to Edinburgh, Ford Cargo van B379CHE seen here at Perth depot was given Stagecoach Rail lettering. (K.A.Jenkinson)

Pictured in Mill Street, Perth in August 1992, Stagecoach Willowbrook-bodied Leyland Leopard 184 (LSK547) which was acquired from Cumberland but was new to United Counties as UVV153W, carried advertising for Stagecoach Rail along its side panels. (K.A.Jenkinson)

banned on all Stagecoach trains whilst the motive power was provided by an electric locomotive from London to Edinburgh and 2 Class 37 diesel locomotive from Edinburgh to Aberdeen.

Property once again featured in the news when Bluebird Northern vacated its depot at Gairn Terrace, Aberdeen in March and moved into part of the premises of Grampian Regional Transport in King Street where the incumbent operator took over responsibility for the cleaning, shunting and fuelling of Bluebird's vehicles. Following in April was the announcement that Cumberland had purchased part of the site previously occupied by the old Leyland Bus factory at Lillyhall upon which it was to build a new depot to replace that at nearby Whitehaven while at Workington the company was to move into a small unit separate from the main depot which was then to be offered for sale. When the new 120-vehicle Lillyhall depot was opened on 26 June, in addition to enabling the old Whitehaven depot to be closed, it also allowed the transfer of a number of vehicles from Workington where space was at a premium following the move to smaller premises. Around this same time, Stagecoach opened a new maintenance base close to its depot on the Inveralmond Trading Estate at Perth, this being equipped with six pits and a body shop and also extended its depot premises and moved from its portakabin accommodation in to a new office complex.

Stagecoach sold its underperforming Magicbus operation in Glasgow to Kelvin Central Buses on 10 April together with 24 vehicles and its depot at Hobden Street, Springburn. Amongst these were a number of Routemasters, some Bristol VRTs which had only a four weeks earlier been acquired from Ribble and, more surprisingly, 6 almost new Alexander Dash-bodied Dennis Darts which had joined the fleet in February. As part of the deal, Stagecoach allowed Kelvin Central Buses to use the Magicbus fleet name and livery for the services acquired for a period of one year and thus, as far as the travelling public was

New to Magicbus in February 1992 and sold with its Glasgow operations to Kelvin Central Buses two months later, Alexander Dash-bodied Dennis Dart J517FPS seen at St.Enoch Square, Glasgow in August 1992 although still painted in Stagecoach corporate livery carries the fleet number (1017) of its new owner on its front panels. (K.A.Jenkinson)

Picking up its passengers in Mill Street, Perth in August 1992, Bristol VRT 105 (FDV816V) still displayed Magicbus fleet names despite having left Glasgow almost a year earlier. Overtaking it is Bristol VRT 099 (NEL117P) which correctly carried a Stagecoach fleet name. (K.A.Jenkinson)

concerned, this change of ownership went largely un-noticed. Interest was then lodged with Strathclyde Regional Council for the purchase of Strathclyde Buses, although this proved unsuccessful with the Labour-controlled Council preferring to sell it to its management and employees in February 1993.

Following its purchase of Greater Manchester Passenger Transport Authority's 49.9% shareholding in National Travel Tokens Ltd. on 3 March which gave it 99.9% of the company, its registered office was moved to Ribble's headquarters at Preston and plans were launched to revamp the token scheme to make it more attractive to participating authorities. These included an increase in discounts and handling commission from 2.75% to at least 3.5% which would be funded by the scrapping of the previous haphazard profit-sharing scheme. Following changes instigated by GM Buses around this time to the Greater Manchester Travel Card scheme to which Ribble subscribed, at the start of May the Preston-based Stagecoach subsidiary launched its own Weekly Travel Card which was available for the Bolton area at a cost of £4.95. Additionally, at the start of the summer term Ribble had joined with Lancaster City Transport to provide improved services to Lancaster University. Branded 'Unisprint', these were maintained by minibuses which were painted in a distinctive black and gold livery and were provided by both operators and with a fare of £1 return - representing a 40% reduction on the previous fare - the service became an immediate success with an increase of 17% usage. This ultimately led to larger vehicles being required and thus the minibuses were replaced by 2 Leyland Olympians and a Leyland National, all of which were adorned with the distinctive black and gold colour scheme. As part of its continuing development plans, Ribble also made a comeback into a market which it had left in March 1988 following the sale to Speake-based Amberline of its coaching activities. Taking up some contracted National Express duties in May on the London to Aberdeen and London to Whitehaven services, it followed these with the introduction of its own limited stop services from Preston to Liverpool and Blackpool which replaced existing local bus services with dramatic cuts in scheduled running times designed to win back passengers from the railways. Meanwhile, Cumberland had introduced a new network of local bus services in the Lake District which included a new summertime 'Lakeland Experience' operation from Kendal branded 'Borrowdale Bus'. This was maintained by a Leyland National painted in the company's apple green & cream Lakeland Experience livery which had since its introduction in 1990 become a familiar sight in this picturesque part of the north-west. Additionally, the existing services to Kendal from Lancaster and Carlisle were branded 'Lakeslink' in order to promote greater awareness amongst visitors to the area.

In his annual report for the year up to 30 April, Brian Souter expressed his delight at the organic profit growth achieved from the company's core operations, particularly in a year when revenue shrinkage was experienced in Eastern Canada and the north west and south of England where the impact of the general economic recession had most affected Stagecoach's business. Having made significant progress towards achieving the target operating margin of 15% seen as being both achievable and essential to enable the substantial and ongoing costs of fleet replacement, the corporate objectives still remained to maximise profit margins at all the company's existing operations and to acquire undervalued or underperforming companies where the potential to improve operating margins to at least 15% of turnover could be identified. At £36 million, the total planned investment in vehicle replacement over the next three years coming on top of £18 million of new UK buses in the previous two years will enable over 750 vehicles to be replaced, equivalent to over 30% of the UK fleet while further substantial investment continued to be made in Malawi and Kenya to reduce the average age of their respective fleets. With greater standardisation on fewer vehicle types, maintenance costs should be further reduced and with the continued commitment shown by the company's management and employees, the year 1992-3 was looked forward to with increasing confidence.

In an attempt to persuade travellers to leave their car at home and travel by public transport, Hampshire Bus marked National Environment Week from 16 to 24 May by offering a new cheap off-peak fare between

The first new bus to be delivered to Kenya Bus Services after its purchase by Stagecoach, and the first to receive the group's corporate livery was Singh-bodied DAF TB2100 605 (KAC145H). (Stagecoach International)

Winklebury and Basingstoke town centre. Charging 50p between 10am and 4pm on Monday to Friday and all day on Saturday instead of the normal 78p, the offer (supported by a door to door leaflet drop in Winklebury) was to run for three months and if successful would then become permanent and extended to other services. Still seeking to improve standards further, Stagecoach placed an order in May for another 150 Alexander-bodied 23-seat Mercedes Benz 709D buses for delivery over the following three years. These were to be used to replace a large number of the van-derived buses currently operated by Stagecoach's various UK subsidiaries which were no longer regarded as being able to provide the standard of passenger comfort desired by the company.

Although much of Stagecoach's activity appeared to be centred on its UK operations, its overseas companies were far from neglected and appreciating that new vehicles were urgently needed for its Kenya subsidiary, 12 new DAF buses were placed in service during April and 48 ERF Trailblazers ordered for delivery in the spring of 1993. Joining Kenya Bus Services as its new managing director on 27 July was Barry Pybis who had previously been operations director at United Counties. The Malawi fleet was also in the process of being upgraded and during the period June 1991 to March 1992 no fewer than 67 new ERF Trailblazers had been placed in service and over 50 older buses scrapped. 44 more ERFs were scheduled for delivery during the year and a new Plaxton Paramount-bodied Volvo B10M coach was ordered together with a number of Volvo B10Ms for its Expressline division whilst on 21 August the first of its 10 new Inter-City tri-axle Dennis Dragon double deckers were placed in service after a launching ceremony attended by Ann Gloag. These were fitted with 108-seat bodied assembled locally by PEW from kits supplied by Duple Metsec. Prior to this, in May another Bristol Lodekka had been received from Stagecoach at Perth where it had been used as a driver training bus. Packed with medical and other supplies, it disgraced itself by having to be towed the last 100 miles to Blantyre following a mechanical failure enroute from Durban and as a result it was not repaired and instead was scrapped to provide spares for the company's original bus of this type.

Following a few weeks of comparative calm, Ribble found itself locked in another new bus war at the end of August when Greater Manchester Buses moved onto its routes in Eccles. After the launch by GMB of a service which directly challenged Ribble's successful M10 route between Brookhouse and Manchester, the Stagecoach subsidiary retaliated by halving its fares and charging senior citizens and children a mere 10p. This move prompted its competitor to respond with a shoppers' return fare of 50p between Brookhouse and Eccles, 5p less than that charged by Ribble and as a consequence, the latter reduced its return ticket to 40p. As the battle continued, Ribble found itself facing a new war with GM Buses on its Bolton to Bury services when the PTE company increased its operations on its routes running through Radcliffe. In addition to halving its fares in an attempt to beat off its competitor, Ribble also advertised for conductors with a view to putting some Routemasters onto the routes from Bolton depot. In preparation for this, Ribble acquired 3 buses of this type from United Counties, although in

Painted in an all-over advertising livery, Stagecoach Malawi Duple Metsec-bodied Dennis Dragon 2005 (BJ4397) is seen here at Blantyre depot prior to its entry into service. (Stagecoach International)

Purchased by Ribble from United Counties in October 1992 but never used, Routemasters CUV122C, ALM60B and WSK219 (originally WLT528) remained in store at the company's Blackburn depot (where they are seen here) until October 1996 when all three were sold. (K.A.Jenkinson)

Inverness Traction's much-travelled ECW-bodied Bristol LH6L 363 (SNU851R) is pictured at Carbost on 9 August 1992 whilst on loan to Sutherland of Glenbrittle for operation on its service to Portree. (Murdoch Currie)

Two former Southdown Leyland PD3/4 Queen Marys still in traditional apple green & cream livery, South Coast Buses convertible open-top 409 (409DCD) and Coastline open-top 3223 (424DCD) await their passengers at Hastings on an enthusiast day in October 1992. (T.S.Blackman)

the event these were never used and instead were placed in store at the company's Blackburn depot. In the meantime, Sussex Coastline Buses was referred to the Monopolies and Mergers Commission after it failed to give an acceptable undertaking to remedy anti-competitive practices carried out against Easy Rider Minicoaches in Bognor Regis which had been the subject of an Office of Fair Trading inquiry earlier in the year.

Other than the purchase of Greater Manchester PTA's share of National Transport Tokens Ltd. in March, no other acquisitions had been made by Stagecoach during 1992 until 25 October when it purchased the remaining operations of Alder Valley from Len Wright's Q Drive group. Although this gave Stagecoach 92 additional vehicles and rented depots at Aldershot and Hindhead, Alder Valley's lucrative Londonlink express coach service was not included in the deal, nor was Q Drive's AVE Berkhof coach dealership. In order to be able to maintain its newly-acquired services until additional vehicles were obtained, Stagecoach temporarily hired a pair of Leyland Lynx single deckers from Q-Drive, although these returned to their rightful owner before the year ended. Although the Alder Valley name had also been purchased, it was not used by its new master who instead adopted the name Stagecoach Hants & Surrey for its newly-gained operations. Almost immediately, several new Alexander-bodied Dennis Darts and Leyland Olympians were added to the Hants & Surrey fleet where they mainly replaced Leyland Nationals and Bristol VRTs, although rather than being withdrawn these were reallocated to other of Stagecoach's southern subsidiaries. Following several delays in the start of production by Volvo of its new B6 chassis, Stagecoach cancelled half of its 200-vehicle order for this model and as compensation gained higher specification mid-engined Volvo's B10M chassis designed for bus rather than coach operation. With the transfer of vehicles between Stagecoach's various UK companies now having become commonplace, it was not unusual to find buses moving from one to another whenever the need arose and in addition to some of the transfer of some Alexander-bodied Leyland Olympians from Bluebird Northern to United Counties, a trio of East Midland Routemasters from East Midland to Stagecoach at Perth and Cumberland's three Dennis Darts to Hampshire Bus, East Midland's tri-axle Olympian Megadekka moved to United Counties on 24 October in exchange for one of its former Bluebird Northern Olympians.

Having achieved expansion in Britain with its acquisition of Alder Valley, Stagecoach almost immediately followed this on 28 October with its purchase of the majority sharholding in Wellington City Transport in

Despite being fitted with Stagecoach Hants & Surrey fleet name vinyls on its cove panels and across its front grille, ex.Alder Valley Leyland Lynx 802 (K802CAN) was only on loan to the Stagecoach South company pending the arrival of some new buses and was later returned to Q-Drive who placed it in its Bee Line fleet. It is seen here at Aldershot bus station in December 1992. (T.S.Blackman)

Seen in Brighton sporting Midland Travel fleet names is Fife Scottish Duple-bodied leyland Tiger 562 (MSU462, originally A506PST) which was used on Midland Travel's tours originating in Scotland. (T.S.Blackman)

Having only recently been acquired with the business of Alder Valley, Plaxton-bodied Leyland Tiger SGS504W although still in its former owner's lemon & two-tone green livery had gained its new fleet number (1298) and Stagecoach Hants & Surrey fleet name vinyls when photographed at Aldershot in December 1992. (T.S.Blackman)

Turning at Lyall Bay terminus is Hawke-bodied Volvo B58/Brown Boverie trolleybus 201 (KA9102) still wearing Wellington City Transport's red & cream livery. (Stagecoach International)

Cityline Hutt Valley Bedford NFMs 59921 (JE5454) and 5992 (JE5455) with coachwork by New Zealand Motor Bodies rest at Lower Hutt depot on 29 October 1992. Used almost exclusively on schools duties, both have since been withdrawn and sold. (Stagecoach International)

New Zealand, taking it into a part of the world where it had previously not had a presence. As well as operating 140 motor buses, Wellington City Transport also maintained a fleet of 88 trolleybuses and held a 67% stake in Harbour City Cable Car Ltd. which operated the Kelburn Cable car between Lambton Quay and the Botanical Gardens in Wellington. The structure of this purchase differed from those of previous acquisitions in that Stagecoach Holdings plc established a wholly-owned holding company in New Zealand named New Zealand Bus Ltd which in turn owned shares in Wellington City Transport Ltd. who additionally owned two subsidiaries, Cityline (NZ) Ltd. and North City Bus Ltd.

Since withdrawn and sold, Wellington City Transport tri-axle Mercedes Benz coach 280 (OT8447) in City Bus Hire livery stands at Kilbirnie depot on 29 October 1992. (Stagecoach International)

Cityline operated in two divisions, one at Papakura, south of Auckland with 35 buses, the other at Lower Hutt, to the north of Wellington with 45 buses, both having formerly been bus operating divisions of New Zealand Railways which were purchased by Wellington City Transport in September 1992, while North City Bus Ltd. was a dormant company which resulted from the earlier acquisition by WCT of another New Zealand Railways bus company. New Zealand had been of interest to Stagecoach since 1989 when, in a similar manner to the UK, its bus services had been deregulated and as such, it was believed that further expansion could eventually be attained as well as British operating patterns being established.

Despite receiving 5 more Bristol Lodekkas from the UK early in the year and introducing a new daily service from Toronto to Boston (Mass) in conjunction with Adirondack Transit Lines, Empire Trailways and Peter Pan Bus Lines at the end of March, Stagecoach's Canadian subsidiary Gray Coach Lines was placed in protective receivership during the summer after continually failing to achieve its potential. The

Painted in Stagecoach corporate colours and displaying Stagecoach Wellington fleet names is Hawke-bodied Volvo B58/Brown Boverie trolleybus 242 (MB7637) seen here at Kilbirnie depot. (Stagecoach International)

Kelburn Cable Car no.2 climbs towards the Botanical Gardens in November 1992. (Stagecoach International)

Painted in corporate livery and wearing Cityline fleet names, Hutt Valley's Hawke-bodied Leyland Leopard 428 (IX3782) joined the fleet from Wellington City Transport in March 1993. (Stagecoach International)

Leaving Manchester's Arndale Centre on an X43 journey to Colne in April 1993 is Ribble coach-seated Alexander-bodied Leyland Olympian 2199 (J199HFR) which carried Mancunian lettering on its upper deck side panels. (T.S.Blackman)

Bristol Lodekkas, which all originated from Stagecoach at Perth and had been converted to offside loading before shipment, were obtained for use of Gray Line's sightseeing tours around Toronto upon which the original bus of this type had already become a familiar sight. Not long afterwards, however, deciding to cut its losses Stagecoach sold Gray Coach Lines to Greyhound Lines of Canada in December, thus ending its brief links with North America and although all its vehicles were included in the deal, the 6 Lodekkas were withdrawn almost immediately by their new owner and offered for sale. In the meantime, Stagecoach suffered another disappointment when it failed in its bid for the franchise of 26 bus routes in Hong Kong which would have required around 200 vehicles, these instead being awarded to local operator Citybus.

After divesting itself of its Canadian interests, Stagecoach almost immediately took an interest in the news that Lancaster City Council was taking the first steps to place its bus operating company on the open market. With its subsidiary Ribble already operating a substantial number of services in Lancaster and Morecambe and a depot in both towns, it was considered that the acquisition of Lancaster City Transport would enable it to achieve further growth and gain greater economies through the rationalisation of services and the consequent need for fewer buses. However, until the full council ratified the recommendations of its finance and resources policy committee, little could be done by Stagecoach to achieve its goal. In the meantime, despite problems with punctuality, traction costs and reliability, and ridership figures which were initially disappointing, Stagecoach Rail extended its joint London to Scotland rail service on 23 October to additionally cover the London to Glasgow overnight route. Under the new agreement, Stagecoach was to provide overnight seating on the London to Glasgow route alongside that offered by British Rail while seated BR accommodation was to be reintroduced to the overnight London to Edinburgh service. Stagecoach dramatically reduced its capacity on the latter from 116 seats to 30 each way in summer and 20 in winter while on the Glasgow service it was to have 60 seats each way in summer and 40 in winter. Although the carriages leased from BR by Stagecoach were to continue to wear Stagecoach Rail livery for the time being and carry a mix of Stagecoach and British Rail passengers, it was decided that it would eventually be phased out on the Aberdeen service at least. Despite the Scottish-based company having some time earlier expressed an interest in the eventual privatisation of British Rail, in the light of the experience it had now gained in rail travel, it was extremely cautious in respect of its future plans, believing that many questions still remained to be answered before any further moves were made.

On the final day of October Ribble launched its Network 2000 group of services with a completely remarketed X43 route from Colne to Manchester which was branded 'the Mancunian'. The first of a number of services which were ultimately to be given a new image by the company, it was operated by coach-seated Alexander-bodied Leyland Olympians which had 8 seats removed to allow added comfort and were manned by dedicated drivers who were issued with new uniforms and had attended a customer care course. Such was the confidence in this new service which had been extended from its old terminus at Blackburn, that additional Sunday journeys were introduced and new tickets were offered as well as the facility of paying for them through standing order arrangements. Another innovative move undertaken in the run up to Christmas was the introduction on 27 November of some experimental night bus services in Inverness which were operated free of charge for the first few weeks to illustrate to the local population that

immediately by their new owner and offered for sale. In the meantime, Stagecoach suffered another disappointment when Stagecoach International (Hong Kong) Ltd., a company it had recently established, failed in its bid for the franchise of 26 bus routes in Hong Kong which would have required around 200 vehicles, these instead being awarded to local operator Citybus.

After divesting itself of its Canadian interests, Stagecoach almost immediately took an interest in the news that Lancaster City Council was taking the first steps to place its bus operating company on the open market. With its subsidiary Ribble already operating a substantial number of services in Lancaster and Morecambe and a depot in both towns, it was considered that the acquisition of Lancaster City Transport would enable it to achieve further growth and gain greater economies through the rationalisation of services and the consequent need for fewer buses. However, until the full council ratified the recommendations of its finance and resources policy committee, little could be done by Stagecoach to achieve its goal. In the meantime, despite problems with punctuality, traction costs and reliability, and ridership figures which were initially disappointing, Stagecoach Rail extended its joint London to Scotland rail service on 23 October to additionally cover the London to Glasgow overnight route. Under the new agreement, Stagecoach was to provide overnight seating on the London to Glasgow route alongside that offered by British Rail while seated BR accommodation was to be reintroduced to the overnight London to Edinburgh service. Stagecoach dramatically reduced its capacity on the latter from 116 seats to 30 each way in summer and 20 in winter while on the Glasgow service it was to have 60 seats each way in summer and 40 in winter. Although the carriages leased from BR by Stagecoach were to continue to wear Stagecoach Rail livery for the time being and carry a mix of Stagecoach and British Rail passengers, it was decided that it would eventually be phased out on the Aberdeen service at least. Despite the Scottish-based company having some time earlier expressed an interest in the eventual privatisation of British Rail, in the light of the experience it had now gained in rail travel, it was extremely cautious in respect of its future plans, believing that many questions still remained to be answered before any further moves were made.

On the final day of October Ribble launched its Network 2000 group of services with a completely remarketed X43 route from Colne to Manchester which was branded 'the Mancunian'. The first of a number of services which were ultimately to be given a new image by the company, it was operated by coach-seated Alexander-bodied Leyland Olympians which had 8 seats removed to allow added comfort and were manned by dedicated drivers who were issued with new uniforms and had attended a customer care course. Such was the confidence in this new service which had been extended from its old terminus at Blackburn, that additional Sunday journeys were introduced and new tickets were offered as well as the facility of paying for them through standing order arrangements. Another innovative move undertaken in the run up to Christmas was the introduction on 27 November of some experimental night bus services in Inverness which were operated free of charge for the first few weeks to promote the service to the local population. Prior to this on 2 November, Cumberland brought its new engineering workshop at Lillyhall into use, this being housed in part of the site previously occupied by the ill-fated Leyland-Volvo bus factory.

FORGET THE REST - TRAVEL THE BEST

It is often said that a year of famine is followed by a year of plenty, and this was certainly true as far as Stagecoach was concerned. While 1992 had proved to be a financially successful year and had witnessed the delivery of a substantial number of new vehicles, it had been a year of consolidation rather than one of great territorial expansion, although this was set to change during the next twelve months. The flow of new vehicles continued at the start of the year with the arrival of the first of 45 new Alexander-bodied Volvo B10M single deckers which were allocated to Cumberland primarily for service in Carlisle. In preparation for an upgrading of services in the city which was to commence on 2 January, Cumberland's 8 Routemasters were all withdrawn from service on 19 December when crew operation came to an end, although one or two continued to put in an occasional appearance until the end of the month. Although Carlisle's route network was not drastically changed, a new colour guide and timetable was distributed door-to-door to provide residents with a greater awareness of the services operated, and in addition frequency and fares information was added to all the city centre bus stops. A further innovative move in this unprecedented investment in Carlisle was the use of 'customer carers' at the main city centre stops from mid-morning onwards each day. In addition to selling tickets to waiting passengers in order to make loading easier and quicker, the 'carers' also kept a watchful eye on timekeeping and were able to provide information for passengers and prospective passengers upon request. Other new vehicles to make their debut at this time were the first of 20 Plaxton Premiere Interurban-bodied Volvo B10M coaches of which 15 were destined to join Stagecoach's Scottish subsidiaries and the remaining 5 were to go to United Counties. Incorporating a number of features specified by Stagecoach, these new vehicles were for use on longer distance services where a higher degree of passengers comfort was desired.

One of Cumberland's original Alexander Dash-bodied Volvo B6s which after only a comparatively short time were permanently returned to Volvo following numerous problems, 274 (J704BRM) passes through Carlisle city centre whilst working local service 63 to Morton Park in February 1993. (K.A.Jenkinson)

Emerging from the shadows into Lowther Street, Carlisle in February 1993 is 742 (K742DAO), one of Cumberland's Alexander-bodied Volvo B10Ms which predominate on the city's services. (K.A.Jenkinson)

Standing in Lowther Street in Carlisle city centre on 19 February 1993 is one of Cumberland's 'customer carers' (extreme right). Complete with cash bag and ticket machine he looks towards the approaching bus having already sold tickets to the waiting passengers. (K.A.Jenkinson)

Later in January, Stagecoach was successful in challenging the reference made by the Office of fair Trading to the Monopolies and Mergers Commission relating to Southdown's alleged anti-competitive practices against Easy Rider Minicoaches in Bognor Regis. Following a High Court ruling that the OFT director general had unlawfully extended the scope of the inquiry, the OFT was faced with having to re-submit its case against Southdown under new terms of reference restricting the geographic area to the original two routes. The ultimate outcome which was announced in June, not surprisingly once again ruled against the Stagecoach subsidiary which then had to give certain undertakings to the MMC in respect of its future behaviour on the two routes. Meanwhile, the OFT was called upon to investigate a complaint made by Moffat & Williamson against Fife Scottish with whom it competed on a number of services in the Glenrothes and Kirkcaldy area. As part of a series of national fares experiments by the Stagecoach group, Fife Scottish had, on 4 January, offered return fares for only 10p more than the single fare on its services around Glenrothes and between that town and Kirkcaldy. This experiment which was continued until the end of February was, according to Moffat & Williamson, anti-competitive in that Fife only appeared to be incurring losses on parallel routes. After resting, unactioned, with the OFT for almost nine months, the inquiry was finally put into motion in September after further complaints from Moffat & Williamson. A similar fares experiment was also undertaken in Malawi between 11 January and 27 February when off-peak discounts were offered by Cityline in Blantyre, Lilongwe and Mzuzu. Here, the definition of 'off-peak' was much easier than in the UK as virtually everyone started work at 7am and finished at 4.30pm or 5pm. Proving extremely successful, the off-peak scheme which applied between 8am and 4pm resulted in improved loadings and took much business from the independent minibuses which were posing an increasing competitive threat in these urban areas.

Continuing to adopt new marketing approaches in order to draw greater awareness to its services, Ribble applied a variety of promotional slogans such as 'Forget the rest ... Travel the best' to the front panels of a number of its minibuses and upgraded its fleet with the addition of 19 new Alexander-bodied Mercedes Benz 709Ds which replaced Iveco 49.10s mainly in Preston and Chorley. These were all given 'Zippy' fleetnames, an identity gained with the acquisition of BET minibus subsidiary United Transport which was taken over before Ribble became part of the Stagecoach group, and it was proposed to use this to rebrand the whole of Ribble's Minilink and midibus operations in the months ahead. Further north, having completed its upgrading in Carlisle, early in March Cumberland introduced 22 new Alexander-bodied Volvo B10M buses in Barrow in Furness, representing the biggest single investment in the town's public transport history. Additionally, the company announced details of a £0.5 million rebuilding programme involving its Hindpool Road depot which had originally been the home of Barrow Borough Transport. The Leyland Nationals replaced by the new Volvos

Seen in Blackburn bus station wearing Zippy fleet names, Ribble Alexander-bodied Mercedes Benz 709D 615 (K615UFR) additionally carries the legend 'Forget the rest - Travel the best!' above its radiator grille as a promotional message to passengers on a service upon which competition was being experienced. (T.S.Blackman)

were, in similar fashion to those displaced at Carlisle, quickly cascaded to Ribble where they were used to oust earlier examples of this type of bus from the fleet.

After placing the first of its new Plaxton Premiere Interurban-bodied Volvo B10M coaches into service at Perth on 14 January and a further 7 with Bluebird Northern in March, Fife Scottish received its 7 in April and used them initially on the X24 service from Dundee to Glasgow. This was one of two new express services inaugurated by Fife on 5 April under the Stagecoach Express banner, the other being the X59 from St.Andrews to Edinburgh which connected with the X24 at Glenrothes. Rather than carry the traditional Fife Scottish fleetnames, however, its new coaches were instead adorned with Stagecoach Express lettering to reflect the new branding applied to the company's improved express service network. Ultimately, the Stagecoach Express name was also extended to several older coaches in the Fife fleet as well as to further new Plaxton Premiere Interurbans delivered later in the year.

Overseas, Stagecoach strengthened its position in New Zealand on 1 February in consequence of a round of Wellington Regional Council tendering when it took over the 'Western Wanderer' (Newtown - Karori Mall) service in Wellington previously operated by Cesta Travel and several routes in the Upper Hutt area from Runciman Motors Ltd., the latter being incorporated into Cityline (Hutt Valley) operations. Although a solitary Hawke-bodied Leyland Leopard was acquired from Cesta Travel, none of Runciman's vehicles, all of which were relatively elderly, were involved in the deal, these instead being retained by their owner for continued use on its non-tendered work.

The only vehicle acquired with the tendered services of Cesta Travel in February 1993 was Hawke-bodied Leyland Leopard JT684 seen here still wearing its former owner's livery and fleet number 25 at Wellington City Transport's Kilbirnie depot. (Stagecoach International)

Only two of the twelve buses acquired from Lancaster City Transport remained in the Lancaster/Morecambe area after the takeover of LCT's services. One of these, all-over advertising liveried Optare Metrorider 450 (K450YCW), passes along Westgate, Morecambe on 23 August 1993, (K.A.Jenkinson)

Back in Ribble's territory, Lancaster City Transport was finally put up for sale in February and, with almost indecent haste, early in April a shortlist of bidders was prepared for the city council's consideration. Surprisingly, Stagecoach had not submitted an offer and instead its subsidiary Ribble launched plans to step up its services in Lancaster and introduce a number of fares cuts and new route initiatives. Although many believed this move was an attempt to weaken the finances of Lancaster City Transport and make the company either unviable or unattractive to prospective bidders, Ribble stated that it was merely protecting its interests in the fear that whoever purchased the council-owned company might be an aggressive competitor. This announcement angered LCT to the point where it launched plans to fight back, indicating the start of yet another bus war which could well prove to be a fight to the death. Meanwhile, Blackpool Transport who was considered to be the most likely operator to take over the Lancaster undertaking was pipped to the post by a more substantial bid submitted by Liverpool-based MTL Holdings who wished to involve the LCT

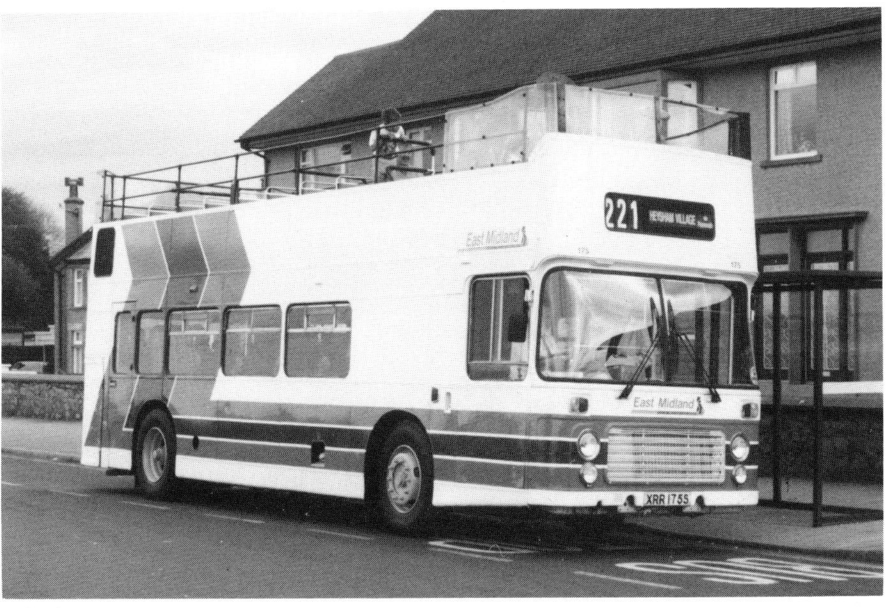

Having not acquired any of Lancaster City Transport's open-top double deckers, Ribble hired a Cumberland Atlantean and an East Midland Bristol VRT to enable it to operate the sea-front service for the remaining few weeks of its 1993 operation. Still wearing East Midland fleet names, 175 (XRR175S) stands at the Happy Mount Park terminus in Morecambe ready to leave for Heysham Village on 23 August 1993. (K.A.Jenkinson)

workforce in its venture, and the situation appeared to be thus resolved. However, following a rejection by LCT staff of the MTL proposal in May, Stagecoach suddenly stepped in with an offer for the undertaking's Morecambe depot and 12 vehicles, thereby transforming the structured sale into an asset disposal. As a result of its acceptance, on 22 August Lancaster City Transport faded into the annals of history and on the following day Ribble began its operations on a new network of services in Lancaster and Morecambe which incorporated all the commercial services previously maintained by both companies. In order to present the area with a new image, the 10 Leyland Atlanteans taken over from Lancaster City Transport were immediately removed to Preston where they were temporarily placed in store and apart from the 2 ex.LCT Optare Metroriders which were both in all-over advertising liveries and a Cumberland open-top double decker, all the buses employed on services in Lancaster and Morecambe were painted in Stagecoach corporate colours. For operation on the former City Transport seafront service from Heysham to Happy Mount Park, Ribble hired East Midland's open-top Bristol VRT and a Lakeland Experience-liveried open-top Leyland Atlantean from Cumberland, both of which retained their rightful owner's fleet names. Having immediately transferred all its Morecambe operations to the former City Transport depot on Heysham Road, Ribble's former depot in the town, which was now regarded as closed, was for a short time used to store the vehicles retained by the council until they were collected by their new owners.

Prior to the Lancaster saga starting to unfold at the beginning of May, East Midland on 30 April sold its Midland Travel coaching operation to Skills of Nottingham together with booking offices at Mansfield and Chesterfield, its National Express agencies and 7 coaches. Additionally included in the deal was the Midland Travel name which Skills intended to develop, although the inherited coaches were to be repainted into their new owner's standard green livery as soon as was practical. Two days earlier, Coastline had begun a new service at Portsmouth between the Continental Ferry Port, city centre railway stations and the Isle of Wight ferry. Operated by a Bristol VRT adorned with a blue centre band and Shuttlebus lettering, this service was unique in that both the French franc and UK sterling was accepted in the payment of the £1 fare and the Wayfarer ticket machine used was adapted to print a ticket showing £1 or 10 FFs. Meanwhile, in the north-west extending the Network 2000 initiative to Cumberland, that subsidiary introduced the premium branding to coincide with the launch of its new X5 Lakeslink express service on 17 May and its existing 555 service running from Lancaster to Carlisle via the Lake District which were thereafter maintained by coach-seated Alexander-bodied Leyland Olympians.

In order to achieve greater efficiency and quality of service, Stagecoach set up its own in-house pension administration department at Perth on 6 April. Headed by Paul Goddard, pensions administration manager who was assisted by Jean Briggs, this gave the scheme more flexibility in deciding how its benefits were communicated to members as well as reducing running costs by as much as 50%. The Group pension fund had a current market value of around £35 million which was managed by professional investment managers appointed by the trustees of the scheme with Standard Life Pension Funds Limited being responsible for investing approximately 85% of the fund and Templeton Investment Management Limited being responsible for the remainder. In setting up the new system it had been necessary to transfer complete records for over 5,000 members, which in itself was a monumental task and in addition the department was responsible for paying monthly pensions to the Group'

SHARES FOR ALL

Without doubt the most important event of 1993 was the flotation of Stagecoach Holdings on the London Stock Exchange in April. Of the 33,505,954 2.5p ordinary shares on offer, 21,778,870 were placed firm while the remaining 11,727,084 were allocated between 44,413 applicants with those offered to the public being almost eight times oversubscribed. The issue price of £1.12 raised £20.6 million and Stock Exchange dealings began on 27 April after which the value of the company's shares quickly started to rise. In preparation for its flotation, external adverts drawing the public's attention to Stagecoach's proposals were affixed to a number of its buses throughout the UK as well as being inserted in the national press. Following its acceptance by the London Stock Exchange, Stagecoach made a number of Group appointments which were to take effect from 1 May. Barry Hinkley who had been appointed to the board of Stagecoach Holdings in October 1992 and was executive chairman of Ribble, East Midland and United Counties relinquished his position of managing director of Cumberland Motor Services to become its executive director was replaced at Cumberland by Paul Southgate who had previously been managing director of Hampshire Bus. Brian Cox who had also been joined the board of Stagecoach Holdings in October 1992 and was also managing director of Stagecoach Rail gave up his position as managing director of Stagecoach South to become its executive chairman, his replacement being Stagecoach South's finance director Debra Topliff. Ben Colson was promoted to the position of Group network analyst and although as a result he relinquished his previous post of commercial director of Ribble and Cumberland, he remained on the board of both companies in addition to being appointed to the boards of United Counties, East Midland, Stagecoach South and Stagecoach Rail. As a result of these changes, Barry Hinkley was able to become more involved in the acquisition and restructuring of future bus company purchases while Brian Cox was able to concentrate more time on rail franchising matters as well as other Group development issues.

After successfully operating an open-top tourist service in Inverness during 1992, this was relaunched on 15 May in conjunction with Guide Friday who had experience in the marketing of open-top services throughout the UK. Although Inverness Traction continued to provide the Bristol VRT used on this operation, it was repainted into Guide Friday's familiar cream and dark green livery and carried promotional lettering with reference to both companies. Another tourist operation to be improved for the 1993 summer season was that around Loch Ness, and in addition to the popular full-day tour which had proved successful the previous year, morning and afternoon tours were introduced along the Loch as far as Urquhart Castle. For operation on all three, Inverness Traction repainted two of its coaches into a special livery which included pictures of the Loch, its surrounding mountains and, of course, the Loch Ness monster! Back on the local bus scene, after a long period of stability, Northampton suddenly seemed set for a new bus war in July when the first shots were fired by United Counties at Northampton

Leaving Blackpool's Talbot Road bus station on a journey to Knott End on 22 April 1993 is Ribble's former Hampshire Bus Duple-bodied Dennis Javelin 1136 (F136SPX) which carried a poster along its side panels publicising Stagecoach's share offer. (T.S.Blackman)

Painted in a special livery for operation on The Grand Loch Ness Tour in 1993 is Inverness Traction Duple Goldliner-bodied Leyland Tiger 431 (1412NE, originally KSL41X). (Campbell Morrison)

Transport after the former registered a number of new competitive services just as the municipal operator was in the process of inviting bids for its sale. Using the same arguments that it used in Lancaster by stating that it was protecting itself against the possibility of an attack by Northampton Transport's eventual new owner, United Counties also introduced a number of new fares initiatives which it claimed were defensive measures to retain its 25% share of its operations in the town. These were quickly matched by the municipal operator who also registered a number of new services against those already operated by the Stagecoach subsidiary, and so the war continued. Looking towards the future, although Stagecoach did not submit a bid for the Northampton undertaking, it registered an interest in the forthcoming franchising of British Rail despite knowing that it would be some considerable time before the Government progressed its rail privatisation plans to the point when bids would have to be submitted.

Despite divesting itself of its 50% share in Hong Kong-based Speedybus Enterprises to Clement Lau on 16 July, Stagecoach still maintained its connections with the Colony where it planned to start bus operations at a future date if it was able to obtain some franchises, whilst at home in its native Perth it could be said that it had finally won its battle with Strathtay Scottish when the latter withdrew the last of its local services in the city and closed its depot on 16 August, leaving Stagecoach to reign supreme.

In its continuing bid to improve its operations with more modern, comfortable and cost-effective vehicles, Stagecoach at the start of August placed an order for a further 280 Alexander bodies for which, two months later, an order for 110 Volvo B6, 120 Volvo B10M and 50 Olympian chassis was confirmed with delivery scheduled to take place during the next two years. In addition an option was placed for an additional 240 Alexander-bodied B6s, B10Ms and Olympians and taking previous orders into account, the company expected to receive a minimum of 490 new Volvo vehicles in the three years commencing 1 January 1993. Meanwhile, the group's year end figures to 30 April 1993 showed that profits had risen to £12.9 million from £8.2 million in the previous year. During that period 299 new vehicles had been delivered to the group's UK subsidiaries with a further 112 to its overseas operations and through prudent management, despite its increase in size, Stagecoach had reduced its overheads from £1.26 million to £1.21 million.

Having invested a large amount of capital upgrading its Cumberland fleet at the start of the year, a similar programme was embarked upon at United Counties during the late summer when a start was made in replacing around 25% of its fleet with new buses and coaches. Coupled with this was a completely revised service network in Bedford which was implemented on 4 September bringing an end to the company's Routemaster operation. All the Leyland Leopards which had been the backbone of United Counties' Coachlinks express services for more than a decade were replaced by new Plaxton Premiere Interurban-bodied Volvo B10M coaches while in Bedford 21 new Volvo B6 midibuses superseded the Routemasters as well as a number of Leyland Nationals and Bristol VRTs. Additionally, 26 Alexander-bodied Mercedes 709D minibuses were received before the end of the year for use at Bedford and Northampton as replacements for Iveco 49.10s as were 21 Alexander-bodied Leyland Olympians which displaced Bristol VRTs in Northampton. Not all of the latter were time-expired, however, and several were swiftly transferred to Ribble for continued use.

Further south, Stagecoach had taken control of East Kent on 7 September, giving it another piece of the jigsaw relating to south-east England. Included in the deal were East Kent Road Car Co. Ltd., East Kent Coaches and EK Worldwide Travel Ltd., 243 buses and coaches and depots at Ashford, Canterbury, Herne Bay, Dover, Folkestone and Thanet. Amongst its operations were numerous local bus routes, some transfer duties at the port of Dover which were undertaken on behalf of various cross-Channel ferry operators, and several National Express contracted services. Despite being a typical former NBC company with its obligatory Leyland Nationals, Tigers and Olympians, Bristol VRTs and Iveco 49.10 minibuses, East Kent's fleet also included some MCW Metrobuses, 3 Optare Delta-bodied DAF SB220s and a handful of single deck MCW Metroliner coaches. Although placed under the control of Stagecoach South for administrative purposes, the company retained its own identity and initially underwent little change except for its buses losing their livery in favour of Stagecoach corporate colours. Its private hire and tours coaches were, however, allowed to retain their existing cream and crimson scheme, thus retaining at least a little of the past. Not surprisingly, both the acquisition of East Kent and the assets of Lancaster City Transport were being considered by the Office of Fair Trading who had in the meantime given clearance to Stagecoach to enter a bid for GM Buses South Ltd. which was in the process of being privatised. Overseas, Stagecoach Malawi was in the throes of updating its fleet and in March took delivery of an ERF Trailblazer bendibus which was followed in August by the first new buses for Cityline for six years, these being rigid ERF Trailblazers which were put into service on the company's flagship service 1 between Blantyre and Limbe upon which they replaced a number of the ex.Kowloon Daimler double deckers which were by this time becoming unreliable. Joining the new ERFs in the Cityline fleet were 4 PEW-bodied Mercedes Benz 812D midibuses which were placed in service on 16 September on route 11 from Limbe to Bangwe which was at this same time converted to one person operation and on 7 November more new ERF Trailblazers were introduced when route 7 (Blantyre to Chilomoni) was also converted to OPO. On 8 September a new burns and plastic surgery unit was opened at the Queen Elizabeth Central Hospital in Blantyre, this being wholly financed and built by Stagecoach Holdings and the inspiration of its

One of United Counties black & gold-liveried Corby Magic Minis Robin Hood-bodied Iveco 49.10s, 64 (G64JVV) rests outside its home depot in June 1996 a few days before its withdrawal from service. (K.A.Jenkinson)

Passing through Corby on its way to Peterborough in June 1996 and wearing Coachlinks fleet names is United Counties Plaxton Premiere Interurban-bodied 160 (L160JNH). (K.A.Jenkinson)

Wearing the pre-Stagecoach crimson & cream livery of East Kent, Leyland National 1346 (PJJ346S) prepares to leave Folkestone bus station for Dover on service 90. (T.S.Blackman)

One of East Kent's three Optare Delta-bodied DAF SB220s painted in the dedicated grey & blue Canterbury park & ride livery, 1401 (J401LKO) passes through the town centre on its way to the Sturry Road parking area. (T.S.Blackman)

managing director, Ann Gloag, who before entering the bus business had been a theatre sister in a burns unit in Perth. The new Malawian unit which comprised a dedicated operating theatre, 26 beds divided into male, female and paediatric wards and was staffed by 13 nurses, 3 patient attendants and 9 hospital servants. Prior to its opening, there had been no specialised burns unit in the country and had it not been for the Scottish-based company, such a facility would undoubtedly still have been little more than a dream. Further afield, Stagecoach expanded its operations in New Zealand when its Cityline Hutt Valley subsidiary acquired an express service between Stokes Valley and Wellington from Stokes Valley Coach Services. In Kenya, the first of 48 new ERF Trailblazer buses was launched at a ceremony in Nairobi on 10 March, although it was 1 May before these buses began to enter service while in Malawi the first of 20 PEW-bodied Volvo B10Ms with coach-type seating had been placed in service in the Expressline. Three of the new Volvos were used on the recently reopened international service from Blantyre to Harare via Tete which connected Malawi with Zimbabwe via Mozambique, closed for several years due to the civil war in Mozambique. The remaining 17 of the new Volvos were used to convert the Expressline service between Blantyre and Lilongwe to one-person-operation on 25 July, running from Chichiri and Lilongwe depots. As more of the new ERF Trailblazer buses arrived they were put onto the Blantyre to Chilomoni service on 13 November at the same time that it was converted to one-person-operation and were followed soon afterwards by 5 allocated to Cityline's Lilongwe depot.

After a less than happy ride, Stagecoach ended its loss-making rail venture in October blaming high traction charges by British Rail and the complexity of selling tickets for through journeys. Nevertheless, the company had gained a great deal of experience through its brave experiment which would no doubt be invaluable when the Government's forthcoming rail franchising plans were eventually put into motion. Meanwhile, early in October in advance of the outcome of its bid for GM Buses South, Ribble registered two high-frequency routes in south Manchester from Piccadilly to Hazel Grove and Stockport to Wythenshawe. Both services, which would compete directly with GM Buses South and were designed to 'test the water' were scheduled to start in January 1994, of which more later. Following a meeting between East Midland and Chesterfield Transport in September, soon after the latter's acquisition of Whites of Calver, the two companies agreed an exchange of routes in the Matlock and Staveley areas. This ultimately took effect on 25 October when Chesterfield's subsidiary Whites became responsible for all the operations centred on Matlock and East Midland gained full control of service 8 from Chesterfield to Staveley and the 81-83 group from Chesterfield to Bolsover. Prior to this, as part of a rationalisation plan, East Midland closed its depots at Clowne and Shirebrook on 1 August after having similarly closed its Harworth premises on 10 January following the loss of several South Yorkshire

One of a pair of Alexander-bodied Scania N113DRBs purchased new by East Kent in 1989, 7781 (F781KKP) had gained Stagecoach corporate colours when caught by the camera enroute to Reculver. (P.Kay)

PTE contracts. Continuing its fleet replacement programme, Ribble took delivery of a further 25 Alexander-bodied Mercedes Benz 709D minibuses, eliminating the last of the company's Iveco 49.10s from Preston, Chorley and Fleetwood depots in the process and additionally

A number of Stagecoach Malawi's ERF Trailblazers are fitted with couplings to allow them to haul freight trailers. One such bus, 863 (BH5863) is seen complete with a trailer at Blantyre in February 1992. (J.Davison)

Displayed at the Bus & Coach Show at the NEC, Birmingham in 1993 was this Plaxton Paramount Interurban-bodied Dennis Javelin. Destined to join the Ribble fleet, it was lettered for the Ribble Valley Mancunian express service. (K.A.Jenkinson)

The 1000th new vehicle to be purchased by Stagecoach was United Counties Alexander Dash-bodied Volvo B6 420 (L420JBD) which was exhibited at the 1993 Bus & Coach Show held at the NEC, Birmingham. (K.A.Jenkinson)

Grimsby Cleethorpes coaching unit Peter Sheffield's Duple-bodied Leyland Leopard 173 (BHO441V) still in its original white livery with purple and blue relief passes through Scunthorpe on a private hire duty in May 1994. (K.A.Jenkinson)

Freshly repainted in Stagecoach corporate colours but yet to receive its new fleet names is Grimsby Cleethorpes East Lancs-bodied Dennis Lance 3 (K703NDO). Standing behind it at Cleethorpes Pier in July 1994 is Roe-bodied Leyland Fleetline 120 (OJV120S) still in GCT orange & ivory livery. (K.A.Jenkinson)

received the first of 23 Plaxton Premiere Interurban-bodied Dennis Javelin coaches purchased for its Network 2000-remodelled longer distance routes. Initially these were put to work on 9 October on the 'Ribble Valley Mancunian'-branded X25 express service from Clitheroe to Manchester for which they were appropriately lettered, and in November they were additionally allocated to the Blackpool to Morecambe service. Prior to this, Stagecoach was able to publicly confirm its commitment to improved standards and massive financial investment when Ann Gloag accepted delivery of the group's 1000th new vehicle, an Alexander-bodied Volvo B6 for United Counties, at the Coach & Bus Show at the National Exhibition Centre, Birmingham on 8 October. Although the Volvo B6 was now proving to be a satisfactory and reliable vehicle, the 5 original examples which had been purchased by Cumberland in 1992, effectively prototypes, continued to prove troublesome and thus, after lengthy negotiations with their manufacturer, were sold back to Volvo during the autumn of 1993.

Still eager for further expansion whenever the opportunity arose, Stagecoach purchased Grimsby Cleethorpes Transport in privatisation on 18 November and immediately placed it under the administrative control of East Midland Motor Services. Included in the deal which gave Stagecoach its first foothold in eastern England north of the Thames, was all the undertaking's bus operations, fleet and depot and its coaching arm which traded under the name of Peter Sheffield. A large part of the 100 vehicles acquired was made up of vehicle types strange to the Stagecoach group such as Dennis Dominator double deckers and Dennis Lance and Falcon single deckers, most of which wore the undertaking's white & orange colours whilst amongst the purple & white liveried Peter Sheffield coaches was a Ford R1114 and several ageing Leyland Leopards. Almost before the ink had dried on the Grimsby Cleethorpes acquisition, on 10 December Stagecoach purchased the 728-vehicle Western Travel group which gave the company its first access to Wales. Western Travel Ltd. maintained services over a large area stretching from Nuneaton and Banbury to Swindon and Aberdare and included twelve different operating companies - Cheltenham & Gloucester Omnibus Co., Cheltenham District Traction Co., Swindon & District Bus Co., Midland Red South; Midland Flexibus Ltd., G & G Travel of Leamington Spa, Vanguard Coaches of Bedworth, Red & White Services, The Valleys Bus Co., Eastern Valleys Bus Co., Western Valleys Bus Co., Aberdare Bus Co. and a 45% share in Circle Line of Gloucester. While the English companies in Western Travel's portfolio operated a mix of typical former NBC vehicles, the Welsh companies had a preponderance of minibuses, the majority of which were of the older van-derived type in need of urgent replacement. Despite all having been under the control of one group, each company except those associated with Red & White employed its own livery and although these were ultimately all to be replaced by Stagecoach's corporate hue, for a time each retained its own identity to provide a wealth of variety. Prior to Western Travel joining the Stagecoach fold, Coastline Buses closed its Havant depot on 27 November and transferred its allocation to its Leigh Park premises, although as there was insufficient space at the latter for its now-increased fleet, several buses had to be parked each night at Havant bus station, a less than ideal site due to occasional vandalism.

Tragedy struck in Malawi on the evening of 20 November when fire swept through the accounts section of Stagecoach Malawi's head office at Chichiri in Blantyre. This sadly claimed the lives of two members of

Wearing Cheltenham District's red & cream livery, Bristol VRT 5088 (NHU671R) seen in Cheltenham was renumbered 927 after becoming part of the Stagecoach group. (J.Whitmore)

One of a pair of Leyland Lynxes acquired with Midland Red South's G & G Travel subsidiary, F660PWK still in pre-Stagecoach livery is seen at Coventry bus station. (J.Whitmore)

staff who had been working late, one of whom was Symon Siula, the company's chief personnel officer, the other, accounts clerk Smart Liwonde. The cost of the damage was estimated at around £115,000 and the entire accounting section had to be temporarily relocated while the future of the building was determined. This was a particularly sad time for John Gould who had only a few weeks earlier taken up the position of managing director of Stagecoach Malawi after moving from a

One of four Alexander-bodied Bristol VRTs purchased by National Welsh from Grampian Regional Transport, 861 (OSR206R) in Red & White's livery of those two colours leaves Chepstow depot to take up a schools duty in March 1994. (K.A.Jenkinson)

One of a pair of 33-seat Wright-bodied Mercedes Benz 811Ds purchased new by Cheltenham & Gloucester in 1993 for its Swindon & District fleet, 802 (K802OWM) is pictured here still wearing its original red & cream livery. (T.W.W.Knowles)

On loan to G & G Travel from West Midlands Travel for operation on service in Leamington connecting the rail station to the town is Freight Rover Sherpa G216EDA seen here at Midland Red's Leamington depot on a frosty day in December 1994.

Midland Red South Dormobile-bodied Ford Transit 378 (F709FKE) acquired from East Kent in 1992 was dedicated to the Avon Shuttle service in Stratford-upon-Avon for which it wore a special white & blue livery and Stratford Blue fleet names. (K.A.Jenkinson)

Resting in Coventry, Midland Red South's green & yellow Easyrider-liveried Leyland National 1051 (KIB8140, originally THX249S) is one of three buses of this type converted for the carriage of the disabled. (J.Whitmore)

Painted in silver livery with blue and red stripes and wearing Metro fleet names, Cheltenham & Gloucester MCW Metrorider 669 (E669JAD) is seen here operating a local Cheltenham service. (T.S.Blackman)

Carrying a yellow & blue livery, G & G Travel 1491 (E99OUH), an ex.Red & White Carlyle-bodied Freight Rover Sherpa, rests in Leamington Spa before taking up its next journey to Whitnash in 1995. (F.W.York)

similar post at Ribble. To fill the position at Preston, Michael Chambers, finance director of Stagecoach (North West) was promoted to managing director of Ribble, the post he relinquished being taken by Robert Harvey who moved from East Midland while David Kirsopp was appointed chief engineer of Cumberland. Meanwhile, at the group's head office in Perth, Keith Cochrane who had joined Stagecoach Holdings in October as financial controller was appointed company secretary on 12 November, thus further strengthening the management team.

Overseas, Stagecoach Malawi on 6 December 1993 began a new Expressline service from Blantyre to Chinteche, a distance of some 375 miles, following the opening of a new tarmac road between these two points and it was planned to extend this further to the northern regional capital of Mzuzu at some time in 1994. Also in Malawi, one-person-operation, which had been introduced in Blantyre in 1993 was further developed in January 1994 when on the 8th of the month route F from Lilongwe to Likuni was thus converted as was the Blantyre to Limbe via Kamuzu Highway service on the 22nd. In New Zealand, the first of 80 new Designline-bodied dual-door MAN 11.190 single deckers were

placed in service in Wellington during February, while on 24 January Stagecoach International (Hong Kong) Ltd. at last inaugurated the first of its two new licensed Resident's services. Numbered 801R, this operated from Pok Hong/Sha Kok Street in the Sha Tin District, New Territories to Wan Chai, Admiralty and Central on Hong Kong Island and was maintained by 5 new air-conditioned Alexander PS-type bodied Volvo B10Ms. Three of these differed from their two sisters in having a slightly longer rear overhang and thus longer overall length (11.49m instead of 11.25m) and as Stagecoach did not have its own garage premises for its small fleet, the buses were parked and maintained at the Fo Tan premises of the Kowloon-Canton Railway Corporation's bus division. A flat fare of HK$16 adult single was charged on route 801R on which travel was not permitted between intermediate points, and the buses were fitted with Hong Kong standard fare boxes with no tickets being issued.

After having failed in its attempt to purchase GM Buses South during the previous year, Stagecoach made a new bid for the company in February 1994 and was confident that it would add this prestigious company to its growing portfolio by the end of March. Its hopes were

Acquired by Red & White from Hampshire Bus in January 1994 and displaying Stagecoach fleet names, Alexander-bodied Mercedes Benz L608D 285 (C808SDY) arrives in Bulwark on a local journey from Chepstow in March of that year. (K.A.Jenkinson)

Awaiting its passengers in Gloucester bus station is Cheltenham & Gloucester Roe-bodied Leyland Olympian 121 (LWS39Y) repainted in corporate livery and complete with Gloucester Citybus fleet names. (Campbell Morrison)

Stagecoach Hong Kong air-conditioned Alexander-bodied Volvo B10Ms 5L (FW7894) and 1 (FW6766) are seen here at Chai Wan on their first day in service, 24 January 1994. The 'L' suffix to the fleet number indicates that no.5 is 11.49m long compared with the 11.25m length of no.1. As can be seen, the fleet name was carried in both Chinese and English. (Stagecoach International)

A route advertising banner for the new 801R service was placed in Sha Kok Street, Pong Hong. (Stagecoach International)

quickly dashed, however, when during the final days of February it was announced that the company had been sold to its management/employees. This was in spite of a move made by the Perth-based giant to woo GMB South's staff by the placing of newspaper advertisements in which a number of attractive promises were made to them and the submission of an even higher bid. Prior to these events, Ribble had set up a new unit in South Manchester which on 29 January began operating a high frequency 7.0am to 7.0pm Monday to Saturday service numbered 192 from Manchester Piccadilly to Hazel Grove via Stockport which it had registered during the previous October and competed directly with GMB South's route bearing the same number. Using the fleet name 'Stagecoach Manchester' and operating from a new base at Bredbury, the service was maintained by 16 new Alexander Dash-bodied Volvo B6s which were adorned with route diagrams and promotional posters. The fares charged were considerably lower than those of GM Buses South with, for instance, 60p from Manchester to Stockport compared with £1.15 by GMS, and as was to be expected this brought a swift response from the incumbent operator who introduced lower return fares, although these were not as low as Stagecoach. So popular did the new service prove, that early in May the original Volvo B6s were supplemented by 6 new Alexander PS-bodied Volvo B10Ms originally intended for Stagecoach South. Meanwhile, early in April GM Buses South retaliated by starting a new half-hourly limited stop service from Manchester to Nelson which competed with Ribble's Network 2000 route X43 and was operated by coaches from its Charterplan subsidiary. In an attempt to counter this intrusion, Ribble introduced additional journeys between Manchester and Nelson on the X43, replaced its Alexander-bodied Olympians with almost new Plaxton Premiere Interurban-bodied Dennis Javelins and cut its fares. Stagecoach Manchester meanwhile registered another new service from Piccadilly to Wythenshawe Hospital which was to start in mid-May, although in the event this was later deregistered without having commenced operation. From Friday 6 May, however, daytime operations on the 192 service were increased from every ten minutes to every four and a half minutes and on 16 June were extended to operate through to midnight on Mondays to Wednesdays, 2.20am on Thursdays

New to Cynon Valley, 391 (GHB146N) is one of three Red & White 1974-vintage ECW-bodied Bristol RESL6Ls to be repainted into Stagecoach corporate colours. (John Probert)

Stagecoach Manchester's new 192 service competed directly with GM Buses South's route bearing that same number. Seen at the Hazel Grove terminus on 5 May 1994 are Alexander Dash-bodied Volvo B6s 251 (L251CCK) waiting to depart to Manchester and 253 (L253LCK) which has just arrived from that city and is successfully blocking the entry to its stand of a GMB South NCME-bodied Leyland Atlantean. (K.A.Jenkinson)

One of the Vauxhall vans operated by Pegasus Express is seen here in its new livery which incorporates Stagecoach stripes. (Stagecoach)

Two of the coaches acquired by Bluebird Buses with the business of Norrie, New Deer, neither of these Plaxton-bodied Volvo B58s - cream & red liveried GSU717N and green-liveried XRP73S were used by their new owner and are seen here awaiting disposal. (Campbell Morrison)

and Fridays and to 3.00am on Saturday night/Sunday morning. The additional vehicles needed to maintain the higher daytime frequencies were 17 new Alexander-bodied Volvo B10Ms which additionally replaced all but 2 of the Volvo B6s.

Elsewhere within the Stagecoach empire, Bluebird Northern early in the year purchased the vehicles and operations of two small family coach businesses less than twenty miles apart in a remote rural area of Grampian. One of these, Norries of New Deer who was taken over in January had 18 vehicles, and although these were taken into stock by Bluebird, all except for 3 minis were immediately withdrawn and offered for sale. The other, Hans Hardy of Aberchirder had 11 vehicles which were all retained for further operation by their new owner after their acquisition in February. Whilst most of the duties gained with these two businesses were of a contracted nature, a small number of local bus services were included and some private hire work. A further development which took place on February 1 was the formation of a joint venture company, Pegasus Express Ltd., between Bluebird Buses and Pegasus Couriers Ltd., an Aberdeen-based express parcels delivery company started in 1980 whose fleet had now grown to 28 vans of varying sizes, 7 of which were leased, a car and an estate car. Incorporated into the Pegasus Express operation was Bluebird Buses Parcels Service and a recently acquired parcel operation in Inverness run by Bluebird Express Parcels giving the new company a budgeted turnover of more than £1 million per year. Operated from Bluebird's depot at Aberdeen and its recently acquired new premises in Inverness, Pegasus was also agents for Red Star in Aberdeen, Elgin and Inverness. Later in the year, on 3 July, Bluebird gained the contract to operate the Speyside Rambler and Ballater - Tomintoul tourist services while Stagecoach at Perth together with Kirkpatricks of Deeside was awarded the contract for the summer Banchory to Pitlochry service. South of the border, on Easter Saturday East Kent launched a new fast service between Broadstairs and Canterbury numbered X81 and branded 'The Pickwick Express'. Marketed as a high quality service upon which children were only able to travel if accompanied by an adult 'to preserve the peace of a bygone age', the Pickwick Express was maintained by coach-seated Alexander PS-bodied Volvo B10Ms adorned with appropriate logos. In a further innovative move, United Counties introduced a new 'Quality Code' to its services on 13 May to confirm its commitment to improving the quality of public transport services within its operating area. Under the 'Quality Code', the company pledged to its customers that should any of its buses arrive at their intended stop more than 20 minutes late due to circumstances within its control, they would receive a complimentary Explorer Ticket allowing them a day's free travel on most of United Counties' services.

As part of its ongoing commitment to its employees, Stagecoach revitalised its ESOP and agreed to allocate up to 3% of pre-tax group profit between eligible employees of all participating UK companies within the group. In effect, there would be two free allocations of shares in each year shortly after the announcement of both the half and full year results and the basis of allocation would be agreed by the ESOP trustees. In addition, Stagecoach agreed to set up a Save As You Earn share option plan which would be available to all employees. Shares to the value of 3% of group profits to the year up to 30 April 1994 were to be set aside for the plan and it was anticipated that the offer would be made around September/October, although in reality it was not until April 1996 that it became operative. Under the Sharesave scheme, shares would be offered at a discount to the prevailing market price which once announced would be guaranteed and did not have to be paid for immediately. Instead, the money needed would be saved regularly by an employee in a scheme managed by a leading UK building society for a period of five years after which a guaranteed tax free bonus equal to nine months contributions would be added. At the end of the five years, all or part of the savings could be used to buy shares at the option price or could be withdrawn in cash. Should employees wish to leave their savings untouched for a further two years, the original bonus would then be doubled.

Amongst the changes made within Stagecoach's management was the appointment on 21 March of Malcolm Stewart, formerly a director and commercial manager of Strathclyde Buses, as managing director of Kenya Bus Services where he replaced Barry Pybis who returned to the UK to take over the position of managing director of East Midland. Alex Boyd, chief engineer of Bluebird Buses was promoted to engineering

Seen at Canterbury bus station in August 1994, East Kent dual purpose-seated Alexander-bodied Volvo B10M 589 (K789DAO), one of a trio acquired from Cumberland in April 1994 carried Pickwick logos and route diagram on its side panels. (D.W.Rhodes)

director of United Counties on 3 May while Allan Fuller, finance director of Stagecoach Grimsby Cleethorpes also took this position at East Midland.

With a target to replace 30% of its entire UK bus and coach fleet within three years, Stagecoach placed forward orders in April for 350 new vehicles for delivery in 1996 with an option for a further 150, following existing orders for 380 vehicles in 1994 and 300 in 1995. Valued at £31.5 million, the new order comprised 50 each Volvo B6s, B10Ms and Olympians and 200 Mercedes Benz 709Ds, all of which were to have Alexander bodywork. Soon afterwards, Stagecoach signed an exclusive bus advertising contract with British Transport Advertising in May which covered 18 of its operating subsidiaries with those outside the deal, Cheltenham & Gloucester, Stagecoach Scotland, Inverness Traction, Midland Red South and G & G Travel who were all involved in existing contracts joining the scheme when these expired later in the year. Two months later, Stagecoach increased its order for new buses for 1996 delivery with 50 Alexander-bodied Dennis Darts, the option on a further 100 and, for Kenya 10 tri-axle Dennis Dragons, the first double deckers to be purchased since 1952/3 when Kenya Bus Services bought a small number of former London Transport Guy Arabs.

NEW PARTNERSHIPS

June too proved to be a month of great activity when in addition to expanding in New Zealand, Stagecoach also made offers for former Scottish Bus Group subsidiary Western Scottish and the Busways Group which until 1988 had been owned by Tyne & Wear PTA. The New Zealand development saw the purchase from Hutt City Council on the first day of the month of the Eastbourne Bus Company, a 20 vehicle undertaking based near Wellington which operated mainly on peak hour commuter routes between Eastbourne and Wellington City and was to be maintained under the title of Eastbourne Buses as part of Cityline Hutt Valley. Meanwhile, back at home Stagecoach on 4 July made an offer under a share exchange deal which, if successful, would give it a 20% shareholding in the South Yorkshire-based Mainline Group which had until November of the previous year been under the ownership of South Yorkshire PTA. Operating in Sheffield, Rotherham and Doncaster under the titles of Mainline, Coachline, Don Valley Buses and Sheafline, it was believed that this company would give the Scottish-based group a new foothold in an area where it had only previously had a minor presence through its East Midland subsidiary. After balloting its shareholders, the company's offer in respect of Mainline was accepted at the start of August soon after those made to Western Scottish and Busways had similarly been. Thus, on 26 July Busways became a part of the Stagecoach group. With 590 vehicles and a wide network of routes in Tyne & Wear, it operated in a number of divisions under the titles of Newcastle Busways, South Shields Busways, Sunderland Busways, Tyne & Wear Omnibus Co., Blue Bus Services, Favourite Services, Economic Bus Services, Welcome Passenger Transport and Armstrong Galley. Each of these units employed its own individual livery and unlike all the previous companies which had been acquired by Stagecoach and had ultimately adopted its corporate colours, there was no immediate plan to extend this to the Busways group which was to retain its existing liveries and fleet names at least for the foreseeable future. Indeed, the only indication of its new owner was the addition of the legend 'Part of the Stagecoach Group' below the fleetname and on certain items of publicity etc. Armstrong Galley, the company's coaching arm, in addition to undertaking an amount of private hire work also operated a number of coaches on contracted National Express services for which they were appropriately liveried. Of the vehicles acquired with Busways, a large proportion were double deckers with the Leyland Atlantean and Olympian reigning supreme but the Fleetline and Scania

One of the vehicles acquired by Stagecoach New Zealand with the business of Eastbourne Buses. (Stagecoach International)

Leaving Sheffield's Transport Interchange is Mainline's yellow & red liveried MCW Metrobus 1927 (B927CDT). (K.A.Jenkinson)

Painted in Shearings Holidays livery for use under contract to that company for its British coach tours, Cumberland Plaxton Paramount-bodied Volvo B10M 157 (WVT618, originally D202LWX) is seen at Lynton, Devon in August 1992. (K.A.Jenkinson)

Approaching Meadowhall shopping complex enroute from Sheffield city centre to Greasbrough is Mainline subsidiary Sheaf Line Leyland National 42 (HNL160N) which began life with Tyne & Wear PTE. (K.A.Jenkinson)

Passing Haymarket bus station in Newcastle is Busways subsidiary Blue Bus Services Plaxton Pointer-bodied Dennis Dart 1744 (L744VNL) which looked smart in its dark blue & cream livery. (K.A.Jenkinson)

Typifying the Busways fleet was the Alexander-bodied Leyland Atlantean, an example of which - 207 (EJR107W) is seen in Newcastle in February 1996 wearing its familiar yellow & maroon livery. (P.T.Stokes)

Purchased by Busways from Grey Green in 1988, Duple-bodied Leyland Leopard 62 (HTY137W, originally FYX820W)) was ultimately transferred to the Favourite Services division and repainted into its orange, brown & white livery. With the legend 'part of the Stagecoach group' added below its side fleet name, it was caught by the camera at the Minster coach park, York in October 1994 whilst undertaking a private hire duty from Wearside. (K.A.Jenkinson)

Stagecoach Economic corporate-liveried Plaxton Pointer-bodied Dennis Dart 1752 (L752VNL) passes yellow, white & blue-liveried South Shields Busways Alexander Dash-bodied Dennis Dart 1741 (L741VNL) at South Shields Market Place. (Terry Wightman)

N113DRB also being represented while the single deckers included Dennis Darts, Leyland Lynxes, Scania N113CRBs, Optare Metroriders, Iveco 59.12s and Renault S56s and S75s. The Blue Bus Services fleet was of particular interest for its immaculate Leyland Leopards, Bristol REs and LHSs while Armstrong Galley, in addition to operating Leyland Tigers and Volvo B10Ms also had a trio of double deck MCW Metroliners.

Following the acceptance on 21 July of an offer made to its shareholders, Western Scottish also became a Stagecoach group company, although unlike Busways, its 340 buses and coaches were to quickly begin to lose their grey, white, red & black livery in favour of Stagecoach corporate colours. In contrast to Busways, Western's fleet was predominantly single deck featuring Seddon Pennine VIIs, Leyland Nationals and Leopards, Dennis Darts and Volvo B6s. A large number of Mercedes Benz and Dodge S56 minibuses were also operated together with a handful of tri-axle Talbot Freeways while the coach fleet comprised Dennis Javelins and Dorchesters, Leyland Tigers, Volvo B10Ms and a few Duple 325s. The only double deckers were 37 Fleetlines and 13 Atlanteans. This acquisition, in addition to making Stagecoach one of the largest bus operators in Scotland, also gave it an operating territory which linked up in its most southerly part with Cumberland Motor Services, providing it with a continuous area through western Britain from the Clyde Coast in the north to Manchester in the south. As well as operating a large network of local bus services, Western Scottish was also involved in Anglo-Scottish express services and thus Stagecoach re-entered the market in which it had started from Perth in 1980.

Following its long battle with Moffat & Williamson and the Office of Fair Trading to whom it had ultimately given a number of undertakings covering a part of Fife not to increase its fares by more than the retail price index, not to reduce frequencies without prior permission and not to register any new commercial routes against tendered services for three years, Fife Scottish suddenly learned that Moffat & Williamson

Approaching Kilmarnock bus station in February 1995 are Western Scottish traditional-liveried Alexander-bodied Volvo B10M AV895 (E865RCS) and corporate-liveried Alexander-bodied Dodge S56 DD283 (D303SDS). (K.A.Jenkinson)

Painted in the Western Scottish white, black, grey & red livery, Alexander Dash-bodied Dennis Dart AN301 (J301BRM) arrives in Ayr bus station in September 1994. In the background is Western's then new corporate-liveried Alexander-bodied Volvo B6 V352 (M675SSX), (K.A.Jenkinson)

Leaving Cumnock depot in September 1994 is Western Scottish Plaxton Paramount-bodied Dennis Dorchester CN142 (VLT272, originally B202CGA) painted in Scottish Citylink colours. (K.A.Jenkinson)

was to dramatically cut its commercial services in Fife to concentrate more fully on its coaching activities. On 4 July, it withdrew 22 of its routes including town services in Glenrothes, Kirkcaldy, St.Andrews and Cupar, although as most of these were already covered by Fife Scottish, only one bus link - Ballingry to Glenrothes - was actually lost. Although this move greatly reduced competition in the area and left the Stagecoach subsidiary in a stronger position, Moffat & Williamson retained around half a dozen town routes in Glenrothes, Markinch and St.Andrews and continued to maintain all its school services and thus did not disappear completely from the area in which it had become increasingly familiar during the previous few years.

During July, in an attempt to set an example to children as well as promote a cleaner, fresher and healthier approach to life, the Stagecoach Group banned alcohol and tobacco advertising from all its vehicles and, having already banned smoking on its buses, saw its latest moves as a natural extension of its existing policy. Although current advertising contracts were to be allowed to run their course, these would not be renegotiated.

One of the first Western Scottish vehicles to be repainted into Stagecoach corporate livery was SV431 (WGB646W), a 1982 Volvo B10M which began life as a coach (WCS121W) and was given a new East Lancs body in 1994. It is seen here about to leave Ayr bus station for Stranraer in September 1994. (K.A.Jenkinson)

In addition to the continuing flow of new buses which were being allocated to almost all of Stagecoach's UK subsidiaries, the number of inter-company vehicle transfers increased dramatically during the summer months to meet new demands and allow the withdrawal of older buses and coaches. Amongst these Ribble cascaded several of its Bristol VRTs to Midland Red South and Red & White in April while during the following month East Midland despatched buses of this type to Perth and Fife Scottish primarily for use on school services. Also moving north of the border to Fife were 4 Willowbrook-bodied Bristol VRTs from East Kent who, in exchange, received 4 of Fife's newer Alexander-bodied Leyland Olympians. 6 more of Fife's Olympians were despatched to United Counties in July where they were joined by 10 cascaded from Bluebird Northern and in August 9 Leyland Nationals were transferred to Red & White from Fife. Perhaps more surprising, however, was the sale by Red & White and South Coast Buses of 20 Alexander-bodied Mercedes Benz L608D minibuses to Stagecoach New Zealand for use in its various fleets. Amongst the new buses placed in service were 5 Northern Counties Paladin-bodied Volvo B10Ms which made their debut in the South Coast Buses fleet at Hastings on 1 August. The chassis of these buses had originally been intended for Stagecoach Malawi and, unlike Volvo B10Ms supplied to Stagecoach's UK companies which had side-mounted radiators, these had them mounted at the front. By now, the group's corporate livery was rapidly being applied to the vehicles of all its subsidiaries except for the Busways units, thus making inter-fleet transfers easier, and the old pre-Stagecoach liveries were diminishing at an alarming rate. Meanwhile, to commemorate Ribble's 75th anniversary, three of its buses, a Mercedes Benz 709D, an Olympian and a Leyland National, were repainted into a special livery of silver-grey with traditional Stagecoach stripes while Cumberland continued to use apple green & cream for its Lakeland Experience vehicles and yellow & tan for its Coachline coaches.

On 17 July United Counties took over the staff bus contracts for the Weetabix factory at Burton Latimer which had previously been provided 'in house', although the Weetabix vehicles were not acquired under this deal and were instead disposed of by their former owner. During the

One of five Willowbrook-bodied Bristol VRTs transferred from East Kent to Fife Scottish for use mainly on schools duties, 1123 (RVB973S) is seen in its new home after being repainted into corporate colours in August 1994. (Campbell Morrison)

Although most of Perth's double deckers carried the Stagecoach fleet name, a couple of ECW-bodied Leyland Olympians were fitted with Perth Panther logos including 020 (TSO20X) seen in Mill Street working the city service to Hillend. (Campbell Morrison)

One of three Ribble buses painted into a special silver livery to commemorate the company's 75th anniversary in 1994, Alexander-bodied Mercedes Benz 709D 591 (G191PAO) is seen here in service in Bolton. (K.S.E.Till)

following month, Stagecoach acquired the remaining 55% share of Circle Line, Gloucester to give it total control of the company while unusually, due to the part closure of the A69 Carlisle to Newcastle road at Warwick Bridge which restricted it to 6ft. 8in. in width, Cumberland hired a Bedford post bus from Royal Mail North West at Crewe from 1 August for operation on route 686 between Carlisle and Brampton until the road was fully reopened on 11 September. One new service worthy of note was that from Cleethorpes to Doncaster which was branded 'Humberline'. Commencing on 17 September and running every 90 minutes on Mondays to Saturdays and three times each way on Sundays, it was maintained jointly by Stagecoach Peter Sheffield (Grimsby Cleethorpes coaching arm) and East Midland.

The quest for further expansion continued, and having stated earlier that it was interested in purchasing the whole of London Buses if it was privatised as a single unit, Stagecoach found that the privatisation ruling applied to the sale restricted each buyer to a maximum of two London Buses subsidiaries. Thus it was still able to gain a substantial foothold in the capital and on 6 September emerged as the new owner of East London Bus & Coach Co. Ltd. and South East London & Kent Bus Co. Ltd. which operated north and south of the Thames respectively. However, under the conditions of sale of all the London Buses subsidiaries, all the buses maintaining services into central London had to remain in a predominantly red livery. With garages at Barking, Bow, Leyton, Romford and Upton Park and an outstation at Stratford, East London was a typical London Buses company with a 590-vehicle fleet comprising Routemasters, Leyland Titans and Scania double deckers, Optare Delta-bodied DAF and Wright-bodied Dennis Lance SLF single deckers and Dennis Dart, MCW Metrorider and Mercedes Benz midibuses. Of particular interest, perhaps, is the fact that East London supplied BBC with the Routemaster (RM1527) which was frequently used on its TV soap 'Eastenders' and continued thus after passing into Stagecoach ownership. Although a number of East London's services penetrated central London, it also maintained a large number of suburban routes on the Essex border and as such had a wide mix of operations. Similarly, Selkent, with 414 vehicles, garages at Bromley, Catford, Orpington and Plumstead and operating Leyland Titan and Olympian double deckers, Dennis Lance single deckers, Optare Metrorider, Mercedes Benz 811D, Dennis Dart and Iveco midi/minibuses

Wearing London's traditional red livery with a cream band at upper deck floor level and gold Stagecoach East London fleet names is Routemaster RML2581 (JJD581D) in central London. (Campbell Morrison)

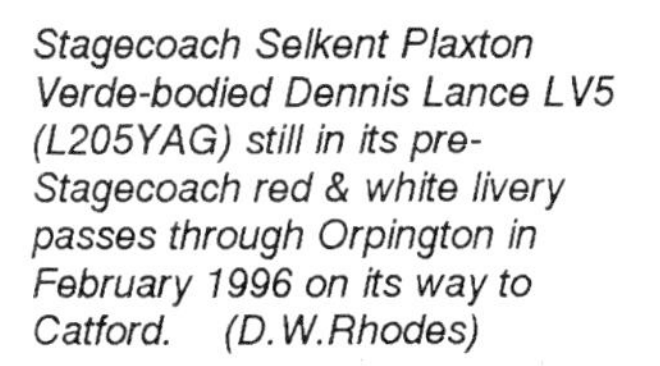

Stagecoach Selkent Plaxton Verde-bodied Dennis Lance LV5 (L205YAG) still in its pre-Stagecoach red & white livery passes through Orpington in February 1996 on its way to Catford. (D.W.Rhodes)

Seen at Farthing Corner services on the M2 motorway whilst undertaking a private hire duty in July 1996 is Stagecoach East London red & silver liveried coach-seated Leyland Titan T63 (WLT890) which began life as a standard bus-seated vehicle registered WYV63T. (D.W.Rhodes)

Although most of East London's fleet is maintained in traditional red livery, a few buses used on services outside central London have been repainted into corporate colours as illustrated by Leyland Titan T233 (EYE233V) seen enroute to Noak Hill. (G.Matthews/J.A.Godwin collection)

and 8 DAF coaches also ran into central London as well as having a number of suburban routes. Both companies quickly replaced the London roundel on their vehicles with standard Stagecoach-style fleet names and eliminated the white band (and in the case of Selkent, also the grey skirt) from the red-liveried buses employed on central London services although East London added a cream centre band to its Routemasters and also gave them gold fleetnames. In order to rationalise its operations Selkent disbanded its small coaching unit at the end of September and transferred its 8 DAFs to Stagecoach at Perth and Bluebird Buses and its coach-seated Leyland Titans to East London who took on the responsibility for all the group's coaching activities in the capital. A further development in the south of England took place on 1 October when East Kent gained the Canterbury City Council contract to operate the park & ride service from Wincheap car park to the city centre. For this duty, East Kent purchased 5 Berkhof-bodied Dennis Lance SLF low-floor buses which it painted in the attractive grey & blue livery used on its Optare Delta-bodied DAF SB220s and an Olympian employed by East Kent on Canterbury's other park & ride service (from Sturry Road) which had commenced in 1991. A couple of weeks prior to this on 17 September, under a recently-gained contract from Hampshire County Council, Stagecoach South began operation on a new Winchester park & ride scheme for which 4 new Alexander Dash-bodied Dennis Darts painted in a special white & green livery were delivered to Coastline Buses. The branding of routes which had now proved to be a successful way of gaining greater customer awareness to particular services was extended to the Penwortham and Longridge areas of Preston on 23 October where Ribble revamped its services under the title of 'Zippy Plus' using Alexander-bodied Volvo B6 midibuses. As the

Resting in Lewisham bus station in March 1995, Selkent Wright-bodied Dennis Darts DW60 and DW61 (JDZ2360/1) illustrate the pre and post-Stagecoach liveries. Whilst DW60 still retains its original grey skirt and old-style fleet names, recently repainted DW61 is all-over red with Stagecoach Selkent names. (G.Matthews/J.A.Godwin collection)

'Zippy' name was already familiar on the company's minibuses in Penwortham, this was a logical extension of the identity which had already achieved an amount of customer loyalty. On this same day, a new initiative under the title 'Stop and Drop' was introduced by Hants & Surrey in conjunction with the Hampshire Constabulary and Rushmoor Borough Council in an attempt to increase passenger safety each evening after dark. Under this scheme, after 7pm passengers could request the driver to stop anywhere along the route (providing it was safe to do so) to enable them to alight as close to their destination as possible. Unlike a hail & ride operation, however, passengers could only board at authorised stops.

Opposite page :
Left column, top to bottom :

East Kent MCW Metrobus 7771 (F771EKM), repainted in Stagecoach corporate livery, travels along St.Georges Lane, Canterbury in August 1995 whilst working the town's park & ride service. (D.W.Rhodes)

Still wearing its old Wellington City Transport colours, Stagecoach Wellington Hawke-bodied Volvo B58/Brown Boverie trolleybus 240 (MB7638) with its trolley booms hoisted down rests at Wellington railway station in May 1995. (P.Puppik)

Painted in Cumberland's Coachline livery, much-travelled Duple Caribbean-bodied Leyland Tiger 1145 (PSU775, originally B148ACK) approaches Bradford Interchange on the X80 service to Leeds. Acquired from Grimsby Cleethorpes Peter Sheffield fleet, it had previously operated for Crosville Wales and was new to Ribble. (K.A.Jenkinson)

New to United Counties and later operated by South Coast Buses, Plaxton Paramount-bodied Leyland Tiger 1084 (C84PRP) is seen here in September 1995 wearing the livery of its current owner, East Kent Coaches. (D.W.Rhodes)

Right column, top to bottom :

Drafted in to the A1 Service fleet at Ardrossan early in 1995, former Bluebird Buses ECW-bodied Bristol VRT 826 (RJT155R) shows off its short-lived orange Stagecoach A1 Service fleet names as it passes through Irvine enroute to Saltcoats on 24 February 1995. (K.A.Jenkinson)

Crossing into Mill Street, Perth whilst working a city service in September 1993 is Stagecoach Routemaster 607 (LDS201A) which began life registered 607DYE. (K.A.Jenkinson)

Still wearing its former owner's colours, Hyndburn Transport East Lancs-bodied Leyland Atlantean 194 (KHG194T) rests between duties in its native Accrington in October 1996 (Travelscene)

Passing through Chadwell Heath on its way to Romford in April 1996 is East London Alexander Dash-bodied Dennis Dart DAL11 (N311AMC) wearing traditional London red livery and sporting East London Hoppa fleet names. (K.A.Jenkinson)

PARK & RIDE
Stagecoach
7771
F771 EKM

Stagecoach
826
RJT 155K

RAILWAY STN
240
VOLVO
BIG RED

STAGECOACH
1
607

X30 LEEDS
Coachline
PSU 775

194
6
FERN GORE
Persil
HYNDBURN
KHG 194T

EK
EAST KENT COACHES
EAST KENT
C84 PRP

ROMFORD STN
East London hoppa
Stagecoach

Taking their Sunday rest at Stagecoach's Perth depot in October 1994 is a line of Routemasters headed by 604 (YTS820A, originally 599CLT) while looking on is Van Hool-bodied DAF K538RJX which had only just arrived from Selkent Travel in London. (Campbell Morrison)

Heading along St.Georges Lane, Canterbury on its way to Windcheap parking area in December 1994 is East Kent low-floor Berkhof-bodied Dennis Lance SLF 1407 (M407OKM) painted in Canterbury's dedicated grey & blue park & ride livery. (D.W.Rhodes)

Commenting upon the first full financial year since Stagecoach's flotation, Group chairman Brian Souter paid tribute to the company's employees and management for their hard work, dedication and enterprise which had resulted in a record pre-tax profit of £18.9 million. In addition to the 650 new vehicles placed in service over the previous three years, a further 680 were on order for delivery during the next two years, thus confirming Stagecoach's commitment to the provision of buses and coaches of the highest quality for its growing number of passengers. Service improvements in several parts of the UK and overseas had generated a healthy increase in passenger numbers with some, such as the Inverness to Aberdeen routes showing a growth of over 100% in passengers and revenue in just twelve months. The restructuring of a number of its operating companies allowed Stagecoach to reduce its costs while, of course, acquisitions brought more potential to the Group in areas where it had not previously been represented.

Returning north of the border, Stagecoach strengthened its market share in the Clyde Coast area on 7 October when Western Scottish purchased Arran Transport & Trading Company, a 24-vehicle company which operated a number of local bus services on that offshore island, Bute, and the Cowal peninsula alongside those of its new owner. Except for one Leyland National which was being used for spares, all the other acquired buses and coaches (13 Bedfords, 4 Mercedes Benz minis, a Plaxton Paramount-bodied DAF, an Optare-bodied Leyland Cub, 3 Leyland Nationals and a Marshall-bodied Dennis Dart) were added to Western's fleet and continued in service, although a number of these were subsequently replaced by Alexander-bodied Dennis Darts and Leyland Nationals transferred from the fleet of its new owner. Meanwhile, across in Perth where Stagecoach had withdrawn from express coaching duties in 1989, the company had now gained a number of contracted National Express workings for which it required 6 coaches. Four of these were Plaxton Paramount 3500-bodied Volvo B10Ms acquired from National Express and until a further 2 arrived, the balance was made up by a couple of the DAFs transferred from Selkent Travel. The services involved were the 383 from Edinburgh to Wrexham via Newcastle, Leeds and Manchester; the 593 Perth - Glasgow - London day service; the 596 Falkirk - Glasgow - London night service and the southbound 957 Perth - Edinburgh feeder route.

Stagecoach's African subsidiaries continued to be the subject of massive investment with improvements being made to their vehicles, services and properties during the latter half of 1994. In Malawi, the company had expanded its workshop facilities at Lilongwe to cope with numerous major jobs which it had previously been unable to tackle and amongst these was the conversion of the only bendibus in the fleet to a conventional rigid vehicle after it had sustained damage in an accident. The depot at Mzuzu which served the company's Northern Region and was some 515 miles away from the head office in Blantyre was completely refurbished and a new depot was opened at Mchinji in the Central Region, the last town before the Malawi/Zambia border. On the operational front, in addition to continuing the gradual conversion of the company's urban services to one person operation, the international

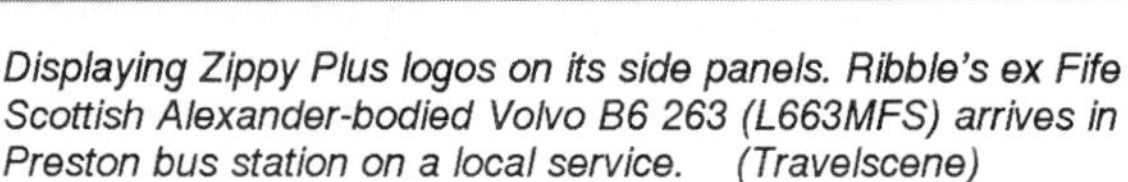

Displaying Zippy Plus logos on its side panels. Ribble's ex Fife Scottish Alexander-bodied Volvo B6 263 (L663MFS) arrives in Preston bus station on a local service. (Travelscene)

Its all-white livery adorned with green Winchester and King Alfred logos for operation on the town's park & ride service is Hampshire Bus Alexander Dash-bodied Volvo B6 403 (M403BFG). (Campbell Morrison)

Taking a break in Middlesbrough bus station is Cleveland Transit green, white & yellow-liveried NCME-bodied Dennis Dominator 222 (C222WAJ). (J.Whitmore)

Next page :
Left column, top to bottom :

Pictured outside Hull's Paragon railway station and bus station in October 1996 are Stagecoach Kingston-upon-Hull eight year-old East Lancs-bodied Dennis Dominator 148 (F148BKH) and recently-acquired ex.Fife Scottish Plaxton Premiere Interurban-bodied Volvo B10M 77 (K577DFS) which had just arrived on the 909 service from South Yorkshire. (K.A.Jenkinson)

MK Metro's Citybus-liveried Robin Hood-bodied Mercedes Benz L608D 114 (D114VRP) leaves Milton Keynes railway station on a journey to Stony Stratford in October 1996. (K.A.Jenkinson)

Bound for Bournemouth in August 1987, Hampshire Bus ECW-bodied Leyland Olympian 201 (A201MEL) seen here in Southampton was amongst the vehicles sold to Solent Blue Line together with Hampshire Bus's Southampton area operations a few weeks later. (Travelscene)

Chesterfield Transport subsidiary Retford & District's Alexander-bodied Leyland Leopard 211 (PRA112R) swings into Retford bus station to take up its duty on the 96 service to Gainsborough. Almost immediately after passing to the Stagecoach Group, this particular bus was despatched to join the Bluebird Buses fleet in Scotland. (K.A.Jenkinson)

Newcastle Busways Alexander Dash-bodied Dennis Dart 1711 (K711PCN) seen here in Wallsend Metro Interchange in September 1994 shows off its yellow, white & maroon livery to good effect. (K.A.Jenkinson)

Right column, top to bottom :

One of the first of the ex.Kowloon Motor Bus Metsec-bodied Daimler CVG6s to enter service with UTM in Malawi was 1002 (BH2628) which is seen here in Blantyre operating the service to Limbe in 1989. (R.Bailey)

Midland Red South Leyland National 604 (NOE604R) swings out of Leicester's St.Margaret's bus station at the start of its journey to Coventry in April 1994. (K.A.Jenkinson)

Once a stronghold of the Bristol RE, Hartlepool Transport's fleet of this type is now greatly depleted as a result of the delivery of a number of new buses. Still hard at work in April 1995, dual-door ECW-bodied 80 (SEF80L) passes along Church Street on the 4A service to St.Patrick's Church. (K.A.Jenkinson)

Now extinct is the livery of Cheltenham & Gloucester's Stroud Valleys company seen here at Stroud in March 1994 on Leyland National 3035 (NFB603R). (K.A.Jenkinson)

Wearing GM Buses South's Charterplan coaching livery, Duple 340-bodied Leyland Tiger no.8 awaits a ferry at East Cowes on the Isle of Wight while undertaking a private hire duty. (J.A.Godwin)

Aquired with the fleet of Cleveland Transit was former Southdown open-top Leyland PD3/4 500 (PRX189B) which is seen here on normal service in Stockton on Tees on a bright summer day. (K.A.Jenkinson)

506 (LAT506V), one of Kingston upon Hull's blue, white & yellow-liveried MCW Metrobuses passes through the centre of its home city on a quiet Sunday in November 1994. (K.A.Jenkinson)

Stagecoach
DON'T CALL ME
BABE!
via Sutton Park
27A
148
HULL
STAGECOACH express
77

501

Citybus
Fires
Fireplaces
114
Citybus

157
MIDLAND RED
MIDLAND RED

We're here to get you there
Hampshire Bus

95

21
Stroud

Wallsend 40B
Busways
1711
Busways

LUXURY COACH HIRE + HOLIDAYS
Charterplan
GREATER MANCHESTER

8
North Sea Lane
DON'T BE CAR LESS
GCT
SECURE
YOUR
CAR
TFU 64T

TO ADVERTISE ON THIS BUS...
0424
433711
21
MALVERN WAY
AND GET RESULTS—FAST!
William Henry Worthington's famous British best bitter
HASTINGS BUSES
BKE 862T

20 Holmleigh Estate
New catalogue Out nOw!
index
LWS 41Y

127
BOLTON MOOR LANE
THE NEW
RIBBLE
RIBBLE
RIBBLE
Solvite. The only one you need.
RIBBLE
JFR 7W
523
BURY
GM buses

48 DRONGAN
WESTERN
AL647
WESTERN
GCS 47V

B64 SCHOOLS
Red & White
578
Red & White

ARMSTRONG GALLEY
PART OF THE STAGECOACH GROUP
Clipper Class

354
BG 154

Awaiting sale at Western Scottish's Nursery Avenue depot, Kilmarnock in February 1995 is former Arran Transport Plaxton Bustler-bodied Bedford YNT E578 (HVY132X) which still wore the livery of its pre-Arran owner, Reynard Pullman of York. (K.A.Jenkinson)

One of the coaches used by Stagecoach at Perth on its new National Express contracted services was Plaxton Paramount-bodied Volvo B10M 623 (J455FSR) which was acquired from Express Travel in 1994. (Campbell Morrison)

service network underwent further expansion when following the Expressline services from Blantyre to Harare and Lilongwe to Dar-es-Salaam, the long-awaited new Coachline service was finally inaugurated on 21 October from Blantyre to Harare. Fleetwise, another 10 locally-bodied ERF Trailblazers were put into service in Blantyre by Cityline shortly before the end of the year, allowing the withdrawal of more of the now elderly ex.Kowloon Daimler double deckers. Also joining the fleet were two Plaxton Paramount 3500-bodied Volvo B10Ms from Ribble Motor Services, both of which were fitted with air conditioning at Perth before leaving their native shores. Following its involvement in an accident in September, Stagecoach Malawi's solitary bendibus was rebuilt to become a standard rigid 51-seat ERF Trailblazer while its Bristol Lodekka was withdrawn from service and scrapped. Meanwhile, in Kenya plans were being drawn up to improve the quality of operations in Mombasa which still fell short of those achieved in Nairobi and moves were being made towards the introduction of one person operation, a totally new concept in the country, in 1995.

Honours were once again bestowed upon the founders of the Stagecoach empire when, in October, Ann Gloag won the top award in the third annual Insider Corporate Elite Leadership Awards, an event jointly conceived by Scottish Business Insider magazine and financial advisers Ernst & Young to recognise individuals who have contributed most to the Scottish economy in the previous year. In addition to taking the overall award, Ann Gloag also headed the Services category in which her brother, Brian Souter was one of the runners up thus confirming the high regard in which Stagecoach was held.

Still wearing Midland Travel fleet names, Plaxton Paramount-bodied Volvo B10M NIB8754 (originally C102DWR) is seen at Perth in October 1993 after being fitted with air conditioning (note the pod on its roof) in preparation for its departure to Stagecoach Malawi. (Campbell Morrison)

Although another year had almost passed, Stagecoach's thrust to enlarge its sphere of operation continued without respite and following an offer made in October, the group gained control of Cleveland Transit and its 51% controlling interest in Kingston upon Hull City Transport on 14 November together with the 49% stake of the latter company held by its employees. Under the terms of the deal it was agreed that both Cleveland Transit and KHCT would retain their current liveries for the foreseeable future and that like Busways, the only indications of the new owner of these two companies would be the addition of 'Part of the Stagecoach Group' below their existing fleet names. In the case of Cleveland Transit, an attractive green, yellow & white scheme was used for its buses, maroon, yellow & white for its Tees Valley unit and yellow & orange for its coaches while KHCT employed a blue, white & yellow scheme for its buses and white, blue & maroon for its coaches which were operated under the Kingstonian name. Bringing a further 252 vehicles into Stagecoach's combined fleet, those inherited from Cleveland Transit included 30 Leyland Lynxes, 12 Plaxton Verde-bodied Volvo B10Bs, 8 Volvo B6s and a quantity of Fleetlines, Dennis Dominators, Renault S56 minibuses and an open-top former Southdown Leyland PD3/4 whilst KHCT contributed Scania single and double deckers, Dennis Dominators, MCW Metrobuses, Iveco 49.10 minibuses and a mixed selection of coaches. Although Transit had a well established and profitable network of services in Middlesbrough and

Previous page :
Left column, top to bottom :

Grimsby Cleethorpes Roe-bodied Leyland Fleetline 64 (TFU64T) passes through the pleasant surrounds of Cleethorpes in July 1994 still wearing its former municipal livery. (K.A.Jenkinson)

Adorned with City of Gloucester blue & yellow livery, Cheltenham & Gloucester Roe-bodied Leyland Olympian 9525 (LWS41Y) was later renumbered 123. It is pictured here standing at the outer terminus of service 20 in April 1994. (K.A.Jenkinson)

Leaving Ayr bus station enroute to Dreghorn in September 1994 is Western Scottish Alexander AY-bodied Leyland Leopard AL647 (GCS47V) which was already fourteen years-old. (K.A.Jenkinson)

Displaying the legend 'part of the Stagecoach group' below its fleet name is Busways subsidiary Armstrong Galley's Plaxton Paramount 3500-bodied Leyland Tiger 14 (644HKX) which began life in 1985 registered B643JAV with Fowlers of Holbeach Drove. (T.W.W.Knowles)

Right column, top to bottom :

Still painted in the blue, cream & yellow livery of Hastings & District but adorned with a corporate Hastings Buses vinyl below its windscreens, ECW-bodied Bristol VRT 762 (BKE862T) circumnavigates Warrior Square, St.Leonards-on-Sea in September 1992. (T.S.Blackman)

Still wearing Ribble's pre-Stagecoach livery, ECW-bodied Leyland Olympian 2107 (JFR7W) approaches Bolton bus station in April 1993 followed by a GM Buses NCME-bodied Leyland Atlantean. (T.S.Blackman)

With exhaust emissions from a sister vehicle having blackened its lower front panel, Red & White Leyland National 578 (NWO494R) leaves Chepstow depot in March 1994 to take up a schools duty. (K.A.Jenkinson)

Painted in UTM's two-tone blue Cityline livery, 1985 vintage Leyland Victory 354 (BG154) awaits its passengers in a Blantyre suburb in 1989. (R.Bailey)

Cleveland Coaches Plaxton-bodied white, orange & yellow-liveried Leyland Tiger 951 (OIB3516, originally YHN451Y) stands in Leeds central bus station whilst undertaking an excursion to the city. (Travelscene)

Cleveland Transit subsidiary Tees Valley used a maroon & yellow livery for its small fleet which included Plaxton-bodied Leyland Leopard 912 (HPY422V) seen here at Stockton depot in April 1995. (K.A.Jenkinson)

Stagecoach Kingston upon Hull's all-white liveried Duple-bodied Dennis Lancet 61 (YAY21Y) adapted for the carriage of disabled passengers carries a corporate-style fleet name on its side panels and a Handyrider name below its windscreens. (K.A.Jenkinson)

Stockton on Tees, KHCT based in Hull had since deregulation suffered badly from increased competition from East Yorkshire Motor Services and several independent operators and had experienced a deal of financial difficulties. Transit had turned it from a loss-making company into a marginally profitable one since it acquired its 51% stake in December 1993, but it was believed that under the ownership of Stagecoach Holdings, this process could be accelerated without the necessity of compulsory redundancies or cuts in basic pay. On the penultimate day of October, Busways absorbed its Welcome Passenger Transport unit which then ceased trading. Another closure was that of Vanguard's base at Bedworth on 23 October after which its fleet was accommodated at Midland Red's Nuneaton depot.

At the same time that Stagecoach gained its two new footholds in north-east England, it was learned that its bid for Darlington Transport Company had failed and that Yorkshire Traction had emerged as the preferred bidder. Busways, which had registered several services in the town in case Stagecoach wasn't successful in the privatisation, quickly set up a new unit under the title of Stagecoach Darlington from a base at Faverdale Industrial Estate and registered the whole of Darlington Transport's service network to commence on 12 December. However, after quickly assembling a fleet of 54 buses (3 Iveco 49.10s from United Counties and 4 from Busways; 6 Leyland Tigers from Fife Scottish and 6 from Bluebird Buses; 9 Leyland Nationals and 6 Mercedes Benz L608Ds from Ribble; 7 Renault S75s and 10 double deck Fleetlines from Busways and 3 Iveco 49.10s from Cleveland Transit), Stagecoach Darlington suddenly began the operation of all its new services on 7 November, running these free of charge in order to avoid the 42 days registration period. A few days prior to this, Stagecoach had been approached by a trade union representative and had offered Darlington Transport's drivers £1,000 each to join the new company in the form of a 'golden hello' as well as giving them guarantees of maintenance of pay, seniority and conditions of service. As a result, seventy of Darlington's eighty five drivers showed their preference for Stagecoach over Yorkshire Traction and on 5 November the municipal operator found itself with only three drivers reporting to work for the late shift. Despite managing to recruit a handful of new staff, it proved impossible for it to maintain its services and those operating outside the Borough were immediately withdrawn. A further consequence of Stagecoach's action was Yorkshire Traction's final withdrawal of its already wavering offer for the undertaking, leaving it in an almost impossible position. Although it struggled on for a few more days, the undercapitalised municipal company which had been on the receiving end of attacks from United

Seen at Chichiri depot, Blantyre prior to its entry into service in 1993 is Stagecoach Malawi Expressline PEW-bodied Volvo B10M 474 (BJ5554). (Stagecoach International)

5
Stagecoach
UWW 4X

23
Burnley & Pendle

X18 COVENTRY
WARWICK-L'SPA
Stagecoach
L451 YAC

Stagecoach
30
CUL 215V

711 Rye Lydd
FOLKESTONE
Stagecoach
VOLVO
602
L602 VCD

Bayline
BUSES
CONGESTION
C492 FFJ

D
Shanklin
003

Stagecoach
Firth Moor 24
803
Stagecoach

Painted in Stagecoach corporate livery, Vanguard Leyland National 2513 (LMA411T) carrying its fleet name in its nearside windscreen had been acquired from Crosville Wales in 1991. (Campbell Morrison)

With 'Free Bus' notices in both its windscreens, Stagecoach Darlington's ex.Fife Scottish Duple Laser-bodied Leyland Tiger 2106 (A942XGG) is seen working a town service during the company's first week of operation. (Campbell Morrison)

Being unable to pick up its passengers at Darlington Transport's stops in the town centre, Stagecoach Darlington had during its first weeks of operation to pick up and set down in Crown Street where congestion became a common occurrence as illustrated by this view on 16 November 1994. Present were two ex.Ribble Leyland Nationals, ex.Busways Daimler Fleetline 802 (OCU802R), former Kingston upon Hull Iveco 49.10 2010 (D604MKH) and an ex.Busways Renault S75. (K.A.Jenkinson)

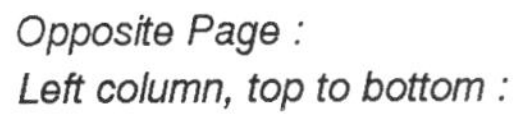

Opposite Page :
Left column, top to bottom :

Having only recently been repainted into Stagecoach corporate livery when photographed in June 1996, Cambus Roe-bodied Leyland Olympian 504 (UWW4X) which was acquired from West Yorkshire PTE in 1987 picks up its passengers in Cambridge. (K.A.Jenkinson)

Enroute to Warwick on the X18 service is Midland Red South 451 (L451LAC), one of six Alexander Dash-bodied Volvo B6s purchased new in 1994. (T.W.W.Knowles)

South Coast Buses Northern Counties-bodied Volvo B10M 602 (L602VCD) at Hythe, Kent in March 1995 catties lettering and a route diagram on its side panels for the Coastliner 711 service. (T.S.Blackman)

The rolling stock employed on the franchised Island Line on the Isle of Wight comprises former London underground trains, one of which is seen here in October 1996 showing Shanklin on its destination screen. (Robert Kenyon)

Right column, top to bottom :

Having acquired Pendle's 50% share of Burnley & Pendle in the spring of 1996, Stagecoach purchased Burnley's share in October of that year. Still in pre-Stagecoach livery, Alexander-bodied Volvo Citybus 109 (F109XCW) is seen here at Accrington. (G.T.W.Carter)

One of a number of former East London Leyland Titans to be acquired by Stagecoach South, 7215 (CUL215V) operated by South Coast Buses and converted tosingle door layout works a local service in Hastings in May 1996. (T.S.Blackman)

One of Bayline's elderly Ford Transit-bodied minibuses, C492FFJ is seen here at work in Torquay on a local service. (K.A.Jenkinson)

Wearing an all-white livery, Stagecoach Darlington's ex.Busways Alexander-bodied Daimler Fleetline 803 (OCU803R) leaves Darlington town centre on a journey to Firth Moor in November 1994. As can be seen, its owner's name was additionally displayed in its destination screen as well as below its windscreen and on its upper deck side panels. (K.A.Jenkinson)

Automobile Services since 1986 and more recently was caught up in the cross-fire between United and Your Bus, had little option but to throw in the towel. During the afternoon of 11 November it ceased its remaining operations and called in an administrative receiver. This left the way open for Stagecoach to consolidate its position in the town and after continuing to run its services free for another couple of weeks, special dispensation was given by the Traffic Commissioner enabling it to start charging fares from 28 November. In a bid, perhaps, to alleviate any hostile publicity following its recent activities in the town, all the revenue generated during the first week of 'normal' operation was donated to charity.

Having withdrawn from local bus operations in Glasgow in April 1992 as a prelude to its failed attempt to acquire Strathclyde Buses, Stagecoach decided to return to the city where it saw an opportunity to develop another urban network of services. After exercising Western Scottish's option to purchase Clydeside 2000's Thornliebank depot for its new operational base and renaming its Perth & District Buses company on 4 November to become Stagecoach Glasgow Limited, it registered a cross-city service from Auchinairn in the north to Castlemilk in the south which was to commence on 19 November. For this, 18 of its new Alexander PS-bodied Volvo B10Ms were given Stagecoach Glasgow fleetnames and plans were made to start additional new services from Drumchapel to Thornliebank and from Easterhouse to Pollock early in 1995 when the fleet was to be increased to some 60 Volvo B10M and B6 buses. In the short term, Clydeside 2000 would continue to base around 30 of its vehicles at Thornliebank until alternative premises could be found. These plans never reached fruition, however, for on 15 November, following an approach by the chairman of Strathclyde Buses, Stagecoach acquired a 20% in SB Holdings Ltd., the parent company of Strathclyde Buses and Kelvin Central Buses, and as a result the 18 new Volvo B10Ms were sold to Kelvin Central Buses, to whom the new service from Auchinairn to Castlemilk was transferred prior to its commencement four days later. Initially the buses concerned retained their Stagecoach corporate livery to which a Kelvin Central Buses red front was added, and thus the new Stagecoach Glasgow operation ended before it began, the Perth-based group having in the meantime gained a share in the company it had sought to purchase two years earlier.

Having already gained experience of the operation of park & ride services in the south of England, Stagecoach Scotland gained the Tayside Regional Council contract to operate its first service of this type in its home city of Perth on Saturdays during November and early

Fitted with Stagecoach Glasgow fleet names and with route details painted on its side windows in preparation for the reintroduction of services in this Scottish city, new Alexander-bodied Volvo B10M 100 (M428RRN) never operated in this form, however, as a result of Stagecoach gaining a 20% shareholding in Strathclyde Buses. (Campbell Morrison)

Still wearing Stagecoach corporate livery but having a Kelvin Central Buses red front and KCB Network fleet names, Alexander-bodied Volvo B10M M768PRS was one of the Stagecoach Glasgow buses sold to Strathclyde Buses as a result of Stagecoach having gained a stake in that company. It is seen here about to take up its duties on the 5 service to Old Kilpatrick which was once the domain of Kelvin's Routemasters. (Campbell Morrison)

Typifying the Strathclyde PTE fleet in which Stagecoach gained a 20% shareholding is orange & black-liveried Alexander-bodied Leyland Atlantean LA1125 (TGG740R) seen in Glasgow city centre. (P.T.Stokes)

One of the newer double deckers operated by Strathclyde Buses low-cost unit GCT was GLO1 (C807KHS), a 1986 Alexander-bodied Leyland Olympian acquired from Kelvin Central Buses in 1993. Wearing its new owner's attractive green & yellow livery with black skirt and centre band it is seen here in 1995 on a private hire duty.

December and on Mondays to Saturdays from 12 December until 7 January. Maintained on a ten-minute frequency by 4 of the company's Alexander PS-bodied Volvo B10Ms, it carried 344 passengers on its first day of operation and 850 on the final Saturday in November.

Coincidental with the news that Mainline, in which Stagecoach held a 20% stake, had acquired a 10% shareholding in Northern Bus of Dinnington and additionally had made an offer for Chesterfield Transport, the Perth-based group strengthened its position in north-east England on 12 December when it purchased Hartlepool Transport Ltd. from its employee owners. Although this company was comparatively small with only 67 vehicles, all of which were single deckers including 33 Bristol RELLs, 12 Dennis Falcons and a number of Leyland Nationals, it nevertheless fitted in well with Stagecoach's other operations in the area, being in close proximity to Cleveland Transit and not too far away from Busways and Darlington. Also included in its fleet were 6 coaches used mainly on private hire duties, although its new owners had no plans to increase this side of the business, its main interest being firmly in the provision of local bus services. Despite the company being maintained as Stagecoach Hartlepool, it was placed under the control of Cleveland Transit for administrative purposes.

During November and December, the arrival of new vehicles and the consequent transfer of older buses between Stagecoach's various UK operating companies continued without respite and at the same time that East London received 15 more new super low-floor Wright Endurance-bodied Scania N113CRLs, Red & White gained its first new coaches - 12 Plaxton Premiere Interurban-bodied Dennis Javelins which it put to use on its Stagecoach 2000 express services. Also gained by the Welsh subsidiary were 3 coach-seated Leyland Titans from East London, more Leyland Nationals from Fife Scottish and 2 Plaxton-bodied Leyland Tiger coaches from South Coast Buses. Upon receipt of more new Volvos, Ribble cascaded a number of its Leyland Nationals to Midland Red South and Cheltenham & Gloucester while Stagecoach Selkent's ex.Green Line Routemaster RMC1490 was transferred to Perth where it saw spasmodic use as a fixed advertisement for the city's park & ride service still adorned in its previous owner's red livery and was also brought into use on rare occasions.

Synonymous with Hartlepool Transport for many years was the ECW-bodied Bristol RELL6L. Here, 70 (MEF70J) stands in its home town's Church Street while working service 11. (T.S.Blackman)

Amongst Hartlepool Transport small coach fleet was 104 (FSL62W), one of a pair of Plaxton-bodied Leyland Leopards acquired from Tayside in 1987. Looking smart in its cream & crimson livery it is pictured here at Beamish Museum on a private hire duty. (K.A.Jenkinson)

Displaying its Stagecoach 2000 fleet name, Red & White Plaxton Premiere Interurban-bodied Dennis Javelin 948 (M948JBO) prepares to leave Cardiff bus station for Abergavenny. (P.Kay)

With Christmas approaching along with thoughts that 1994 was now almost at an end, it was with some surprise that an announcement was made to the effect that Stagecoach and Volvo had joined with Corporacion Financiera Del Transporte of Colombia to form a new company under the title of Sistema Metrobus de Bogota (SMB) to carry out a feasibility study with a view to operating a new mass transit system in the Colombian capital. Stagecoach and Volvo who together owned a 50% share of the new company were respectively to provide the management and vehicles for this new four-corridor bus operation, much of the mileage of which would be run on exclusive Busways financed and built by SMB without financial support from the Colombian government. Although some of the 400 bi-articulated and articulated buses to be built by Volvo in Brazil for use on the new system would be owned by SMB, the majority would be owned by local operators contracted to the system. Due to the amount of work required to prepare the infrastructure, build the vehicles and plan their operation, it was not envisaged that the system would become operational until 1998, but nevertheless, it gave Stagecoach its first opportunity in South America where it saw possibilities for further development in the future.

Ending the year on a high note and further consolidating its position in south-west Scotland, Stagecoach at the end of December reached agreement with the Ayrshire bus co-operative A1 Service of Ardrossan to purchase its operations. A1 was unusual in that it was owned by nine separate owners, not all of whom originally wanted to sell their businesses, but although the decision was taken by a majority vote, it was decided that all the members would sell to Stagecoach. Although all A1 Service's local bus operations and 67 vehicles were included in the deal, all of the co-operative's members retained their premises except for Parkhouse bus station at Ardrossan which was included in the deal, and those who additionally ran coaches kept these too. Indeed, a few even retained a handful of their buses in order to maintain some contracts held in their own rather than A1's name. The co-operative's fleet was mainly made up of double deck buses (mostly Leyland Atlanteans and Olympians, Fleetlines and Ailsa Volvos), although a small number of minibuses and single deckers were also included, the newest of which was a two month old Wright Endurance-bodied Volvo B10B. After taking control of the company on 29 January 1995, it was renamed Stagecoach (A1 Service) Ltd. on 9 February and placed under the administration of Western Scottish. Having no base from which to operate, the company rented the former Western Scottish depot near

Used as a mobile hoarding to promote Perth's park & ride service which was operated by Stagecoach, former Selkent Routemaster 600 (490CLT) still in its London red livery is seen performing its duty at St.Johnstone football ground, Perth in December 1994. (Campbell Morrison)

Still wearing its former owner's blue & white livery and displaying its old A1 Service fleet name in addition to its new Stagecoach A1 Service names is Alexander-bodied Ailsa Volvo 956 (NSP338R) seen at Parkhouse bus station, Ardrossan on a dull day in February 1995. (K.A.Jenkinson)

Picking up its passengers in Saltcoats during torrential rain on 24 February 1995 is Roe-bodied Leyland Olympian 904 (EWY74Y) which had recently received Stagecoach corporate livery and blue Stagecoach A1 Service fleet names. (K.A.Jenkinson)

Approaching Kilmarnock bus station on 24 february 1995 and still wearing the red livery of its former owner, East London, is Stagecoach A1 Service Leyland Titan 947 (OHV684Y). (K.A.Jenkinson)

Freshly repainted in corporate livery, Stagecoach A1 Service ex.Ayrshire Bus Owners Plaxton Derwent-bodied Volvo B10M 599 (G569ESD) is seen here at Parkhouse bus station, Ardrossan in February 1995. (K.A.Jenkinson)

Still sporting Stagecoach Manchester fleet names and a route diagram for the 192 service on its side panels, Alexander-bodied Volvo B10M L345KCK had gained its new fleet number (665) when seen at Silverhill depot, Hastings in October 1994 immediately after being transferred to South Coast Buses. (T.S.Blackman)

Ardrossan Harbour from its new owner Clydeport and additionally housed a number of buses at Western Scottish's Kilmarnock depot and, to compensate for the vehicles retained by various ex.A1 Service members and several buses which were immediately withdrawn, a total of 39 buses were drafted in from other Stagecoach group companies. These comprised 7 Seddon Pennine VIIs, 5 Fleetlines, 3 Renault S56s and 2 Mercedes Benz L608Ds from Western Scottish; 13 Leyland Titans from Stagecoach East London and 9 Bristol VRTs of which 4 came from East Midland, 1 from Inverness Traction and the remainder from Bluebird Buses. Several of these still retained pre-Stagecoach liveries and all the ex.London Titans were red, thereby providing a sea of different colours in Ardrossan and its surrounds for a few weeks. During the months which followed, the familiar blue livery of A1 diminished rapidly and many of the vehicles inherited were replaced by more arrivals from within the Stagecoach group. The London Titans were all gradually transformed into Stagecoach corporate colours and were ultimately joined by more of their type while several of the Western Scottish buses returned 'home' after being superseded by 6 ex.GM Buses Fleetlines and 5 more Bristol VRTs from Cumberland and East Midland. Looking to the future, Fife Scottish in November borrowed a coach-seated Leyland-DAB bendibus from Mainline at Sheffield in order to test its suitability on Stagecoach Express services. Used on a variety of routes and proving popular with passengers during its three month stay with the company, its success ultimately led to the purchase of a number of bendicoaches which entered service in 1996.

Furthering its philosophy that strong management was an essential ingredient in the future success of the company, Stagecoach continued to reshuffle and promote staff to new positions believing that fresh eyes often saw what others missed. To this end, during the latter months of 1994 and early in 1995 several managerial changes were made throughout the UK and overseas. Amongst these, Colin Brown joined the staff at the Group's headquarters in Perth as financial accountant responsible for the consolidation of quarterly, half-yearly and annual

accounts while Mike Clayton, formerly finance director at Selkent moved to Stagecoach (North West) in November as its finance director. East London engineering director Peter Duff assumed line responsibility for all engineering matters, Paul Southgate moved from his position of managing director of Cumberland where he was succeeded by Les Warneford of Midland Red to become managing director of Selkent on 1 October and Trevor Gilbert was promoted from operations manager to manager of Cityline Auckland in New Zealand. Other moves within the Group around this time found Busways finance director John Conroy promoted to the company's managing director, David Kirsopp moving from Cumberland to Busways as chief engineer, Alex Carter taking over the general managership of Midland Red South, Heath Williams becoming general manager of Hants & Surrey and Mark Threapleton taking up the post of operations director with Selkent. Leaving the board of Stagecoach Holdings on 31 January 1995 was non-executive director Muir Russell who was replaced on 1 March by Robert Spiers, the group finance director of The Royal Bank of Scotland.

Following the introduction by Stagecoach Kenya of 10 new 11m. long ERF Trailblazer buses in October and November 1994, the first of 50 new 12m.long buses of this make were placed in service early in January as part of a comprehensive upgrading of the company's operations in Nairobi and Mombasa. Fitted with air suspension, fully automatic transmission and bodied by Labh Singh Coachworks of Nairobi, special authorisation had to be obtained for the operation of these buses on Nairobi local services due to their increased length. As a result of a net service increase of 24 buses, only 20 of the older Leyland Victory single deckers were withdrawn.

FURTHER INVESTMENT AND EXPANSION

In its native Scotland, Stagecoach launched what was believed to be the first-ever January Sale to be held by a bus company when on 9 January, Fife Scottish offered day return tickets for the price of a single fare across the whole of Fife and throughout the rest of its network of services. The scheme which was to run until 29 January was available to passengers travelling between 9am and 5pm on Mondays to Fridays and at any time on Saturdays and Sundays and in addition the company announced that the annual fares increase due in February had been postponed until further notice. As well as introducing this innovative scheme, Fife Scottish also provided a total of 3,000 free three-course lunches at the Glen Pavilion, Dunfermline for senior citizens and their friends during January following a survey of their opinions about local bus services. Survey forms were distributed on Fife's buses and from the company's offices with those returned becoming part of the free lunch prize draw.

After a comparatively quiet February, the following month witnessed a return to peace after the year-long head-to-head battle between GM Buses South, Ribble and Stagecoach Manchester. Following a review of their competitive services by the companies involved, GMB took the decision to withdraw its Manchester to Burnley X43 service which had been initiated in retaliation to the introduction by Stagecoach Manchester of its 192 service to Hazel Grove. The latter, who had been running the 192 with 23 Alexander-bodied Volvo B10Ms upon which the fares charged were lower than those of GMS, decided that the only way to get the returns it required from this operation was to reduce it to 13 buses and implement fare increases, although these would still be lower than those charged by its competitor. Similarly, in Darlington the two surviving operators, United and Stagecoach Darlington, reached an agreement to reduce competition following a series of county council-led discussions aimed at reducing congestion in the town. Under this new treaty, Stagecoach agreed to take off its country services which had been launched by Darlington Transport against United's longer distance routes while United responded by withdrawing its additional minibus duplication which it had introduced against Your Bus and Darlington Transport. With the above moves and the additional reduction in the activities of both companies on town services from 26 March, Stagecoach Darlington was able to reduce its peak vehicle requirement from 47 to 37 buses in March and thus lower its overheads. Following this move, responsibility for Stagecoach Darlington was transferred from Busways to Cleveland Transit on 1 May soon after it had received a number of youthful Volvo B6s from Ribble as replacements for its assortment of elderly Leyland Nationals and some of its Fleetline double deckers. In exchange, Ribble received 10 of Busways' Alexander-bodied Volvo B6s which, after only four weeks, it despatched onwards to East London who also gained 5 buses of the same type from East Midland. Before ending its battles in Manchester and Darlington, Stagecoach had turned its attention to Hull where it had suffered from competition offered by East Yorkshire and a number of independent operators. The result of discussions between the two main rivals led to them exchanging a number of services in the city from 26 February as well as co-ordinating frequencies, and under this agreement KHCT gained a net increase of 12 peak-hour vehicles and had around a 50% share of the city traffic as opposed to its previous 35%. In order to maintain its increased operations, 10 of Ribble's Stagecoach Manchester Alexander-bodied Volvo B10M single deckers were drafted into the KHCT fleet on a temporary basis pending the delivery of 15 new Northern Counties-bodied Volvo B10Ms. Upon receipt of the latter in April, the Stagecoach Manchester Volvos were despatched to East London where they enabled the ex.Busways/Ribble Volvo B6s to be returned to Ribble. Following the new agreement reached between East Yorkshire and KHCT, the two companies introduced citywide Smart Card ticketing early in April based on Wayfarer 3 equipment, thus restoring inter-operator co-operation which had been absent since KHCT expelled East Yorkshire from its CrownCard scheme in September 1992. Following the closure of its engineering activities at Kilmarnock, Western Engineering Ltd was renamed Stagecoach Western Scottish Ltd. in 1 March, although major overhaul work for Western's fleet continued to be undertaken at its Nursery Avenue premises. As a consequence of the closure of London Underground's East London line for refurbishment, Stagecoach was awarded the contract to provide long-term replacement bus services starting on 23 March from Whitechapel to Shoreditch and Whitechapel to Surrey Quays. For this purpose, East London repainted 16 of its 26-seat Optare StarRider into an orange & white livery to which appropriate lettering and route diagrams were added before loaning 7 of them to sister company Selkent who was to operate the Surrey Quays route. Early in May, however, this service was passed to East London who regained the vehicles concerned, allocating them to Stratford garage from where both services were then operated. Upgrading its fleet and ousting a number of its Bristol REs, Hartlepool received its first new buses since becoming part of the Stagecoach Group - and indeed for ten years - when 10 Northern Counties-bodied Volvo B10Ms were placed in service in April while Cleveland Transit also took delivery of 15

Painted in a special orange and white livery and lettered for operation on Underground replacement service ELT, Stagecoach East London's Optare StarRider SR107 (G107KUB) leaves Surrey Quays on its way to Whitechapel in May 1996. (D.W.Rhodes)

buses of this same combination.

Despite its undisputed success within the bus industry both in the UK and overseas, Stagecoach lost battles as well as won them and despite challenging a ruling from the Corporate Affairs Minister, Jonathan Evans, in April that it must divest itself of its 20% share in Mainline, it reluctantly agreed in July to accede to this demand by offering to sell its shares to FirstBus, making a 60% profit in the process. Across the Pennines, despite its earlier failure to purchase Manchester-based GM Buses South, Stagecoach still hoped to add it, or at least a part of it, to its portfolio at some time in the future and thus it did not come as a great surprise when in April 1995 it leased to it 20 of its almost-new Alexander Dash-bodied Volvo B6s including the 5 which had been on loan to East London from East Midland. In what it described as a 'no strings attached commercial venture' the buses concerned were leased for a twelve month period after which GM Buses South would have the option to purchase them.

After being instructed to divest itself of its shareholding in Mainline, early in May Stagecoach was given a similar order by the Minister of Corporate Affairs to dispose of its stake in SB Holdings within three months. As could be expected, this command was received with a deal of anger and immediately the Perth-based company set out to consider its options. While a number of smaller Strathclyde area operators welcomed the instruction, others felt that if Stagecoach had to sell, this might provoke a new bus war along the banks of the Clyde, especially as British Bus, owners of Clydeside 2000 was quick to state that it might increase its activities in Glasgow if this were to happen. Meanwhile, Stagecoach was involved in another battle, this time with BBC Scotland who had in its television programme 'Frontline' criticised its alleged aggressive tactics and ruthlessness in the bus industry and particularly in Fife. Most of the programme was heavily biased against Stagecoach and contained numerous inaccuracies, and in response the company placed £60,000 worth of advertisements in leading Scottish newspapers attacking BBC Scotland for 'questionable' production methods. In subsequent adverts Stagecoach suggested that the television programme was a sensationalist bid to knock a successful firm and pointed out that the company employed 19,500 people, had bought 2,000 new buses between 1988 and 1995, and offered a service costing 20% per mile below Department of Transport industry averages. Additionally, in an open letter by Brian Souter published in the Sunday press, he stated that 'of 541 complaints about bus services made to the Office of Fair Trading since 1987, Stagecoach had only been involved in 24 of them and, with the exception of 2 cases, Stagecoach had been cleared of predatory accusations'. On a lighter note, planning application was granted by Perth and Kinross District Council for the conversion of Stagecoach's former premises on the fringe of the city at Walnut Grove into a 60-bed, four star hotel. This property, which had been sold by Stagecoach to Express Travel in 1989 had recently been vacated by the latter company when it withdrew from the area.

After spending some time investigating projects in Asia, Australaisia, North and South America, Africa and Continental Europe, Stagecoach at the end of May entered into a joint venture with Montagu Private Equity to buy part of the Rodoviaria de Lisboa (RL) in and to the north of Lisbon, Portugal, encompassing the Cascais, Estoril and Sintra areas, and under this deal, Stagecoach held the option to purchase Montagu's shareholding at a later date. Having first to gain approval and the transfer of route licences from RL, it was to be some time before Stagecoach gained control of its 25% slice of this important company despite it registering Stagecoach Portugal Ltd. in England on 7 June. This, however, was but one notch in Stagecoach's overseas developments, for in New Zealand it had acquired the operations of Runcimans Motors whose bus services were incorporated into Cityline Hutt Valley's operations while its contract and coaching activities were maintained as a separate company. In the meantime, Stagecoach Hong Kong received 6 new 110-seat dual door Alexander-bodied tri-axle Volvo Olympian double deckers in April to enable it to start the second of its residents' services on 16 May. Numbered 802R, this was identical to the 801R except that it started at Sha Tin Wai/Yi Shing Square in the Sha Tin district. Away from bus operation, Stagecoach pledged a £40,000 donation towards the building of a new hospital in Malawi where it had already invested in a new burns unit and annually donates £20,000 to the Queen Elizabeth Central Hospital.

New for Kenya Bus Services and painted in Stagecoach Express livery is Singh-bodied ERF Trailblazer 901 (KAE837V). (Stagecoach International)

Back at home, Stagecoach also supported the less able bodied when its subsidiary, Cleveland Transit, provided 10 free Shopmobility vouchers offering the use of wheelchairs and scooters to the mobility impaired among concessionary bus users. As well as saving those concerned around £10, it also included discounts to Stockton shops and cafes, Shopmobility newsletters and a number of social events. Furthering its expansion, Stagecoach through its subsidiary Busways purchased the old-established business of Jolly of South Hylton on 26 June on Mr.Jolly's retirement. Although the company's operations, including its main route running into Sunderland, were included in the deal, Jolly's 8 Bedford buses were retained by their original owner and were replaced by Dennis Darts from the Busways fleet. Prior to this, in May A1 Service had purchased the small business and 2 Freight Rover Sherpa minibuses of Hamilton of Maybole who operated a service from its home village and Ayr and also maintained a few Strathclyde PTE contracts.

Stagecoach Hong Kong's dual-door Alexander-bodied tri-axle Volvo Olympian 8 (GK3194) passes through Hong Kong Central whilst working a residents' service in the autumn of 1995. (D.Bentley)

Carrying 'The Dickensian' promotional lettering on its side panels and the legend '£3.80 Return' in its foremost side window, East Kent Plaxton Premiere Interurban-bodied Dennis Javelin 1105 (M105CCD) awaits its departure from Canterbury bus station on the X64 service to the Medway Towns. (P.Kay)

Painted in a green & cream livery for operation on a park & ride service in Coventry, Midland Red South Alexander-bodied Mercedes Benz 709D 332 (M332LHP) stands at Coventry Memorial Gardens in June 1995. (J.A.Godwin)

Following the success of its 'Stagecoach Express' network of services in Scotland and south of the border, Kenya Bus also adopted this brand name in May for some of its longer distance services while back at home, Coastline introduced a new service under this banner jointly with Southampton Citybus on 4 June running between Brighton and Bournemouth via Worthing, Chichester, Portsmouth and Southampton. Numbered X27 and operating on an hourly frequency and with attractive low fares, it was maintained by new Plaxton Premiere Interurban-bodied

Painted in the yellow, white & blue livery of its former owner, Chesterfield Transport, Volvo-engined Leyland National 101 (KHT121P) is seen here at Sheffield Transport Interchange. (T.S.Blackman)

Having just arrived at Clarence Pier, Portsmouth on the 747 service, Coastline Plaxton Premiere Interurban-bodied Dennis Javelin 1103 (M103CCD) was operated by Southampton Citybus to whom it was on loan for use on the joint X27 service, hence the Citybus Express fleet name upon its Stagecoach corporate livery. (J.L.Hobbs)

Volvo B10Ms crewed by specially trained drivers. However, in order to enable standardisation of quality etc., two of Coastline's Plaxton Premiere-bodied Dennis Javelins were loaned to Southampton for its share of the service and, although painted in standard Stagecoach colours carried Citybus Express fleet names. At this same time, operation of the highly successful park & ride operation in Perth was extended from 4.20pm to 6.0pm while Bluebird Buses once again was involved in the operation of a number of Regional Council-supported tourist services within its area. Later, towards the end of July Ribble launched its new Stagecoach Express network with services Manchester to Blackpool and Southport to Lancaster which interlinked at Preston together with services running from Chorley, Bolton and Blackpool while early in May East Kent had begun a new express service branded 'The Dickensian' from Canterbury to Rochester via Gillingham and Chatham. Furthering Stagecoach's philosophy on providing its customers with value for money, East Midland launched a new ticket under the name of 'MegaRider' which was sold on its buses and gave a week's unlimited travel in the Mansfield area for £3. This proved so successful that it was soon afterwards extended to the company's Chesterfield area where a MegaRider silver ticket at £2.99 allowed a week's unlimited travel throughout the inner zone and a MegaRider gold ticket at £4.99 was similarly available for the outer zone.

Sadly, in the eyes of some, a decision was taken at the behest of the company's employees in June to discontinue the distinctive yellow Busways livery together with the blue & cream of Blue Bus Services and maroon & cream of Economic and replace them with Stagecoach's corporate colours feeling that the time had now come to portray a new, crisper image on Tyneside. The existing liveries of Armstrong Galley and

Chesterfield Transport Roe-bodied Leyland Fleetline 142 (NKY142R) seen leaving the town enroute to Clay Cross typified the former municipal operator's double deck fleet. (D.J.Stanier)

Acquired with the business of Chesterfield Transport, Whites Travel's Duple 320-bodied Dennis Javelin F243OFP seen in its original white & blue livery on a private hire duty at Cleethorpes was soon transferred to Stagecoach's Red & White fleet in which it has been numbered 953. (K.A.Jenkinson)

Wearing National Express Air Link livery is Armstrong Galley Plaxton Excalibur-bodied Volvo B10M 86 (KSU463, originally J422HDS) which was acquired by Busways from Park of Hamilton in 1993. (Stagecoach)

Favourite were, however, to remain unchanged, at least for the foreseeable future while the other existing fleetnames were to be replaced by Stagecoach Busways (which encompassed the Newcastle, Sunderland and South Shields divisions), Stagecoach Economic and Stagecoach Blue Bus Services. Although a number of new vehicles were on order for the Busways fleet, these were still awaited when Cleveland Transit received its first new double deckers since deregulation in the form of 5 Northern Counties-bodied Volvo Olympians, a further 3 of which were sent to Hull to join KHCT.

Having been instructed to withdraw from Mainline, Stagecoach made a bid for neighbouring Chesterfield Transport in an attempt to retain a presence in South Yorkshire/North Derbyshire and was successful in gaining control of this company on 28 July. Included in the deal was Chesterfield's subsidiaries Retford & District and Whites of Calver, the latter being the undertaking's coaching arm. The inherited 112-vehicle fleet, whilst being predominantly single deck and containing 58 Leyland Nationals, also included 23 double deckers in the form of 17 Fleetlines, 2 Olympians and 4 Atlanteans and 19 minibuses plus 9 Leyland and Bedford coaches. Although East Midland assumed responsibility for the newly-acquired companies, immediately closed its own depot in the town and moved into that acquired with Chesterfield Transport, confirmation of the integration of both companies' services in the area had to be put on hold in the light of a Monopolies and Mergers Commission inquiry into the takeover. This also held up the repainting of the recently acquired vehicles into Stagecoach corporate colours and thus the undertaking's attractive yellow & blue scheme was given a reprieve with only the usual legend 'Part of the Stagecoach Group' being applied below the existing fleetname. Not wishing to continue Chesterfield Transport's loss-making coaching activities, Stagecoach attempted to find a buyer for its Whites of Calver subsidiary, but after failing to do so, this operation was closed down in September. Changes also took place in the north-east when Busways coaching division Armstrong Galley became the sole operator of National Express service 230 from Newcastle to Heathrow and Gatwick Airports. As a consequence, the coaches employed on this route were repainted into the attractive National Express Airlink livery and were adorned with lettering appropriate to their operation. Meanwhile, during June East Kent had relocated its Ashford depot to new premises on the Cobbs Wood Industrial Estate which had potential for future expansion.

Despite being a progressive, forward thinking company, Stagecoach has never forgotten its past and, having a soft spot for old buses and coaches, has preserved some of the examples it had operated in its formative years. In addition, it had inherited several historic buses with its numerous business acquisitions over the past few years and had even repurchased a Leyland PS1 which had originally operated for McLennan of Spittalfield. Although a number of these make the occasional appearance at old vehicle rallies each summer in various parts of the country, it is rare to find any of them operating in a revenue-earning capacity and thus it came as something of a surprise when on 4

Amongst Stagecoach Scotland's preserved fleet is GRS343E, an Alexander-bodied Albion Viking which was delivered new to Alexander Northern in 1967 and is now restored to its original cream & yellow livery. (D.W.Rhodes)

Although several Bristol REs were taken over from Delta of Stockton in exchange for Cleveland Transit's coaching operation, none were operated and were instead quickly sold. Seen in Delta's red & grey livery is MVT210K which began life with Potteries Motor Traction. (K.A.Jenkinson)

One of 21 new Alexander-bodied Volvo Olympians purchased for the A1 Service fleet as replacements for many of the elderly vehicles acquired with the Ayrshire Bus Owners business, 914 (M492ASW) seen in September 1996 shows its new style fleet name and additionally carries Stagecoach logos at each side of its dot-matrix front destination screen. (D.Robinson)

Acquired by National Welsh from Eastern National in 1988, Red & White's Dormobile-bodied Ford Transit C902LEW has been converted into a recovery vehicle and numbered RW18. Seen at Chepstow bus station complete with an amber beacon on its roof, it has been repainted into corporate Stagecoach colours. (Des Thorne)

Sold very soon after being acquired by Midland Red South with the business of David Grasby, former London Country Duple-bodied AEC Reliance EPM134V stands in Cirecncester whilst operating a local service. (K.A.Jenkinson)

Parked in the yard of Midland Red South's Leamington Spa depot in October 1995 is G & G Travel's two-tone blue & red liveried Bristol VRT 1930 (LHT724P) and Grasby's yellow liveried ex.London Fleetline 3968 (KUC968P). (K.A.Jenkinson)

July the McLennan single decker was put back into service on the Perth Tourist Board 'Trundler' service between Callender and Crieff. Providing its passengers with unhurried views of some of Scotland's most beautiful countryside, it maintained this service until 12 September, proving a popular attraction in times of increasing standardisation. Additionally, Western Scottish borrowed Bluebird's preserved 1967 Alexander-bodied Albion Viking for use on a tourist service on Arran upon which it also made use of its own ex.MacBrayne's 1960-vintage 21-seat Duple-bodied Bedford C5Z1.

Stagecoach also undertook an exchange of operations on Teesside on 27 July which rid it of its Cleveland Coaches activities. Under this deal, Cleveland Transit disposed of its unprofitable coaching unit and its 14 vehicles to local independent Delta Coaches of Stockton who in exchange passed all its local bus operations and a similar number of Bristol RE buses to Transit. Being elderly and of a type not operated by Cleveland Transit except in Hartlepool where they were being progressively replaced, the inherited buses were not operated by their new owner and instead were immediately sold for scrap. After dispensing with its coaching operation, Cleveland Coaches Ltd. was renamed Tees Valley Ltd. on 4 September. Meanwhile, in south-west Scotland, A1 Service had planned to join forces with AA Buses, Clydeside and Clyde Coast Services to start a new service between Ayr and Greenock via Ardrossan and Largs in competition to an identical service which had been introduced by Ashton Coaches. Although the new operation was given service number 585 and branded under the title of 'Coastline', following court action by Ashton, the consortium renumbered the service 535 and gave it the name 'Coastlink', although this was subsequently altered to 'Clydecoaster'. To assist Ardrossan-based Clyde Coast Services with its share of this operation, Western Scottish loaned it one of its Volvo B10Ms which had been repainted white with green stripes and special branding for this purpose. Additionally, following the loan from late April of one of A1 Service's Ailsa Volvos to Clyde Coast Services to assist it with its contract duties, this was joined by a further 6 buses of this type from 30 June. After starting operations on the Clydecoaster service, A1 Service passed its share of the operation to Clyde Coast on 24 July, lending it 3 more special-liveried Volvo B10Ms for this purpose and on 4 September took over all that independent's six local bus routes to allow it to concentrate all its resources on the 535 service. As part of this deal, 6 of the Ailsa Volvos which had been on loan to Clyde Coast since 30 April were sold to that company for operation on its various contract duties whilst transferred to A1 Service were 3 of its Mercedes Benz minibuses. Before the aforementioned moves, on 24 July A1 Service had taken over three services in the Dalry/Irvine/Kilmarnock area which had previously been operated by the Valley Bus Co. prior to its licence being revoked by the Traffic Commissioner.

Continuing its support of various charities, Stagecoach teamed up with the Imperial Cancer Research Fund in a national fundraising campaign aimed at passengers and staff. Starting on 30 June upon which day the company donated one penny for every passenger travelling on its

Cheltenham & District Alexander-bodied Volvo B10M 404 (N404LDF) is seen here in its home town carrying dedicated route lettering along its side panels for the 94 service from Cheltenham to Gloucester. (G.T.W.Carter)

Given a blue band at upper deck floor level and lettering on its upper deck side and front panels for the Shuttlebus service between Portsmouth Harbour and the City Centre, Coastline ECW-bodied Bristol VRT 367 (JWV267W) performs its usual duty in Portsmouth city centre in the summer of 1996. (F.W.York)

buses, it concluded on 3 August when collecting buckets were positioned throughout Stagecoach's operations across Britain. During the intervening four weeks, 40,000 specially-designed badges bearing the familiar image of a Stagecoach bus had been sold at £1 each at the company's depots, bus stations and offices as well as on the buses themselves and together these initiatives raised a total of £101,423 for the Fund, much to the delight of everyone involved. Additionally, Stagecoach allowed one of its East London Routemasters (RMC1485) to be used on a week-long Bus-a-thon in July to raise money for The Foundation for Children with Leukaemia. Travelling 3,000 miles around the coast of Britain, the bus was sponsored by several well-known companies including Ford, Bus & Coach Week and Pontin's and was crewed by volunteers from East London's Romford garage. During 1994, Stagecoach who donates 0.5% of its pre-tax profit to charities each year contributed £95,000 while in the previous year it had gifted £64,000.

Continuing to believe that Britain's rail network would provide it with a wide range of new opportunities without risk to its existing bus business, early in the summer Stagecoach entered 'indications of interest' in the first three franchises to be offered for Great Western Train Company Ltd., LTS Rail (the London, Tilbury and Southend line) and South West Trains which it was expected would be taken over by the private sector in the spring of 1996. While the company waited, with fingers crossed, to learn which of these, if any, it had been awarded, a further development in the national Stagecoach Express network was achieved early in July with the launch of a new service running from Grimsby to Sheffield which was an upgraded, quicker version of the established Grimsby to Doncaster route. The new 909 service was operated hourly using Plaxton Premiere Interurban-bodied Volvo B10Ms (1 from East Midland and 4 from Grimsby Cleethorpes) and in addition Kingston-upon Hull City Transport provided a feeder link from Hull via the Humber Bridge. Indeed, such was the popularity of this new operation that in October its frequency was doubled with a departure every 30 minutes. Seeking to improve its services in the Stroud Valley, a major revision of services was undertaken in Cirencester on 7 August and at this same time the fleet name 'Stagecoach Cirencester' was applied to the vehicles used on the new network. This, however, was only regarded as a local identity, the buses concerned still being owned by Cheltenham & Gloucester's Stroud Valleys division. In a bid to enhance its operations

Resting in Glenrothes bus station is Fife Scottish 399 (N141VDU), the company's solitary low-floor Alexander-bodied Volvo B10L. (Campbell Morrison)

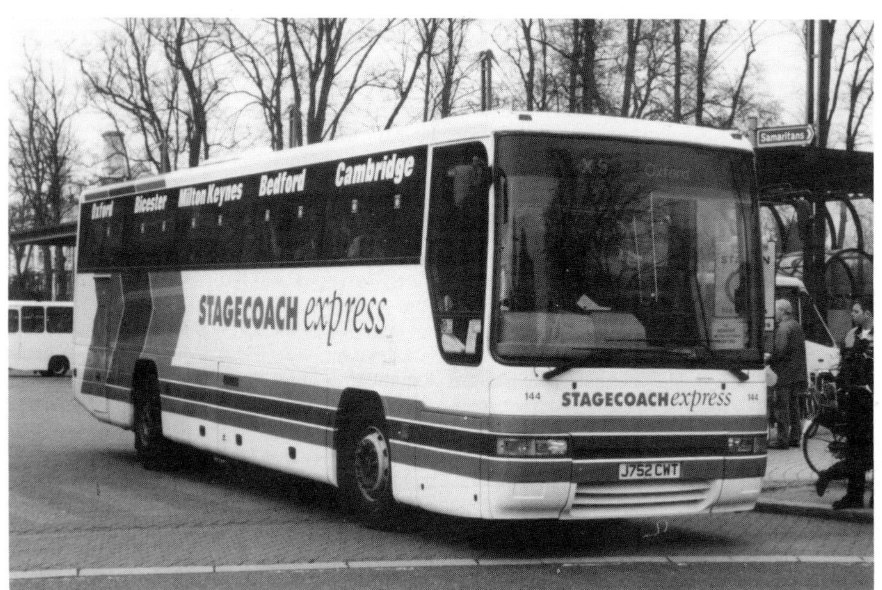

Leaving Drummer Street bus station, Cambridge in April 1996 at the start of its journey to Oxford on the Varsity Express service is United Counties Plaxton Premiere-bodied Volvo B10M 144 (J752CWT) which was acquired from Wallace Arnold Tours in 1995. (K.A.Jenkinson)

One of thirteen Wright-bodied Mercedes Benz 811Ds acquired by Stagecoach Transit from Selkent in 1995, 313 (HDZ2613) is seen in corporate livery at Stockton displaying its new fleet names. (M.Templeton)

in Ayrshire acquired with the A1 Service co-operative, the first of 21 new Alexander-bodied Volvo Olympians were put into service at Ardrossan in July where they replaced the last of the Bristol VRTs and Ailsa Volvos, and all had been delivered by the start of September. However, despite this massive improvement in vehicle quality, Stagecoach was still awaiting the decision of the Monopolies & Mergers Commission who, at the request of the OFT had been investigating the takeover of A1 Service. When this was eventually announced in November, it fortunately stopped short of ordering Stagecoach to sell its new Ayrshire subsidiary but laid down a number of measures in the form of behavioural undertakings regarding fares and frequency of competitive services which the company decided to agree to. Stagecoach was prevented from increasing fares which it had reduced to compete for a period of three years and additionally it was unable to decrease frequencies where these had been increased, withdraw newly-registered services or register timings in front of its competitors. Additionally, Stagecoach was ordered to release former A1 staff from 3-year undertakings which prevented them from competing with the company on local bus services. Tendered services and coach operation were always allowed within the 3-year period. Meanwhile, in September Bluebird Buses purchased the 12-coach business of Scotravel of Elgin which until 1994 had operated as Dunbar's Coaches. Of the vehicles acquired, 5 were immediately offered for sale and 4 were placed in Bluebird's reserve fleet while the remaining 3 (a 25-seat Mercedes Benz 608D and 2 Duple-bodied Volvo B10Ms) were retained in service, although the Mercedes Benz was sold a month later. As neither Scotravel's taxi business or depot were included in the deal, the company's contracts and private hire operations were incorporated into those of Bluebird's Elgin depot.

Looking towards the future and seeing an increasing need for better transport provision in Nairobi where a growth in population and private

Stagecoach Selkent Carlyle-bodied Dennis Dart DT28 (49CLT, originally G28TGW) carried Roundabout fleet names for operation on the Orpington network of services, the tender for which was later sadly lost. (J.A.Godwin)

The first new double deckers to be purchased by Stagecoach Busways were Alexander-bodied Volvo Olympians, one of which - 725 (N725LTN) picks up its passengers in Newcastle in February 1996. (P.T.Stokes)

vehicles was causing increased congestion and pollution, Kenya Bus Services put forward plans for a new mass transit system. This would create a network of Busways which would centre around three major routes into the city centre and thus attract more people to use public transport for their daily journeys and met with a positive response from the Kenyan government and the World Bank. Indicating the progress which had been made by Stagecoach Malawi towards improved standards, no fewer than 412 of its employees were presented with safe driving awards which ranged from one to twenty three years and with the company having carried 53 million passengers over 19 million miles during the previous twelve months, its accident ratio was one for every 31,250 miles travelled. Back in England, Stagecoach's expansion continued with the purchase by Midland Red South of the small business of David Grasby Coach Hire of Oxhill on 2 September. Included in this deal were 11 coaches (3 Volvo B10Ms, 2 DAF MB200s, 4 AEC Reliances, 1 Ford R1014 and 1 Ford R1114) and a former London DMS-type Fleetline double decker, 5 local bus services which worked only on occasional days and 6 school contracts. Although Grasby's was to be retained as a separate operating unit within Midland Red South, its garage was not purchased and on 16 September the acquired vehicles were dispersed to their new owner's Banbury and Leamington Spa depots for continued operation. Amongst the service changes undertaken by Stagecoach's English subsidiaries, East London relaunched its Monday to Saturday 723X service from Stratford to Lakeside Shopping Centre in September while on the 25th of that month United Counties began a new Stagecoach Express service branded 'Varsity Express' from Oxford to Cambridge using 6 Plaxton Premiere 350-bodied Volvo B10M coaches purchased from Wallace Arnold. This significantly undercut the fares charged between these two cities by National Express and Cambridge Coach Services who immediately adjusted their prices in order to remain competitive.

Reconfirming its commitment to improving the quality of its vehicles, Stagecoach in October placed a massive order for 1,120 new buses and coaches amongst which were 10 articulated inter-urban Volvo B10M coaches, 8 of which were to have Plaxton Premiere bodies and the remaining 2 Berkhof bodies. The remainder of the order comprised 150 Northern Counties-bodied Volvo Olympians; 60 Plaxton Premiere Interurban-bodied Volvo B10Ms; 400 Alexander-bodied Mercedes Benz 709Ds; 100 Alexander Dash-bodied Dennis Darts; 60 Alexander PS-bodied Volvo B10Ms and 100 Alexander RS-bodied Volvo Olympians for distribution between the various UK subsidiaries and 50 Scania L113s for Portugal, 70 MAN midibuses for New Zealand, 10 Volvo B10Ms for Malawi and 110 ERFs for Makawi/Kenya which were all to be bodied locally. This massive investment ensured that Stagecoach's ongoing policy of reducing the overall age of its massive fleet continued on target and when all these new buses and coaches were delivered during 1996, their arrival would allow the withdrawal of a similar number of vehicles which were becoming time expired. So much for the next twelve months, but what of the present time? Making its debut at the Coach & Bus 95 Show at Birmingham's National Exhibition Centre in October was a new Alexander Ultra-bodied low-floor Volvo B10L for Fife Scottish which was placed in service at Kirkcaldy soon after the Show had ended. This,

Three of Kenya Bus Services' new Metsec-bodied tri-axle Dennis Dragons are seen here at their official launch in Nairobi in October 1995. (Stagecoach International)

Carrying a school bus sign and a board for the 256 service to Stratford in its windscreen, G & G Travel's blue & white liveried Duple 320-bodied DAF 59 (A6GGT) is seen at Midland Red South's Leamington Spa depot in October 1996. (K.A.Jenkinson)

however, was a 'one-off' bus obtained for evaluation and no further examples were expected to join the Stagecoach group until it had proved itself in service. Amongst the other new buses to enter service at this same time were 27 Alexander Dash-bodied 9.8m Dennis Darts which joined the Stagecoach East London fleet. Painted in an all-over red livery and adorned with 'East London Hoppa' fleet names, these were used to replace a number of ageing minibuses. Additionally, all 16 of Selkent's Alexander-bodied Dennis Lances were transferred to East London at around this same time, losing their attractive red & white livery in favour of unrelieved red in the process. Busways received its first new double deckers for five years when 40 Alexander-bodied Volvo Olympians took to the road in the autumn together with 17 new Volvo B10M single deckers while in Kenya the first of 20 coach-seated Metsec-bodied tri-axle Dennis Dragon double deckers entered service in October. A more unusual addition to the Kenya fleet was a 25-seat Mitsubishi Canter minibus which was used solely as a staff bus, a vehicle much needed especially by cashiers who had previously to travel by service bus to the bank with the company's takings! As a result of the fleet growing from 305 to 361 buses during 1995, Kenya Bus Services depot at Eastleigh had now become greatly overcrowded with a number of buses needing to be parked at a nearby rented site. In order to overcome this problem, a brand new depot was constructed at Riruta which in addition to having offices, washing facilities and an excellent maintenance workshop, provided parking for around 100 vehicles.

Having failed to secure GM Buses South when it was sold by Greater Manchester PTA, Stagecoach set about preparing the way for a future bid for this company by selling its small Stagecoach Manchester operation to EYMS Group subsidiary Finglands on 13 October. Passing with the 192 service and its outstation at Bredbury were the 13 Alexander PS-bodied Volvo B10M buses which maintained this operation, and apart from having their fleet names replaced by those of their new owner, as part of the deal they retained Stagecoach corporate livery until the early summer of 1996. Further south, in order to create further operating economies, Stagecoach Hants & Surrey closed its Hindhead depot on 28 October and transferred its allocation to its Aldershot premises. In order to save dead mileage, however, four new outstations were opened at Guildford, Haslemere, Lindford and Petersfield, each of which was no more than an open parking area able to accommodate a small number of vehicles.

Having gained considerable success with its Stagecoach Express services in various parts of Britain, the network was further strengthened in mid-October when Western Scottish began new services under this banner from Ardrossan to Edinburgh and Glasgow to Sanquhar. At this same time, most journeys on the existing Glasgow to Ayr Express service were extended to Girvan and a few through to Stranraer. Seeing a demand for late night services around Aberdeen, Bluebird Buses experimentally introduced a number of journeys operating after midnight on a few routes, and so successful did these prove, in December they were increased with one even radiating out as far as Ellon. Meanwhile, following an agreement reached between Cleveland Transit, Tees & District and Teesside Motor Services, the routes of all three companies were recast in the Stockton and Middlesbrough areas in order to eliminate wasteful competition. After the first phase undertaken on 13 August which greatly reduced Transit's presence in the Langbaugh area and eliminated it from all its former Teesside Railless Traction Board routes, the reorganisation was completed on 29 October when further exchanges took place and all the area's services were renumbered.

With its rear engine cover stowed in its doorway, United Counties corporate-liveried ex.Cleveland Transit NCME-bodied Leyland Fleetline 980 (GAJ125V) receives attention at Corby depot in June 1996. (K.A.Jenkinson)

Transferred from Grimsby Cleethorpes to East Midland and repainted into corporate livery, Roe-bodied Fleetline 126 (XFU126V) is seen in Chesterfield working the 81 service to Bolsover. (G.T.W.Carter)

Despite still wearing Stagecoach corporate livery and a route diagram for the 192 service, former Stagecoach Manchester Alexander-bodied Volvo B10M M417RRN had gained the fleet name of its new owner, Finglands when photographed in Piccadilly in December 1995. (K.A.Jenkinson)

Acquired with the business of Miller, Foxton in 1993, Cambus subsidiary Premier Travel Services Plaxton Paramount 3500-bodied Scania K112CRB 410 (F947NER) named Broadsman is seen while working a Travelscope holiday tour. (T.W.W.Knowles)

Viscount's spotlessly clean coach-seated ECW-bodied Bristol VRT VEX291X in pre-stagecoach yellow & white livery was caught by the camera at Peterborough in June 1996. (K.A.Jenkinson)

During the following month, South Coast Buses gained under short-term contracts most of the East Sussex County Council tendered services previously operated by Bexhill Bus Co. following that company's withdrawal from the local bus scene, although the latter was then free to concentrate on its coaching activities and retained contracts operated under the County Rider scheme for disabled travellers. In a new round of re-tendering in the capital, Selkent suffered a major blow when it lost all of its Orpington services which it had maintained with minibuses under the Roundabout banner for several years. With CentreWest winning four of its routes and Londonlinks and Crystals the other two, it had little option but to close its Orpington base when the new operators took over on 2 December, having no other services in that area of Kent.

Indicating its continued success, Stagecoach was able to report a 43% increase in its pre-tax profits for the 24 weeks up to 14 October, the first interim period to reflect its London acquisitions. During this time, the group's turnover had increased 50% to £189.7 million while its passenger numbers across its UK subsidiaries had grown by 1%. Indeed, only Stagecoach South had failed to show increased revenue and profits during this period, although this, it was stated, was caused mainly by the hot summer, delays in the delivery of new vehicles and as a result of increased staff turnover. Within the core UK businesses, the key objective in addition to meeting profitability targets continued to be to identify and develop opportunities for increased passenger numbers and organic revenue growth and this continued to be pursued with unfaltering vigour. Further strengthening its management team, Mike Britten was appointed chief engineer at Cumberland while in Africa Steven Hamilton moved from his post of assistant chief engineer at Kenya Bus Services to become chief engineer of Stagecoach Malawi where he was joined by George Thuo, also from Kenya Bus Services, as finance controller.

As another year drew to a close, Stagecoach purchased Cambus Holdings Ltd. on 6 December, thus further expanding its area of operation. Included in this deal was Cambus, Viscount Bus & Coach Company, Peterborough Bus Company, MK Metro (which operated under the Road Car fleet name), Milton Keynes City Bus and Premier Travel Services with routes in and around Cambridge, Peterborough, Milton Keynes and Bletchley. With the exception of Premier Travel, all the other companies had until their privatisation been part of the National Bus Company who had separated Milton Keynes Citybus from United Counties. The acquisition of CHL added around 370 more buses and coaches to Stagecoach's combined fleet as well as providing it with a new and important area of operation and in the short term, at least, it was proposed to maintain the companies involved as independent subsidiaries. Before too long, however, all were placed under the administrative control of Cambus at its Cambridge headquarters, although each company retained its own local management for its day to

Still in the pre-Stagecoach two-tone blue & white colours of Cambus, Roe-bodied Leyland Olympian 505 (UWW8X) stands alongside recently repainted, corporate liveried sister bus 503 (UWW3X) at Cambridge in April 1996. Both buses were acquired from West Yorkshire PTE in 1987. (K.A.Jenkinson)

Parked at Kilmaine Close depot, Cambridge in April 1996 are two of Cambus subsidiary Premier Travel's Plaxton-bodied Volvo B10Ms. On the left is dark blue Travelsphere-liveried 428 (K458PNR) which was acquired from Supreme, Hadleigh in 1994 whilst alongside it is white Eurolines-liveried 437 (J702CWT) which came from Wallace Arnold Tours in 1994. (K.A.Jenkinson)

Adorned with a special white, red and light blue livery and lettering for Cambridge's City Rail Link service, Cambus Marshall-bodied Volvo B6 167 (L667MFL) picks up its passengers near Drummer Street bus station in June 1996. (K.A.Jenkinson)

Leaving Drummer Street bus station Cambridge in June 1996 on its way to Sawston Village College is Cambus Leyland National 304 (PEX620W) painted in Millerbus cream & red livery but having received Stagecoach Cambus fleet names. (K.A.Jenkinson)

Recently replaced by new Alexander-bodied Volvo B6s on Cambridge's park & ride service. Cambus Leyland Lynx 311 (F168SMT) in cream & red livery with Millerbus fleet names is seen on this operation in June 1996 in Cambridge city centre. (K.A.Jenkinson)

day operational purposes. Despite the NBC origins of these companies who typically operating a large number of Bristol VRTs, many of which had been purchased secondhand, only 6 Leyland Nationals were included in their combined fleet which contained numerous Mercedes Benz, Optare City Pacers, MCW/Optare Metroriders, a handful of Leyland Olympians and 3 Leyland Lynxes inherited in 1992 with the business of Millers of Foxton. Although most of Premier Travel's coaches were Volvo B10Ms, 4 Scanias and a Toyota Coaster were also included in their number. The liveries used were almost as varied as the buses themselves with Cambus and Premier Travel both using white & two tone blue, Viscount yellow & white, Buckinghamshire Road Car dark green & cream and Milton Keynes Citybus cream & red.

Throughout the whole of 1995, but particularly during the latter months of the year, inter-company vehicle transfers had escalated dramatically, partly as a consequence of the delivery of new vehicles and partly due to the increased needs of some subsidiaries. Amongst the buses involved were a number of Busways Leyland Atlanteans and Fleetlines which were surplus to requirements following the arrival of 40 new Alexander-bodied Volvo Olympians. Several of the former were given a new lease of life with their transfer to Red & White and Fife Scottish while 4 of the Fleetlines were despatched to United Counties along with 7 buses of this type from Cleveland Transit. Following the closure of Chesterfield's Whites of Calver operation, its fleet was dispersed to Busways, Red & White and Western Scottish while 3 of Grimsby Cleethorpes Peter Sheffield Tigers were transferred to Cumberland, a further 21 of Selkent's Leyland Titans joined Stagecoach South, 8 of Chesterfield's Leyland Leopards were moved to Western Scottish who also received some Selkent Leyland Titans, Ribble Volvo B10Ms and East London MCW Metroriders and Mercedes Benz 811Ds, Cleveland Transit gained 10 Mercedes Benz 811Ds from Selkent, and 11 Cumberland Mercedes Benz 608Ds were despatched to join East Midland who also received a number of Grimsby Cleethorpes Daimler Fleetlines ousted by new Volvo Olympians. In order to provide the extra coaches needed for its enhanced express service network, 10 former Wallace Arnold Volvo B10Ms were purchased for use by East Midland and United Counties while a further 3 coaches of this type were acquired from the same source for East London's coaching unit and 2 Volvo B10Ms were obtained from Dorset Travel for the Western Scottish fleet. As well as reshuffling over 150 vehicles between its various subsidiaries, Stagecoach was able to rid itself of a large number of its time expired buses with the arrival of more than 500 new vehicles.

Following the decision during the summer of 1995 to phase out most of the Busways liveries in favour of Stagecoach corporate colours, a similar move was made in January 1996 in respect of Cleveland Transit

Operating the Walnut Street circular express service X19 in Milton Keynes is Citybus 109 (D109VRP) in cream & red livery and complete with Metro Express fleet names leaves the new town's railway station in October 1996. (K.A.Jenkinson)

Only ten full size buses remained in the Milton Keynes fleet in the autumn of 1996. One of these, 3019 (CBV19S), an ECW-bodied Bristol VRT acquired from Ribble in 1993, is seen in Road Car's cream & dark green livery at Milton Keynes in October 1996. (K.A.Jenkinson)

The first new buses to be allocated to Cambus following the company's purchase by Stagecoach were Alexander-bodied Mercedes Benz 709Ds diverted from Western Scottish, one of which - 210 (N643VSS) - passes Drummer Street bus station, Cambridge in April 1996. (K.A.Jenkinson)

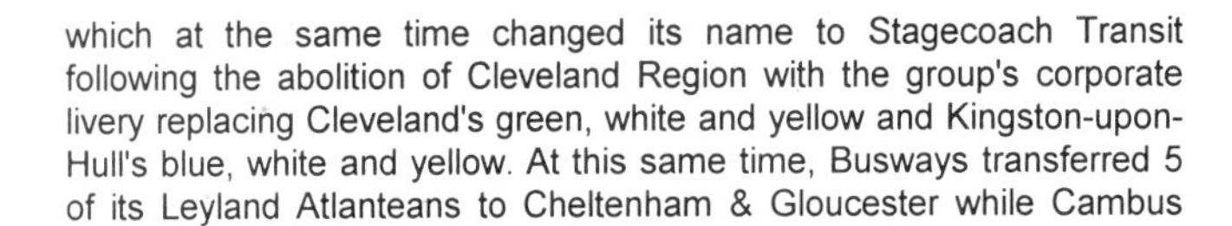

which at the same time changed its name to Stagecoach Transit following the abolition of Cleveland Region with the group's corporate livery replacing Cleveland's green, white and yellow and Kingston-upon-Hull's blue, white and yellow. At this same time, Busways transferred 5 of its Leyland Atlanteans to Cheltenham & Gloucester while Cambus and Viscount both received their first new vehicles, these arriving within weeks of CHL's purchase by Stagecoach. Comprising 12 Alexander-bodied Mercedes Benz 709Ds, these were diverted from a batch originally intended for Western Scottish with whom 4 had already spent a few days in service before travelling southwards.

TRAINS, TRAMS, AND MORE BUSES

Shortly before 1995 ended, Stagecoach received the news that under the British Rail privatisation scheme it had gained the 7-year franchise to operate South West Trains who operated a network of urban and mainline passenger services from London Waterloo to over 200 stations largely in south-west London, Surrey, Hampshire and Dorset. South West Trains used 1022 vehicles, mainly electric multiple units and Class 159 diesel railcars and covered an important commuter area from which many of those working in London travelled daily. Prior to taking over the operation of its new rail network on 4 February, Stagecoach tendered two Rail Link services from Romsey to Winchester and Bordon to Liphook which allowed other operators to run Stagecoach vehicles on Stagecoach routes, the vehicles and ticketing equipment for which would be provided by the Perth-based group. In the event, although bids had been submitted by seventeen companies, both tenders which were for a one year period were awarded to Stagecoach group subsidiaries with the former being gained by Hampshire Bus and the latter by Hants & Surrey. For the operation of these, Hampshire Bus received 2 Optare Delta-bodied DAF SB220s on long term loan from East London while Hants & Surrey gained a pair of Alexander Dash-bodied Dennis Darts from Busways and prior to taking up their new duties, all were repainted into a special new livery to which dedicated lettering was added. Pledging to spend £3 million during the next four years on improving SWT stations in addition to £2.6 million for their maintenance, Stagecoach for the first month provided passengers on its two feeder bus services with free travel for the bus part of their journey in a move to encourage people to try the service and discover exactly what it had to offer. Under the terms of the franchise, however, the responsibility for maintenance of the track and signalling etc. remained with Railtrack.

The new year began with the completion on 1 January of the negotiations to secure licences for approximately 22% of the former Rodoviaria de Lisboa in Portugal of which mention has been made earlier. In partnership with City of London fund managers HSBC Montagu Private Equity, Stagecoach acquired 150 vehicles ranging from Volvo midibuses to UTIC-AEC Reliance single deckers and Volvo bendibuses together with operations based at Cascais and Aboboda, both located around 25kms from Lisbon. Amongst the operations was a small coaching unit which is undergoing review before any decision as to its future is made. Included in the deal were two depots, a couple of outstations and workshops in Cascais as well as the historic 900mm gauge Sintra vintage tramway and the concession to run a service to the coast. As the tramway had been allowed to fall into a state of disrepair over a number of years, only 2 of its 14 trams had operated on a small section of the line during 1995 and thus steps quickly needed to be taken if this was to survive. To this end, Stagecoach persuaded Sintra Council to rebuild some of the track it had ripped out previously while the company set about attending to the 1903 trams to bring them back to usable condition. The objective is to extend the line a few hundred metres to the historic city itself and build up tourist traffic on the whole of its length, while on the innovative front, Stagecoach has joined a submission from Sintra Council for Thermie funding from the EC for an

Showing off its new livery at Waterloo station, London is South West Trains 2402 77383 which carries the legend 'A Stagecoach Company' below its windows. (Stagecoach)

One of a pair of dual-door Optare Delta-bodied DAF SB220s transferred on long term loan from Stagecoach East London to Hampshire Bus for operation on its South West Trains Rail Link service, 5001 (472YMF) is seen here adorned with its new livery and fleet names in July 1996. (F.W.York)

Amongst the vehicles inherited by Stagecoach Portugal from Rodoviaria del Lisboa were Caetano-bodied Volvo B58s, an example of which is seen here in its original orange & white livery. (J.Bentley)

electric bus park and ride scheme in the city. Immediately renamed Stagecoach Portugal, the group's first European venture obviously needed a massive investment in terms of fleet improvement with much of its fleet dating from the 1970s and although 50 new Marcopolo-bodied Scanias were on order at the time of the company's purchase, more are obviously needed in order to reduce the fleet's average age.

In compliance with the directive given by the Department of Trade and Industry some six months earlier, Stagecoach finally sold its 20% equity stake in Mainline to FirstBus in January at the same time that the Consumer Affairs Minister, John Taylor, accepted assurances from the Monopolies and Mergers Commission that Stagecoach's acquisition of Chesterfield Transport did not act against the public interest. This enabled the long-awaited rationalisation of services in Chesterfield to be confirmed with a considerable saving in vehicles and mileage and also allowed a vehicle repainting programme to commence to eliminate the acquired undertaking's yellow and blue livery in favour of Stagecoach's corporate image.

Illustrating the old and the new, Stagecoach Portugal's Sintra Tramway car no.12 stands alongside a recently delivered new Marcopolo-bodied Scania L113 in corporate colours in 1996. (Stagecoach International)

February began with the acquisition by Stagecoach of the outstanding minority interest in its New Zealand Bus subsidiary to give it total control of the company whilst back home on 19 February it purchased Exeter-based Devon General Ltd. and Torquay-based Bayline Ltd. from Transit Holdings. Devon General, from which Bayline was born, had been the first NBC company to be privatised when, in 1986, it was sold to its management providing the foundations for Harry Blundred's Transit empire which ultimately spread to Oxford, Portsmouth, London's Docklands and parts of Queensland in Australia. Together, the Devon General and Bayline companies brought 311 additional vehicles into the Stagecoach fold, of which all but one were minibuses, as well as giving it access to a part of Britain where it had previously not had a presence. Soon after their acquisition, on 7 March both companies were merged under the title of Stagecoach Devon and became part of Stagecoach West.

Unbelievably, February witnessed yet another takeover bid when an offer made by Stagecoach to the employee shareholders of the former Greater Manchester PTE company GM Buses South Ltd. was accepted on the 27th after a number of assurances had been given to that company's staff in respect of their future employment etc. To be operated as an autonomous business from its present headquarters at Stockport, Stagecoach stated that it had no immediate plans to repaint the familiar orange buses into its corporate livery, although in the event it

Wearing Bayline's cream & maroon livery, Dormobile-bodied Ford Transit 491 (C491FFJ) seen here at Exeter is typical of the many minibuses of its type operated by the company. (J.L.Hobbs)

Repainted into Circle Line green & cream livery, former Cheltenham & Gloucester Leyland National 309 (SAE754S) is seen in Cheltenham working a schools service in November 1996. (G.T.W.Carter)

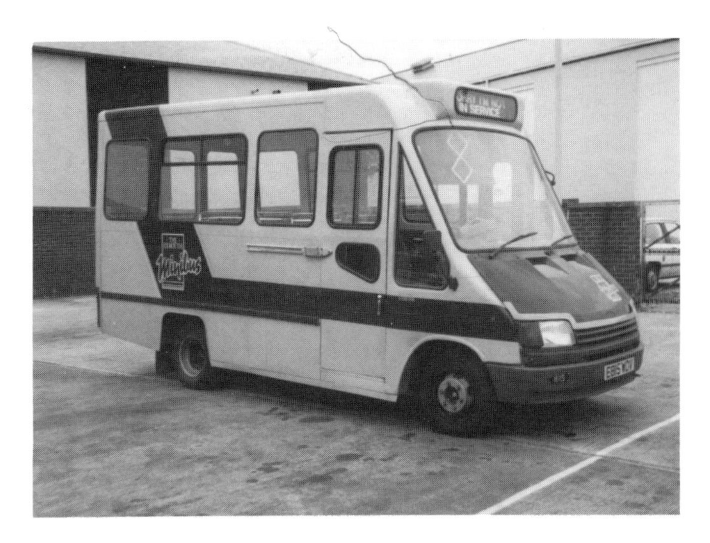

Painted in grey & red livery with Exmouth Minibus fleet names is Stagecoach Devon Mellor-bodied Ford Transit 815 (E815WDV) seen at Exeter in March 1996 before it was renumbered 266. (J.L.Hobbs)

Working a duty on the X38 service to Plymouth is Stagecoach Devon Reeve Burgess-bodied Mercedes Benz 709D 408 (F720FDV) still wearing Devon General cream & crimson livery and fleet names. (J.L.Hobbs)

was only a matter of a month or so before Stagecoach's striped scheme began to appear and the announcement was made that this was to be the company's new standard. Bringing a further 744 vehicles into the group's combined fleet including coaches operated under the Charterplan banner, this acquisition gave Stagecoach a major foothold in Manchester where since its sale of Bee Line Buzz it had operated only a handful of vehicles. With two depots in Stockport and one each at Hyde Road and Princess Road, Manchester and at Glossop, GMB South maintained a wide network of services to the south and east of Manchester although a large number of these were not without competition from other operators. The buses acquired with this company were predominantly double deckers comprising Leyland Atlanteans, Olympians, MCW Metrobuses, Dennis Dominators and Falcon Vs and Scanias while the remainder of the fleet included MCW Metrorider, Dennis Domino, Mercedes Benz 811D and Dodge S56 and S75 minibuses, Leyland National single deckers and various Leyland, Volvo and Setra coaches. Despite both Charterplan and GMS Training retaining their existing titles, the trading name of the bus-operating company was changed to Stagecoach Manchester on 18 March when the first new buses to join the fleet made their debut, these being 15 Alexander-bodied Volvo Olympians originally intended for Stagecoach South.

Towards the end of February, one of Stagecoach's longest serving employees retired. Joining the company shortly after its inception, Isabel Peters who had been personal assistant to Brian Souter and Ann Gloag had watched Stagecoach grow from a small express coaching business into one of the world's largest providers of public transport, taking an active part in its development in a number of ways. To mark her retirement, a farewell lunch was held at the Royal George Hotel in Perth which was attended by many of her friends and colleagues and in addition to being presented with a set of luggage, a gold chain and a cheque from staff within the Group, she was also given a new Peugeot 206 car as a mark of appreciation for her many years of loyal service.

Unlike February which had proved to be a month of great expansion, March saw Stagecoach experience mixed fortunes. Having failed in its attempts to gain a larger share of the franchised Hong Kong bus market and believing that no franchise opportunities were likely to arise before the handover of the Colony to China in 1997, Stagecoach ceased the operation of its two residents' services on 31 March, passing them to Kwoon Chung Motors who took them over on the following day. Although Stagecoach Hong Kong's 6 Volvo Olympian double deckers were sold to Citybus on 22 April, its 5 Volvo B10M single deckers were retained and placed in store pending a decision on their future. Ultimately they were exported to Stagecoach's New Zealand subsidiary later in the year. On the same day that Stagecoach withdrew from Hong Kong, it purchased Pendle Council's 50% share in Burnley & Pendle Transport who operate around 120 vehicles on services close to the Yorkshire/Lancashire border and maintain a coaching unit trading as Viscount Central. Unable to persuade Burnley Council to sell its share in the company, Stagecoach was reconciled to a joint venture with the remaining municipal authority. Indeed, so incensed was Burnley Council at its partner's sale to Stagecoach Holdings that, as owners of the undertaking's bus depot at Queensgate, Burnley which additionally Ribble had used as an outstation for a number of years, it threatened to evict Ribble, leaving it to find alternative accommodation in the town.

Following a rationalisation of its recently-acquired Cambus Holdings group, Premier Travel had moved during January from its base at Kilmaine Close, Cambridge to the Cambus depot in the city at Cowley Road, although the former Premier depot was retained and used for storage and overnight parking of some vehicles. A month later, on 18

Having only just arrived at Exeter from Busways, Newcastle are Stagecoach Devon Reeve Burgess-bodied Mercedes Benz 709Ds 492, 488, 490 and 497 (D409/4/8/7TFT), all of which still retained the liveries of their former owner and were awaiting repainting into corporate colours prior to their entry into service. (J.L.Hobbs)

Freshly repainted in corporate colours, Stagecoach Devon PMT-bodied Mercedes Benz 814D H889NFS seen at Exeter bus station originated with Gray of Fochabers in Scotland. (J.L.Hobbs)

Amongst the first new buses to be added to the Stagecoach Devon fleet was Alexander-bodied Mercedes Benz 709D 480 (N511BJA) which was diverted from a batch originally intended for Stagecoach Manchester. (J.L.Hobbs)

During the autumn of 1995 Grimsby Cleethorpes received a number of new Alexander-bodied Volvo Olympians to replace some of its elderly Roe-bodied Fleetlines. One of these, 138 (N138AET) collects its passengers in Grimsby bus station in March 1996. (D.Robinson)

February, most of the daytime services of Milton Keynes Citybus and MK Metro were recast to provide a new network maintained mainly by minibuses and as a result a large number of those companies Bristol VRT double deckers and Leyland National single deckers were able to be withdrawn to leave only 10 big buses in the fleet. At this same time, both these companies lost their identities in favour of Stagecoach Milton Keynes which was adopted for the whole of their operations. Meanwhile, it was learned that the bid submitted for the acquisition by Stagecoach Holdings of the franchise for British Rail's Intercity East Coast operation was not to be referred by the Secretary of State for Trade and Industry to the Monopolies and Mergers Commission should it be accepted by

Typifying the GMS fleet is NCME-bodied Leyland Olympian 3087 (B87SJA) seen in Piccadilly bus station, Manchester in its pre-Stagecoach orange livery. (K.A.Jenkinson)

Amongst the coaches operated by GMS's Charterplan subsidiary was Setra S215H 24 (J73VTG) which had joined the fleet from Bebb, Llantwit Fardre in 1994. (K.S.E.Till)

Depositing its passengers in Piccadilly bus station, Manchester in September 1996 is GMS Leyland National 257 (SIB4558, originally CFM352S). Still painted in its pre-Stagecoach orange, black & white livery and with its route details on its side windows, it carried Campus LInk logos and the legend 'A Stagecoach Subsidiary) below its GMS Buses fleet names. (K.S.E.Till)

Amongst the first former GMS buses to be repainted into Stagecoach corporate colours was Northern Counties-bodied Scania N113DR 1465 (H465GVM) seen in Manchester city centre in September 1996. (K.S.E.Till)

the director of passenger rail franchising. In the event, this was academic as Stagecoach did not emerge as the successful bidder with Sea Containers gaining control of the lucrative East Coast line.

Despite its general success in the operation of its Stagecoach Express services in various parts of Britain, the showcase X27 from Brighton to Bournemouth which had been operated jointly from Coastline's Chichester and Southampton CityBus's Portswood depots was discontinued from 9 March as a consequence of disappointing passenger numbers. On the previous day, however, better fortunes were experienced by Western Scottish when it commenced operation of two new services to Butlin's Wonderwest World from Ayr bus station and the town's railway station. Under contract to Butlin's and each running on a half-hourly frequency, both services had in previous years been operated by Keenan of Coalhall who mainly used buses painted in all-over advertising liveries for Butlin's, as now did Western. During April, a major service reorganisation was undertaken by Hampshire Bus at Andover on the first day of the month and at the same time Western Scottish passed its operation of the X34 service from Ardrossan to Glasgow to Ashton Coach Hire with whom it operated jointly on the 585 Coastline service from Ayr to Greenock. Further changes were made to Stagecoach's express network in south-east England when East Kent's 'Dickensian' service from Canterbury to Rochester was reduced from an hourly to two-hourly frequency while on a more optimistic note, the company introduced a new route (X65) branded 'Sheppey Express' running from Canterbury to Minster. Other operational changes of note to take place during April were those at Northampton and in the Lake District. On the 14th of the month, after reaching an agreement with Northampton Transport, services in that town were rationalised to reduced wasteful mileage while on the 28th. Cumbria County Council published its Lakeland Explorer timetable which detailed the tourist services which were to be operated by Cumberland during the summer months. This included the Coachline Dalesman services from Ambleside to Leeds and Keswick to York and several 'Rambler' routes around the Lake District, some of which had been operated during the previous summer and some of which were new. Wishing to increase its summer open-top service in Torbay and only owning one such vehicle, Stagecoach Devon acquired a pair of open-top Bristol VRTs from Coastline during March along with a pair of Plaxton Premiere Interurban-bodied Dennis Javelin coaches required for operation on an express service between Torquay and Exeter.

After being evaluated by United Counties since 1992, Stagecoach

One of three Leyland National 2s acquired by Burnley & Pendle from National Welsh in 1988, 70 (BUH240V) picks up its passengers in Rawtenstall.

Acquired by Western Scottish with the business of Arran Transport, Duple Dominant II-bodied Bedford YMQ MCS139W later passed to Midland Red South for use as a driver training bus. Numbered T5, it prepares to leave Leamington depot in October 1996 under the watchful eye of the company's driving instructor. (K.A.Jenkinson)

One of a number of former Newcastle Busways Alexander-bodied Leyland Atlanteans transferred to Midland Red South, 982 (AVK174V) still in its former owner's yellow, white & maroon livery albeit with Midland Red fleet name vinyls rests at Leamington Spa depot in October 1996. (K.A.Jenkinson)

Passing through Lewes town centre is East Sussex County Council green & yellow-liveried Wadham Stringer Vanguard-bodied Leyland Swift G92VMM, one of two such buses which were operated on its behalf by South Coast Buses who had given it fleet number 2892. (T.S.Blackman)

found the installation of Fleet Activity Control Technology' software to be invaluable in monitoring/managing its fleet maintenance programme and took the decision to enter into a contract worth potentially up to £1million over three years to install this system throughout most of its subsidiaries. This, it was believed, would save the company large sums of money through accurate warranty control and time/lost management and would show a good return on investment. Further economies were also being achieved by Gloucester Citybus who had implemented a programme of vehicle refurbishment which could extend the lives of several types of buses by up to ten years as well as provide passengers with a better, more modern environment in which to travel. In addition to undertaking such work for Stagecoach group companies such as Stroud Valleys and Swindon & District, Gloucester Citybus also made its service available to other operators not connected with the Perth-based group.

Being more concerned with profitable bus operation rather than often unprofitable coaching activities, it came as little surprise when towards the end of April Stagecoach sold its GMS Buses subsidiary Charterplan to the Hull-based EYMS Group who had a year earlier bought Ribble's Stagecoach Manchester bus operations. Rather than integrate its new business and its 27 acquired coaches into its Manchester subsidiary, Finglands, EYMS chose to incorporate Charterplan into its East Yorkshire Travel operation while Stagecoach renamed its Charterplan Tours Ltd. company on 1 July to become GMS Coaches Ltd. Although Charterplan's Charles Street, Stockport base was to be retained by

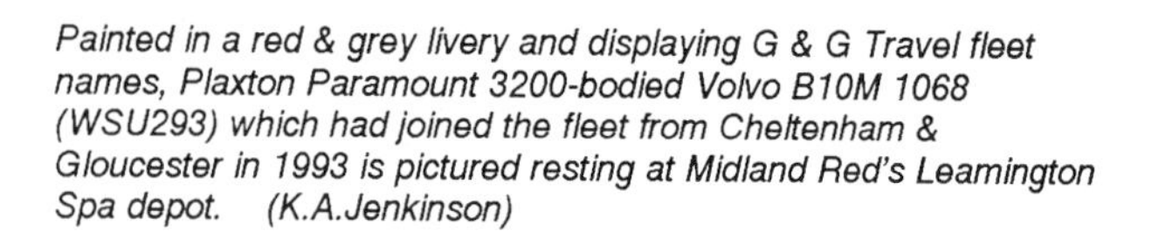

Painted in a red & grey livery and displaying G & G Travel fleet names, Plaxton Paramount 3200-bodied Volvo B10M 1068 (WSU293) which had joined the fleet from Cheltenham & Gloucester in 1993 is pictured resting at Midland Red's Leamington Spa depot. (K.A.Jenkinson)

Sporting a Spire Sprinter fleet name on its side panels East Midland is Alexander-bodied Mercedes Benz 709D 96 (E96YWB) which still wore the livery of its former owner, Chesterfield Transport. (P.T.Stokes)

Operating from the soon to be sold Huntingdon depot of United Counties, ECW-bodied Bristol VRT 731 (FDV809V) acquired from Devon General in 1988 hurries towards Cambridge on the 74 service from its home base in June 1996. (K.A.Jenkinson)

One of the first Cambus vehicles to receive Stagecoach corporate colours was Optare Metrorider 966 (K966HUB) seen here leaving Drummer Street bus station, Cambridge on a Sunday service in April 1996. (K.A.Jenkinson)

Standing at Stagecoach Malawi's Chichiri depot at Blantyre are corporate-liveried 1990 ERF Trailblazer 880 (BH5752) and 1989 AVM Dahmer 437 (BH1897) which carried Expressline names. Note the length of the rear overhang of 437. (J.Davison)

Stagecoach Manchester, agreement was reached for its continued use by East Yorkshire Travel until it could find new premises in the area. Early in the following month after the purchase by FirstBus of Strathclyde Buses, Stagecoach complied with the instruction by the Office of Fair Trading and sold its 21.7% stake in the Glasgow-based company to FirstBus on 3 June, making a £15 million profit in the process. Meanwhile, following its acquisition of Cambus Holdings and negotiations with the Office of Fair Trading, Stagecoach was advised by the Minister for Competition and Consumer Affairs, John Taylor, that if it was to avoid an investigation by the Monopolies and Mergers Commission, it must divest itself of its Milton Keynes operations and its United Counties depot at Huntingdon within six months. The request (instruction) relating to the latter was particularly odd in view of the fact that this was not part of the Cambus acquisition and indeed had been owned by Stagecoach since November 1987 and in an attempt to appease the Minister, Stagecoach offered instead to divest itself of Viscount Buses. This was, however, not accepted and rather than face yet another lengthy inquiry, the Perth-based group decided to accede to the original request and began looking for buyers for its Milton Keynes and Huntindon operations. As a consequence, the repainting of the two Milton Keynes fleets into Stagecoach corporate colours never got underway and instead all the buses concerned retain their existing liveries.

In the company's report to its shareholders for the year ended 30 April 1996 it was pleasing to find that despite the impact of adverse weather and fuel duty increases, margins on Stagecoach's core bus businesses rose from 17.0% to 17.4% and the company now had a 17% share of the UK bus market. Its major investmet in new buses had reduced the average age of its overall fleet from 9.1 years to 8.7 years (the industry average was 11 years) and it was predicted that this would reduce further to 8.1 years by 30 April 1997 after the delivery of another 990 buses and inter-urban coaches. In addition to the new vehicles, improved frequencies and lower fares had enabled passenger numbers to be increased and additionally, as a result of extended manufacturers' warranties and standardisation of vehicle types it had been possible to reduce expenditure on engineering materials and labour, although staff costs accounted for approximately 49% of turnover. Further cost

Transferred to Stagecoach Kingston-upon-Hull from A1 Service, Ardrossan in 1996, East Lancs-bodied Scania 800 (C100HSJ) approaches its terminus at Bransholme at the end of its journey from Hull city centre in October 1996. (K.A.Jenkinson)

Pictured at Canterbury bus station enroute to Dover in summer sunshine is Stagecoach East Kent Plaxton Premiere Expressliner-bodied Volvo B10M 8916 (M916WJK) painted in National Express corporate colours. (D.W.Rhodes)

Busways solitary Optare Sigma-bodied Dennis Lance 1204 (M204DRG) is pictured here wearing the all-yellow MetroCentre Shuttle livery for operation on service 100 from The Monument, Newcastle to Gateshead MetroCentre. (Campbell Morrison)

Having been cascaded by Fife Scottish to Red & White, Leyland National 512 (RSG824V) is seen here already to leave its depot to take up a duty on the 53 service to Brynmawr. (Campbell Morrison)

reduction measures undertaken included the integration of the administration offices at Aberdeen, Kilmarnock and Kirkcaldy into one central unit in Fife, thus saving £120,000 annually and similarly Cambus and Chesterfield Transport's administration were merged with that of East Midland at Chesterfield.

During the first half of 1996, the flow of new vehicles had continued unabated and as had become customary, their arrival led to the cascading of several older members of the fleet to pastures new within the Stagecoach empire. In order to upgrade the Devon fleet and allow the withdrawal of a number of its elderly Ford Transit minibuses, early in June a number of Iveco 49.10s were transferred from Red & White who had received a quantity of new Mercedes Benz 709Ds whilst also despatched to Devon were a couple of Mercedes Benz 811Ds and an 814D from Bluebird Buses and 16 Mercedes Benz 709Ds from Busways. Prior to these moves, Stagecoach Midland Red had renumbered its G & G, Grasby and Vanguard vehicles to bring them into line with its own fleet and had throughout the year been progressively replacing its Iveco and Ford Transit minibuses with new Mercedes Benz 709Ds and its Bristol VRTs and Fleetlines with Leyland Atlanteans acquired from Busways. Used mainly on school contract duties, these retained the bright yellow livery of their former owner and merely had their fleet names replaced with Midland Red vinyls prior to being placed in service mainly at Leamington Spa and Stratford on Avon depots. In the meantime United Counties at the end of June replaced all its

One of the new Northern Counties-bodied Volvo B10Ms purchased by Stagecoach for its Kingston-upon-Hull fleet, 707 (M707KRH) still in its original blue, yellow & white livery travels along Holderness Road, Hull on its way to the city centre in October 1996. (K.A.Jenkinson)

Painted in Viscount Central colours, Burnley & Pendle Alexander-bodied Volvo B10M 114 (H114ABV) is seen at Accrington in November 1996. (Travelscene)

Resting at the bus park adjacent to Hull bus station is Stagecoach Kingston-upon-Hull's Kingstonian coaching unit's Plaxton Paramount-bodied Volvo B10M 50 (IIL1319) which was originally registered C50FRH. (K.A.Jenkinson)

remaining Corby Magic Minis-liveried Iveco 49.10s with new Alexander-bodied Mercedes Benz 709Ds painted in standard Stagecoach colours. Amongst the other new vehicles to arrive were 5 Berkhof-bodied Dennis Lance SLF low-floor buses for Ribble which were part funded by a grant from Greater Manchester PTE for operation on the M10 service which linked Manchester with Eccles and Brookhouse. As part of its bid to further reduce the average age of the Stagecoach Malawi fleet, 36 secondhand Leyland Victory single deck buses were purchased from Durban City Transport in South Africa and after being overhauled and repainted into corporate colours by their new owner, these replaced a number of older buses of this type inherited with UTM in 1989.

Fife Scottish Alexander-bodied Leyland Leopard driver training bus GSU839T has been given a version of Stagecoach's corporate livery with its upwards stripes at the front rather than at the rear and carries a fleet name reading 'Stagecoach Fife Number 1 in the Kingdom'. (D.Robinson)

Repainted in Guide Friday's green & cream livery and appropriately lettered for the Hastings Tour operated in conjunction with Stagecoach South is South Coast Buses open-top ECW-bodied Bristol VRT 7623 (UWV623S). (Stagecoach)

Stagecoach Midland Red Alexander-bodied Mercedes Benz 709D 360 (N360AVV) with Stratford Blue Shuttle fleet names stands in Stratford on Avon town centre in November 1996. (K.A.Jenkinson)

Seen awaiting sale at Kilmaine Close depot, Cambridge is Cambus Toyota Coaster 424 (K96OGA) painted in grey livery and still carrying Millers of Cambridge fleet names. (K.A.Jenkinson)

As the flow of new vehicles continues apace to all the various Stagecoach group companies, so older buses and coaches are sold - some for further use by other operators, others for scrap. Destined for the breaker's torch is this heavily cannibalised Ribble Leyland National seen making its way along the M62 motorway to Carlton behind a DAF recovery wagon of breaker Trevor Wigley. (K.A.Jenkinson)

On the operational front, for the whole of May East Kent offered its passengers in the Thanet area a range of cheaper fares. Promoted as 'May Madness', most of the fares concerned were cut by up to 50% and such was the success of this offer that ridership increased by almost 30%. As a result, from 9 June a whole new package of fares was introduced with concentration being given to simplicity and return tickets and included in this scheme was the 'Megarider' which was a value for money network ticket which offered unlimited journeys for just £3.99 and was based on the successful concept pioneered earlier by East Midland, Busways and Stagecoach Scotland. North of the border, Fife Scottish's St.Andrews town services were completely revised from 13 May when the vehicle requirement was able to be reduced from 3 to 2 buses while a week later on 21 May Western Scottish introduced a new open-top double deck service on the isle of Bute, running this on an hourly frequency. Five weeks later, on 29 June, yet another open-top service was launched, this time in Perth under the title of 'The Perth Experience'. Using a Bristol VRT and running hourly seven days a week, this took in all the sights in and around the city and quickly gained popularity amongst visitors to the area. Earlier, on Tuesday 4 June Winchester City Council promoted a 'Car Free Day', encouraging people not to bring their cars into the city centre. Supporting this, Hampshire Bus for that day reduced its fares by 50% for all journeys within the Winchester Freedom Ticket zone and to publicise this initiative, most of the company's buses carried large posters in their rear window on the first three days of the month. Prior to the above, several companies within the Stagecoach group had launched various initiatives which rewarded passengers using their services as well as promoting bus travel. Amongst these schemes was that adopted by Busways in South Shields under the title of 'Collect'n'Save' whereby pensioners could exchange their bus tickets for gas, electricity, telephone or TV stamps, and one by Stagecoach South entitled 'Ride & Save' which gave discount at selected local shops on the production of bus tickets. Red & White introduced a 'Stagecoach Club' where regular passengers could earn vouchers which could be redeemed at various retail outlets or be used towards TV licence stamps while Travelclubs were set up by Stagecoach Transit and shoppers' Budget Card tickets were promoted by Busways which offered similar incentives to passengers.

Under a reorganisation in Scotland, Ayrshire Bus Owners (A1 Service) Ltd. changed its name to Stagecoach A1 Service Ltd. on 13 May at the same time that non bus owning Clyde Island Buses Ltd. was renamed Stagecoach Express Ltd. and on the penultimate day of the month Western Scottish Buses Ltd. changed its title to Western Buses Ltd. At this same time, Western moved its head office from its old-established base at Nursery Avenue, Kilmarnock to a vacant property at Sandgate bus station Ayr in order to allow the redevelopment of part of the Nursery Avenue site. Soon afterwards, A1 Service on 16 June moved from its cramped depot off Princes Road, Ardrossan to the former P & O Pandoro premises at Ardrossan Harbour where more space was available for its fleet. Meanwhile, earlier in the year the front part of East Kent's Westwood depot at Thanet was leased to LIDL for use as a food store, leaving the back section still serving its original purpose with access now being gained by a roadway on the northern side of the site. Back in Scotland, following the closure of the railway between Aberdeen and Ballater earlier in the year, Bluebird Buses had provided transport for the Royal household between Aberdeen and Balmoral on the occasions of visits by the Royal Family to the castle. This was acknowledged in June when Bluebird was granted the Royal Warrant of Appointment to Her Majesty the Queen as suppliers of bus and coach

Proudly displaying the Royal Crest aft of its fleetname is Bluebird Buses Plaxton Premiere Interurban-bodied Volvo B10M 583 (N583XSA) seen here in September 1996. (D.Robinson)

On the day the two gas-powered Optare Metroriders operated by Cambus were introduced on the Cambridge city centre shuttle service, appropriately registered 81 (GAZ4381) is overtaken outside Kings College by MCW Metrorider 002 (D648NOE) which was on long term loan from West Midlands Travel and was performing one of its last duties before its return to its rightful owner. Both buses carried the special green & yellow livery dedicated to this service. (K.A.Jenkinson)

One of Fife Scottish's new Jonckheere Mistral-bodied Volvo B10M bendicoaches, 562 (N562SJF) poses near the Forth Bridge for this publicity shot. (Stagecoach)

Specially purchased by Kenya Bus Services for staff transport is this 25-seat Mitsubishi Canter minibus registered KAE453Y. (Stagecoach International)

services after which the Coat of Arms was proudly applied to some of the company's vehicles.

In an innovative move supported by Cambridgeshire County Council, Stagecoach Cambus launched two new compressed natural gas powered Optare Metroriders on Cambridge's free city centre shuttle service on 11 June upon which they replaced two conventional MCW Metroriders on loan from West Midlands Travel for the past eighteen months. Painted in the special green and yellow livery worn by their predecessors and adorned with Stagecoach, British Gas and County Council logos, the new buses were fitted to DpTAC specification and were chosen for their potential environmental advantages. These were not the only new type of vehicle to be introduced by Stagecoach, however, for on Friday 12 July, Fife Scottish placed two new high-floor Jonckheere Mistral-bodied Volvo B10M bendicoaches in service on its Stagecoach Express X27 route between Anstruther and Glasgow. Seating 72 passengers, these 18m long coaches were the first of their type to be operated in Britain and with double glazed windows and reclining seats, each of which was fitted with a belt, they were indeed luxurious in every respect. Joining them within the Stagecoach group early in August, were the first two of Ribble's four Plaxton-bodied Volvo B10M bendicoaches which were initially used mainly on the service running from Southport to Lancaster, although following the arrival of the remaining two they were transferred to the routes running into Manchester from Blackpool and East Lancashire. Additionally, two Plaxton-bodied Volvo B10M bendicoaches joined Fife Scottish in October/November for work between Anstruther and Glasgow or Edinburgh alongside the two Jonckheere-bodied examples and a further two are expected before the end of the year together with two more which are yet to be allocated. In the meantime, Stagecoach Kingston-upon-Hull had towards the end of July joined forces with East Yorkshire Motor Services to introduce a completely new hourly service between Hull and Leeds which was marketed as the 'Ridings Express'. For its share of this operation, East Yorkshire repainted two of its Leyland Royal Tiger Doyen coaches into Stagecoach corporate livery complete

Arriving at Preston bus station during its first week in service is Ribble's Plaxton Premiere-bodied Volvo B10M bendicoach 101 (P973UBV) which had still to receive its Stagecoach Express fleet names. (Travelscene)

One of two East Yorkshire Leyland Royal Tiger Doyens painted in Stagecoach corporate livery for use on the joint X62 service from Hull to Leeds, 8 (508DKH) is pictured at its terminal outside Hull Paragon railway station in November 1996. (K.A.Jenkinson)

Repainted into an all-red livery for its new Speed Link operation and adorned with all-over advertising is Stagecoach Malawi PEW-bodied ERF Trailblazer 974 (BJ9558). (Stagecoach International)

with both Stagecoach fleet names and EY logos while Stagecoach Kingston-upon-Hull interworked its vehicles with the 909 service to Sheffield and in order to provide the necessary additional vehicles KHCT obtained a pair of Plaxton-bodied Volvo B10Ms from Fife Scottish and two new coaches of this type. Back in Scotland, A1's service network underwent major revision on 12 August when several new services were introduced, three were withdrawn and a number were given improved timings. As a consequence of these changes, the old-established Parkhouse bus stance at Ardrossan which had been acquired with the co-operative in January 1995 was closed and offered for sale, thus removing yet another trace of the old A1 operation. However, in November the last former A1 bus to retain its former owner's blue & cream livery, an Alexander-bodied Leyland Atlantean, was surprisingly repainted in this scheme and was soon afterwards joined by one of the company's most recent Alexander-bodied Volvo Olympians which was similarly treated, thus keeping the memory of the Ayrshire Bus Owners co-operative alive. Earlier in the autumn, Fife Scottish had repainted its open-top Leyland Atlantean into the all red scheme used by W.Alexander for its Fife fleet in days long gone, illustrating that Stagecoach stripes were not mandatory after all!

With winter approaching, several seasonal services were withdrawn for the duration and in addition A1 Service ceased its operations on the 585 ClydeCoaster route between Largs and Greenock on 5 October when they were taken up by Clydeside Buses. From 17 November, however, A1 Service introduced Sunday services on several of its routes including those from Irvine Cross to Broomlands and Lowtherbank and additional journeys on its X36 between Ardrossan and Glasgow for the run up to Christmas, although all were scheduled to cease after 22 December while Fife Scottish launched a new 'Nightliner' service on 22 November with two journeys each way from Kirkcaldy to Edinburgh (11.30pm and 2.00am from Kirkcaldy, returning at 12.45am and 3.15am from Edinburgh) on Friday, Saturday and Sunday nights. It was not only in the UK that new branded services were being launched, however, for in Malawi a new network of routes was being progressively launched under the name 'Speedlink' in order to meet changing travelling needs. The first of these was between Blantyre and Lilongwe where, by streamlining the number of stops on the Intercity routes, Speedlink was an hour quicker than competitors' services but charged the same fares. Initially using 11 of the company's newer ERF Trailblazers which have been repainted into a new all-over red livery, no fewer than 42,000 travelled on Speedlink during its first four weeks of operation and such was its success that it is soon to be extended to other routes in the country.

Having considered several possible opportunities for further development in Europe, on 24 July Stagecoach made a bid for Swebus AB, the 3,450 vehicle subsidiary of the Swedish state-owned railway company, SJ. The largest bus company in the Nordic region, Swebus in addition to providing contractual public bus services to the council public

The timetable leaflet for Fife Scottish's Nightliner service.

The oldest bus in the Hyndburn Transport fleet was twenty one-year old East Lancs-bodied Leyland Leopard 41 (JFV294N) which is seen here in October 1996 still in its erstwhile owner's red, grey & navy blue livery with the legend 'A Stagecoach Subsidiary' added above its front and below its side fleet name. (Robert Kenyon)

Amongst the trains owned by Stagecoach Porterbrook Limited are 317 diesel High Speed Trains of the 125 type, thus designated by their maximum speed of 125 mph, although in reality they rarely exceeded 100 mph. Initially use on British Rail's InterCity East Coast line between London Kings Cross and Edinburgh and on services from London to Bristol and South Wales, 43075 is seen here approaching Doncaster station on a Kings Cross to Leeds working prior to the line's electrification. Each '125' had a powered driving unit at both front and rear. (Travelscene)

Left : CRZ196, one of Swebus of Sweden's Van Hool-bodied Scania coaches. (Stagecoach International)

The most recent addition to Stagecoach's preserved vehicle fleet is ECW-bodied Bristol MW6G HFM561D which was delivered new to Crosville in 1966. Although bought as a source of spares for Stagecoach HDV639E, its future has yet to be decided. (D.Robinson)

transport authorities throughout Sweden also had operations in Finland, Norway and Denmark, all countries in which bus services had already been deregulated, and thus was viewed with great importance as the next potential addition to Stagecoach's ever-growing empire. Around 90% of the company's vehicles were commuter buses of which 87% were operated in Sweden, and in 1994 members of the Swebus group had acquired two companies in Finland which were then merged under the name of Oy Swebus Finland Ab. Later that year the Swedish company had purchased Poldan Tours A/S of Denmark, which it renamed Dania Tours A/S while in 1995 it further expanded with the acquisition of Danish operator Jens Faber and Norwegian companies Vestoppland Bilsellskap AS, Litra Bus AS, AS Hamar og Oland Bilruter and HOBAS AS. Swebus's operations could, perhaps, be likened to those of Stagecoach in northern Scotland where large rural areas are interspersed with a number of towns of various sizes and in a similar fashion to Bluebird Buses and its associated Pegasus Express, Swebus also undertook the carriage of parcels and packages etc. Upon conclusion of the negotiations with SJ and Konkurrensverket (the Swedish competition authority), Swebus was purchased on 1 October by Stagecoach Europe Ltd. (which had been renamed from Stagecoach Portugal Ltd. on 21 August) and thus took the Perth-based group to yet another part of the world in which it had not previously had a presence. Meanwhile, in the southern hemisphere Stagecoach, in addition to continuing to successfully maintain its operations in New Zealand, was also investigating franchising opportunities in Vietnam, Australia and other Pacific Rim countries where it believed there might be openings for future development.

At the same time that Stagecoach was negotiating with Swebus, it also made an offer in July for Porterbrook Leasing Company MEBO Ltd., one of the three UK railway rolling stock companies who owned 3,774 railway vehicles which it leased to 16 of the 25 train owning companies. These vehicles comprised 1,572 electric multiple units, 698 diesel multiple units, 317 High Speed Trains (125s), 169 locomotives, 619 hauled passenger vehicles and 345 hauled freight vehicles. Although it was a comparatively new company which had been purchased from the Department of Transport on 8 January 1996, it had operated since 1 April 1994 when most of British Rail's rolling stock had been placed under the control of the three ROSCOs (rolling stock companies). When the Government announced its privatisation plans for these companies in March 1995, despite seeing the benefits in participating, Stagecoach was not at that time able to bid for Porterbrook and instead, early in October 1995, joined what proved to be an unsuccessful bidding group for one of the other ROSCOs, Angel Train Contracts. Thus, its acquisition of Porterbrook on 28 August 1996

Of the five Leyland Leopards operated by Sussex Bus, only SSU780W carries Duple Dominant bodywork. Acquired from Graham of Paisley in 1990, it is seen here in its owner's white & red livery some six years later passing along South Street, Chichester on its way to Old Bosham on the 56 service. (J.L.Hobbs)

The wind of change blowing through Accrington in late-October 1996 can be witnessed by this photograph at Hyndburn's depot in the town. Only two members of Hyndburn's fleet are to be seen amid a sea of Ribble Leyland Olympians which had ousted a number of the erstwhile council-owned company's Atlanteans. (N.Larkin)

provided it not only with a firm platform on which to continue to build its railway interests, but also with a significantly enlarged portfolio which included fleet management contracts with West Yorkshire PTE and West Midlands PTE. In order to finance its purchase of Porterbrook, Stagecoach introduced an innovative scheme to transform corporate debt into bonds which could be sold to international investors. The scheme, called securitisation, involved £545 million which would be secured on lease payments for trains provided by Porterbrook to the various train operating companies. The bonds were considered particularly low risk investments as around 80% of the leases are guaranteed by the government. Securitisation allowed companies to remove assets from their balance sheets which frees up capital and provides more funding sources. Arranged by UBS, Stagecoach will provide an average interest rate of 7.4% on the bonds, thus reducing its own interest costs from those first envisaged when it announced the Porterbrook deal and providing it with an additional £25 million surplus which it expects to use in its investment programme. On 13 September the newly acquired company was renamed Stagecoach Porterbrook Limited.

Continuing its quest for further consolidation in northern Scotland, Bluebird Buses on 5 August took over the business of Marshall & Mitchell who traded as Eastons Motor Services at Inverurie. In addition to providing it with three services, two of which operated only on school days, this also brought five more coaches into the Stagecoach fold. Only two of these, both Volvo B10Ms were placed in service by their new owner, however, the remaining three (2 DAFs and a Mercedes Benz 609D) being added to Bluebird's reserve fleet for early disposal.

Never content to stand still and always eager to further expand its operations, Stagecoach on 11 September purchased the 65 vehicle fleet and operations of Hyndburn Transport following the withdrawal of a bid made earlier for the former municipal undertaking by Blackpool Transport. Although the company's depot at Accrington was not included in the deal, a six month lease was obtained for its continued use to allow time for its operations and those of Ribble to be merged. Rather than be retained as a separate subsidiary, the newly-acquired company is to be fully absorbed by Ribble who will then maintain its Accrington area services from its existing depots at Blackburn and Clitheroe and its outstation at Burnley. In the meantime the legend 'A Stagecoach Subsidiary' was added to the Hyndburn fleet name on all the acquired vehicles which initially continued to operate in their existing livery. Some of these, however, were destined to have an extremely short life and upon the arrival of several new Northern Counties-bodied Volvo Olympians with Ribble which allowed the transfer of some of its older ECW-bodied Leyland Olympians to Accrington, a number of Hyndburn's older Leyland Atlanteans were withdrawn from service and despatched to Perth pending their disposal. The repainting of the erstwhile council-owned company's vehicles which were to be retained began in earnest with the Leyland National Greenways being the first thus treated, these emerging with Stagecoach Ribble fleet names and renumbered into Ribble's scheme.

Seen in Accrington on a dull afternoon in late October 1996 is the first former Hyndburn Transport vehicle to be repainted into Stagecoach corporate livery. East Lancs-Leyland National Greenway AFM1W which began life with Crosville has been numbered 901 in the Ribble fleet and given that company's fleet names. (P.Kay)

In the midst of Stagecoach's expansion since the start of 1996, numerous new initiatives were introduced in an attempt to encourage an increase in ridership, some of which have been mentioned earlier, and indicating that all areas of the potential market were being targeted. Early in September Stagecoach Manchester launched a new scheme aimed at university students in the city. After introducing an experimental £5 weekly ticket at the beginning of April on its routes operating along Wilmslow Road which served the seats of learning, at the start of the new University year the company repainted 17 of its 'standard' Leyland Atlanteans into an all-over blue livery, branded them under the title of 'Magic Bus' with no reference to their Stagecoach ownership, and put them to work on routes 142 and 143 upon which low fares were charged. Coupled with this innovative move, Stagecoach Manchester replaced all its orange-liveried buses on the Wilmslow Road services (which were rebranded as the 'Q Service Network) with ones painted in Stagecoach colours in order to present its new corporate image. Unusually, considering that both the Magic Bus double deckers and Stagecoach single deckers are under the same ownership, each applies a differing fare scale with that of Magic Bus ranging from 25p to 90p and that on the corporate-liveried buses starting at 35p and rising to £1.30. Additionally, a third student fare scale was introduced which is capped at 60p and there is also a new term-time ticket priced at £49 which allows students to travel system-wide. Aimed at reducing competition from the large number of operators travelling along the Wilmslow Road corridor, it will be interesting to see whether or not this new venture achieves the success it is designed to gain.

One of a number of Stagecoach Manchester NCME-bodied Leyland Atlanteans to receive an all-over blue livery and Magic Bus fleet names for operation on two services travelling past Manchester University, 4725 (A725LNC) picks up a healthy load of passengers at Piccadilly bus station in September 1996. (K.S.E.Till)

Having just arrived at Ashton bus station at the end of its journey from Manchester, Stagecoach Manchester's new Alexander-bodied Volvo B10M 838 (P838GND) takes a short rest before resuming its duties. (K.S.E.Till)

In an attempt to make Stagecoach's future development less susceptible to any single area of business risk, the company set up a new UK Bus Management Board on 6 September which will function separately from the two railway company boards and have no common directors. Under this move, South West Trains is chaired by Brian Cox who was joined by Ann Gloag, Barry Sealey and Derek Scott replacing Brian Souter, Barry Hinkley and Keith Cochrane who joined the board of Porterbrook which is chaired by Sandy Anderson. The newly created UK Bus Management Board in addition to Stagecoach's executive directors Brian Souter, Brian Cox and Barry Hinkley was joined by three of the group's senior managers, each of whom represented a specific area of the group's UK activities - Tony Cox for the former NBC companies, Roger Bowker the London Buses franchised operations and John Conroy the former PTE's. Although standing down at his own request from his position as group finance director in September, Derek Scott retained his position as company secretary after which Keith Cochrane took over the role of finance director. Other changes within Stagecoach's senior management team included Ian Manning who joined the company from Buckinghamshire County Council in August to become managing director of Stagecoach Portugal who had gained Roger Bowker as its chairman. Following his three year posting to Stagecoach Malawi as its managing director. John Gould returned to the UK to take up the post of managing director of Cumberland while Les Warneford moved from Cumberland to become managing director of Stagecoach Manchester where he was joined by Alan Fuller as finance director. Ian Mackintosh became general manager and a director of Bluebird Buses with Tom Wileman taking up these duties at Western Buses. In the meantime, Busways Marketing, the company's design, publicity and print facility which undertook work for outside customers as well as for several Group companies changed its name to Stagecoach Graphics in order to more easily identify with its role.

In October, Bluebird Buses further consolidated its position when it purchased the business of J.S.Gordon of Dornoch in the Highland Region. Although this operators 6 coaches were included in the deal, none of them were used by their new owner and instead were immediately put up for sale. Soon afterwards, on the 19th of that month Stagecoach purchased the 11 vehicle business of Sussex Bus of Chichester. Despite placing it under the control of Coastline Buses, it is to retain its existing identity and white & red livery and will continue to maintain its own established services. More importantly, however, Stagecoach gained full control of Burnley & Pendle Transport following a meeting of Burnley Council on 30 October when it reluctantly decided to sell its 50% share in the company to its partner after finding itself unable to increase its investment in the company. Although the decision is, at the time of writing, still subject to ratification by the Department of Transport and the Director General of Fair Trading, and is currently drawing protests from trade unions, members of the public and Burnley councillors, three of whom resigned in protest at the decision, within ten days of the announcement being made, one of the company's Alexander-bodied Volvo B10M double deckers emerged in Stagecoach corporate livery complete with Stagecoach Burnley & Pendle fleet names! Meanwhile, the divestment of Milton Keynes and United Counties' Huntingdon depot has still to take place, although at the start of November a shortlist had been drawn up of three prospective buyers, one of whom could itself face an OFT investigation if it was the successful contender. North of the border, Bluebird Buses opened a new airport-style waiting room in November at its Aberdeen bus station where members of Bluebird's Commuter Club - who have electronic key cards to enter - can enjoy free hot drinks and soups during its opening hours from 6.30am to 9.0pm and read the newspapers which are provided.

On 13 October, Stagecoach had gained a further foothold in the railway network when it commenced operation of a five year franchise to operate the Isle of Wight's eight and a half mile Island Line. This franchise was unique in that Stagecoach was responsible not only for running the trains but also for the maintenance of the track (which is not owned by Railtrack) and other infrastructure. Under the terms of the franchise it is committed to continuing to operate the service at its existing or an improved level as well as introducing a local residents' travel scheme and testing other discounted fares. Maintained by former London Underground rolling stock, the Island Line differs considerably from the mainland railways and presents a new challenge to the company as well as taking it to an area of England in which it has not previously had a presence. Instead of being placed under the control of South West Trains as perhaps might have been expected, the island line has been incorporated into Stagecoach South's operations for greater convenience, this presenting no problems in view of Brian Cox being chairman of both SWT and Stagecoach South. Also taking place on 1 September was the closure by Stagecoach Kingston upon Hull of its Lombard Street depot which was adjacent to Ferensway bus station, its allocation being relocated to new purpose-built premises at Stoneferry, away from the city centre. This was not the only new bus depot to be built by Stagecoach, however, and although construction work had yet to commence, a site had been acquired on the A27 road near Portsmouth where Coastline planned to build a new depot to replace its cramped Leigh Park facility. Similarly, land had been purchased on the White Lund Trading Estate at Morecambe where it was proposed to build a new depot early in 1997 which would enable the closure of the present premises in both Morecambe and Lancaster.

Despite its critics, Stagecoach's no-nonsense and sometimes unusual business style has proved highly successful. Layers of unnecessary and expensive administration have been sliced away and everyone is expected to do their bit for the company from the chairman down. Its dynamic and innovative management continually seek new ways for developing the business and generating increased profits. Although on occasions being ruthless with its competitors, Stagecoach has also

One of the Isle of Wight's Island Line ex.London underground trains awaits its departure to Shanklin at Ryde station. (F.W.York)

This official postcard shows a selection of buses in service in Stockholm with Swebus including Scanias and Volvos.

shown that it can comfortably work with others where its own income is not jeopardised and has reached territorial agreements in some areas where it does not feel under threat. Although all major acquisitions are undertaken by Stagecoach Holdings, all its operating companies are given the autonomy to purchase smaller operators or services where they regard these to be beneficial in terms of expansion or as a means of reducing competition and thus, for instance, Bluebird Buses has taken over several companies in this manner during the past few years. More than any of the other major bus operating groups, Stagecoach has supported the UK bus manufacturing industry during its period of recession and despite its fleet only accounting for one sixth of the UK operating industry, its orders have accounted for one third of its production. By ordering such large quantities of new buses and coaches, however, the company has been in a strong negotiating position in relation to prices and delivery dates and similarly has been able, through its massive purchasing power to secure substantial savings on all kinds of other purchases. Amongst its priorities is the injection of new, more comfortable buses into all of its fleets both at home and overseas and in particular at an early stage into the companies it has recently purchased. In addition to boosting staff morale, it again confirms the company's commitment to its customers without whom it could not survive. Although Stagecoach has appeared to be anti-coaching on several occasions, selling its activities in this field to other operators, this is not so and where it is profitable it is retained and developed. Unlike many operators who arguably seek only to maximise turnover (a throwback to nationalised industry or municipal ownership where management status was a function of turnover size rather than return on capital and profits growth), Stagecoach follows a simple rule of maximisation of long-term shareholders wealth. In defence of its corporate livery, while this may not be to everyone's taste, it has not only promoted a unified image and made the transfer of vehicles between its different operating companies easier, but has also been the most durable of any of those introduced since 1980. Despite the general belief that 'stripes must be painted on everything', although the corporate livery is recommended to all its local managers, they nevertheless are given the freedom to retain existing or introduce new liveries where this is believed to be in their company's best interest and this can be illustrated by Cumberland with its Coachline and Lakeland Explorer schemes, Circle Line at Gloucester which retains its green & white colours and Armstrong Galley etc.

Lined up at Selkent's Catford garage in September 1996 prior to their entry into service are nine of its new Alexander Dash-bodied Dennis Darts numbered 615 to 623 (P615-23PGP). (G.Matthews/J.A.Godwin collection)

Truly a story 'from rags to riches', Stagecoach has always ensured that everyone employed within the company would share in the rewards of its success. Long gone are the days when Ann Gloag and Brian Souter collected the coupons from tea packets in an attempt to save enough for a new car, and one which they would have to share at that! Now, according to the mass media, Ann Gloag who has purchased Beaufort Castle, the ancestral home of the Frasers of Lovat is reportedly the second richest woman in Britain after the Queen. Additionally, it has recently been stated that she and her brother Brian Souter are the two highest earners in Scotland, but despite this neither of them have ever lost sight of their humble beginnings. Their business philosophy has always been to treat others as they themselves expect to be treated and although this may be hard to understand in instances such as the Darlington saga. Nevertheless, they have always maintained their belief that it is teamwork that has created their success and that without the strength of a superb management team and workforce, this would have been impossible to achieve.

Looking to the future, Stagecoach has already gained the 1997 contract for the Perth city park & ride service which is to be extended to run six days each week from April and has plans to further expand its Stagecoach Express network during the early months of the new year. Additionally, upon learning that Dundee-based Tayside Public Transport Company was being offered for sale, Stagecoach submitted a bid in mid November 1996 which was given consideration alongside offers from FirstBus and Yorkshire Traction, all of whom regarded the company as a valuable addition to their portfolio. As both Stagecoach and Yorkshire Traction already have a presence in Tayside, this could perhaps attract interest from the Office of Fair Trading if either are named as the preferred bidder when the announcement is made in December. Meanwhile in November Stagecoach was shortlisted to acquire a further four rail franchises : ScotRail Railways, North West Regional Railways (which includes Merseyside Electrics), InterCity West Coast and Central Trains whilst at this same time it placed an order for 625 more new buses for delivery in 1997 together with a secured option for a further 250. Somewhat surprisingly in view of Stagecoach's policy of banning cigarette advertising on all its vehicles, its subsidiary South West Trains was approached by a major tabacco company in November with a proposal to paint smoking carriages in colours associated with different brands of cigarettes. In order to judge passenger reaction, SWT invited passengers on its long-distance services to complete a questionnaire which asked whether they thought it was acceptable for a tobacco company to thus sponsor smoking carriages. In a statement made by SWT at that time, it pointed out that it was a long way off making a decision and added that if it eventually went ahead, it would first want to explore things such as air filters in smoking carriages etc. and that there would be no increase in the number of these carriages. Indeed, SWT currently did not allow smoking on any of its suburban trains and had no plans to alter this.

Despite the changes which might be implemented following the general parliamentary election in 1997, Stagecoach continues to look confidently towards the millennium and expects to add more companies both at home and overseas to its ever growing empire. Aiming to attain a £2 billion turnover by the year 2000, gain a 25% market share in UK buses, UK trains and a further proportion overseas and to become a FT-SE 100, global company in terrestrial transport as British Airways is in aviation, Stagecoach sees an exciting future ahead. Its firm commitment to investment in new vehicles, service enhancement and improvements in the quality of its operations are priorities it intends to achieve and with, hopefully, a larger share of Britain's rail network, it foresees some integration of rail and road public transport. Its past success within the public transport industry can be measured in its shares which since its flotation in April 1993 have risen from 112p to five times that amount and its growth from 1 bus in Scotland in 1980 to over 12,000 buses and nearly 4,000 rail units worldwide in 1996. This proves that with strategic vision, leadership, expert management and a dedicated workforce small acorns can, in a comparatively short space of time, grow into large forests.

Both Cambus and Viscount received delivery of new Northern Counties-bodied Volvo Olympians during October 1996 as replacements for elderly Bristol VRTs which have been the backbone of the double deck fleets of both companies for many years. This view shows Cambus 529 (P529EFL) at Haverhill during its first week in service. (M.H.A.Flynn)

FRONT COVER PHOTOGRAPHS

Stagecoach Kingston-upon-Hull Plaxton Premiere Interurban-bodied Volvo B10M 80 (P180PRH) picks up its passengers outside Hull railway/bus station in November 1996 at the start of its journey to Leeds on the X62 service. (K.A.Jenkinson)

Leaving Waterloo station, London is one of Stagecoach's South West Trains electric units painted in the company's corporate style livery. (Stagecoach)

BACK COVER PHOTOGRAPHS

Left column, top to bottom:

Travelling along Morecambe's promenade on 23 August 1993 is Cumberland's Lakeland Experience-liveried open-top Leyland Atlantean 1928 (ERV251D) which was on loan to Ribble for operation on the former Lancaster City Transport sea-front service from Heysham Village to Happy Mount Park. (K.A.Jenkinson)

Seen in Peterborough in June 1996 is Viscount Alexander-bodied Mercedes Benz 709D 200 (N614VSS) which was diverted from Western Scottish when new. (K.A.Jenkinson)

With its destination blind already set for its return journey to Whitehaven, Cumberland Alexander-bodied Leyland Olympian 1030 (K130DAO), complete with wheel trims, arrives in Carlisle in February 1993. (K.A.Jenkinson)

Right column, top to bottom:

Passing through Piccadilly Circus, London, on its way to Plumstead in May 1996 is Stagecoach Selkent Northern Counties-bodied Volvo Olympian 303 (M303DGP) painted in London's traditional all-red livery. (D.W.Rhodes)

Stagecoach's standard full-size single decker is the Alexander PS-bodied Volvo B10M, an example of which is seen here in Red & White ownership (768 : M768RAX) in Cardiff city centre in April 1996. (T.S.Blackman)

New Zealand subsidiary City Line Hutt Valley's dual-door Coachwork International-bodied Hino RK176 7252 (NL7833) is seen here fresh from the paint shops after receiving Stagecoach corporate livery. (Stagecoach International)

511 (J511FPS), one of Inverness Traction's Alexander Dash-bodied Dennis Darts purchased new in 1992 picks up its passengers in the centre of its home town. (Campbell Morrison)

STAGECOACH COMPANIES INCORPORATED OVERSEAS

Incorporated in Denmark:
* Swebus Denmark A/S.

Incorporated in Finland:
* Oy Swebus Finland Ab.

Incorporated in Hong Kong:
Stagecoach (Hong Kong) Limited.

Incorporated in Kenya:
Kenya Bus Services Limited.
Kenya Bus Services (Mombasa) Limited.

Incorporated in Malawi:
Halls Transport Services Limited.
North Charterland Transport Company Limited.
PEW Limited.
Stagecoach Malawi Limited.

Incorporated in the Netherlands:
KHCT Eurogroup BV.
Kivitz Reizen BV.
Stagecoach International BV.

Incorporated in New Zealand:
Cityline (NZ) Limited.
Harbour City Cable Car Limited.
New Zealand Bus Limited.
North City Bus Limited.
Wellington City Transport Limited.

Incorporated in Norway:
* Vestopplands Bilselskap AS.
* Vestopplands Bilselskap Eiendomselskap AS.

Incorporated in Ontario, Canada:
Skipburn Limited.

Incorporated in Sweden:
* Billingens Trafik AB.
* Harlstadbuss AB.
* Swebus AB.
* Swebus Fastigheter AB.
* Swebus Handel AB.
* Swebus Service AB.
* Swebus Sverige AB

** Owned by subsidiary holding company Stagecoach Europe Limited incorporated in England.*

OTHER COMPANIES OWNED BY STAGECOACH HOLDINGS plc

Busways Trustee (No.1) Limited.
Busways Trustee (No.2) Limited.
Chesterfield Transport E.B.T. (Number 1) Limited.
Chesterfield Transport E.B.T. (Number 2) Limited.
Chesterfield Transport PST Limited.
Cleveland Transit Trustee (No.1) Ltd.
Cleveland Transit Trustee (No.2) Ltd.
Cleveland Transit Trustee (No.3) Ltd.
East Kent Nominees Limited.
GM Buses South (E.B.T.) Limited.
GM Property Services (Manchester) Limited.
Hartlepool Transport (EBT 1) Limited.
Hartlepool Transport (EBT 2) Limited.
KHCT (ESOP) Limited.
KHCT Trustee Limited.
Stagecoach APS Trustee Limited.
Stagecoach ESOP Trustee Limited.

ASSOCIATED COMPANIES

Nicecon Limited.
SMT1 Association Limited.

Incorporated in Portugal:
Rodovarios LDA.

Incorporated in the Republic of Ireland:
Routemaster Reinsurance Limited.

The first shall be last, as is often said and it is perhaps thus fitting that the last photograph in this book should be of the very first vehicle to be purchased new by Stagecoach. Now numbered 650 and part of the company's preserved vehicle fleet, Volvo B10M FES831W was purchased in February 1981 and fitted with a 50-seat Duple Dominant III fitted with an onboard toilet facility. body. After giving yeoman service on the company's Anglo-Scottish services, it was given a new Duple Dominant body with bus seating for 59 passengers in July 1987 and demoted to local bus operation from Perth until January 1994 when it was finally retired. (D.Robinson)